THE LAST OF THE
DRUIDS

THE LAST OF THE
DRUIDS

The Mystery of the
Pictish Symbol Stones

IAIN W. G. FORBES

AMBERLEY

To my loving wife Susan
and my children, Neil, Lyndsay and Colm

Many thanks to my parents, Mima and Bill Forbes, and my wife Susan, who have continually encouraged me in all my endeavours and have supported me throughout this project. My father for his enthusiasm for the subject and my mother for proofreading this book. I would also like to thank Jane Dormon for contributing her illustrations, which were invaluable. A special mention also for Theo Zawadzki for accompanying me on field trips and also to Briain Wilson and Ceri Davies for leading me astray on one memorable Pictish stone forage. Finally, I would like to thank all my other friends and family who have had to put up with me enthusing about the Picts!

First published 2012

Amberley Publishing
The Hill, Stroud
Gloucestershire, GL5 4EP

www.amberleybooks.com

Copyright © Iain W. G. Forbes 2012

The right of Iain W. G. Forbes to be identified as the Author
of this work has been asserted in accordance with the
Copyrights, Designs and Patents Act 1988.

British Library Cataloguing in Publication Data.
A catalogue record for this book is available from the British Library.

ISBN 978 1 4456 0230 1

Typeset in 10pt on 12pt Sabon.
Typesetting and Origination by Amberley Publishing.
Printed in the UK.

CONTENTS

INTRODUCTION

The stars,
That nature hung in heaven, and filled their lamps,
With everlasting oil, to give due light
To the misled and lonely traveller.

John Milton (1608–1674)

The Enigmatic Picts

In the past it was easy to dismiss the Dark Age people of northern Europe as simply barbarian savages with little to offer except resistance to the legions of Rome. However, we now know that the disparate tribes that dominated North West Europe before, during, and after the Roman Empire, were much more sophisticated than many have given credit for in the past. Archaeological excavations continue to reveal exquisitely fashioned artefacts, including weaponry and gold jewellery, which provide information on their technological and artistic prowess. As a result we have a greater insight into the world that these so-called 'barbarians' lived in. We also know that their societies were complex and ordered with highly developed social structures. There is even evidence that the Celts, for example, had sophisticated legal and belief systems, an interest in astronomy and placed great emphasis on poetry. These aspects of life were regulated by a theological order, known as the druids, who appear to have operated at a trans-tribal level, with novices perhaps even travelling considerable distances to study at specific locations (the Isle of Anglesey for example). While the culture of many of these Celtic peoples and tribes have become increasingly familiar to us, there would appear one major exception: the Picts of northern Scotland. This vanished people remain as mysterious as ever, with scholars unable to agree on many basic issues including what language they spoke and their cultural origins. Without a single surviving decipherable sentence written in Pictish there is no consensus on whether they were even Celtic or represented a much older indigenous people with little relation to the rest of European mainstream culture.

   It is hoped that this book will shed considerably more light on the Picts, emphasise their considerable achievements and help place their culture firmly in the Celtic mainstream.

Picts: First Contacts

In the first century AD, Roman legions pressed northwards into the land we refer to today as Scotland. There they encountered what to them must have been just another 'barbarian' people. Although it is clear that attempts were made to subdue these northern tribes, the Romans were never to occupy this territory permanently, and the native population was destined to remain outside the empire. The Romans initially referred to these indigenous tribes by various names including the *Caledonians*, *Dicalydones*, and *Maeatae*. Later they were to drop these terms in favour of the collective and more familiar name 'Picti' or 'Picts'. In AD 142, during the reign of the emperor Antoninus Pius, an attempt was made to establish a permanent defensive wall. The wall ran across southern Scotland between the rivers Clyde and Forth for nearly 40 miles, and featured forts stationed every 2 miles along its length. The rationale behind this massive project would appear to have been the isolation of the Pictish tribes to the north. However, after just twenty years the Romans had retreated from this Antonine Wall to what is known today as Hadrian's Wall, some 60 miles further south. This even larger construction project represented the Romans' most fortified frontier, complete with forts and mile castles, and would become the northernmost boundary of the empire until the fifth century. Beyond the wall there was nothing that the Romans considered to be of value.

To us the term 'barbarian', particularly in the context of the Picts, may conjure up images of mindless, naked, and tattooed savages bent on wanton destruction, and this indeed is the sort of image that many people may still associate with the ancient peoples of Scotland. To the Romans it had a wider definition; it included any peoples that had not embraced Rome and its ways and therefore their civilisation. Is it fair for us to continue to use such a term in connection with the various peoples who inhabited territory beyond the northern confines of the Roman Empire? Is it possible that these largely forgotten peoples of Europe actually had well-developed societies with a level of sophistication that would surprise us? Disappointingly, if the Romans recorded anything about the Caledonians and other tribes, their customs, their culture, or any languages they spoke, very little has survived the centuries. What has survived relates principally to Roman military campaigns into their territory. We cannot even be sure what they called themselves. It is thought by many scholars that the very name 'Picti' was coined by Roman soldiers, and referred to the purported custom of Caledonian warriors painting or tattooing designs on their bodies.

One of the earliest and perhaps most important Roman texts relating to these people is a biography of the Roman general and emperor Agricola. The text *Agricola* was written by the military author Tacitus (who also happened to be Agricola's son-in-law) and contains a substantial description of the Roman campaign through northern Scotland in AD 83 to 84, including a speech attributed to one of the leaders of the Caledonians, Calgacus. However, both the biography and Calgacus' speech reveal little about the Caledonians or their society. The speech was supposedly delivered to some 30,000 Caledonian warriors prior to the battle of *Mons Graupius* in AD 84, which was probably fought in Aberdeenshire in the north-east of Scotland. The Romans in previous years had suffered a number of serious setbacks at the hands of these tribes, including perhaps the humiliating loss of a legion. The Roman general on this new campaign was Agricola, and he had amassed a considerable force of some four legions, 8,000 auxiliaries, and 5,000 cavalry, before marching them deep into Caledonian territory. The battle according to Tacitus was a terrible defeat for the native tribes. Calgacus' own fate is unknown, but it is probable that many Caledonians were captured and taken to Rome for public humiliation and execution or sold into slavery. Despite this considerable setback for the Caledonians, in the longer term they were able to re-establish themselves, and remain a thorn in the imperial foot for the duration of the Roman occupation of the island of Britain.

Whether or not the transcript of the speech presented in *Agricola* by Tacitus is wholly fictionalised or indeed carries some essence of a genuine speech by Calgacus, it nonetheless transmits a sense of geographical isolation beyond the boundary of empire, and seems to question the morality of further Roman expansion. By suggesting that this is one 'glorious victory' too far, it perhaps even provides something of an excuse for the Romans, and Agricola in particular, for not having consolidated their victory with occupation and annihilation of their foes. However, it undeniably places in the mouth of a so-called 'barbarian' an oration that carries a sense of nobility, courage, and intelligence.

> Now, however, the furthest limits of Britain are thrown open, and the unknown always passes for the marvellous. But there are no tribes beyond us, nothing indeed but waves and rocks, and the yet more terrible Romans, from whose oppression escape is vainly sought by obedience and submission. Robbers of the world, having by their universal plunder exhausted the land, they rifle the deep. If the enemy be rich, they are rapacious; if he be poor, they lust for dominion; neither the East nor the West has been able to satisfy them. Alone among men they covet with equal eagerness poverty and riches. To robbery, slaughter, plunder, they give the lying name of empire; they make a desert and call it peace.

It would be some time before another writer would treat the northern tribes with such respect and dignity.

Pictish and Celtic Stereotypes

Following the collapse of the Roman Empire in the fifth century, new kingdoms emerged in northern Britain. The kingdoms of the Picts were principally located in the north and east of Scotland. Neighbouring the Picts were now Welsh, Gaelic (Scottish), and Anglian kingdoms. All of these different peoples were destined over the next few centuries to war with the Picts. It is therefore hardly surprising that in any relevant surviving documents written by their neighbours, the Picts are usually mentioned only in passing, in a derogatory sense, and mainly in relation to battles. As with the Roman accounts, once again we get little sense of the Picts or their culture. Towards the end of the first millennium a new political unit emerged, one that resulted from a union between the Scots and the Picts. This union created the new Gaelic-speaking kingdom of Alba, later to be known as Scotland. At this point or shortly afterwards, all mention of the Picts stops. They simply seem to have vanished from the face of the earth, apparently leaving little behind; to all intents and purposes entering a world of mystery and mythology.

It was not until some eight centuries or so after their disappearance that interest in this long-forgotten people was rekindled, albeit on a limited scale. Nineteenth-century antiquarians started to investigate what records remained, to excavate, and document Pictish sites and monuments. They generally regarded the Picts as a Celtic tribe, although other more exotic origins were proposed, and unsurprisingly given the lack of historical sources they were enthusiastically linked to words such as 'mysterious' and 'enigmatic'.

While antiquarians in the nineteenth century, and subsequently archaeologists in the modern era, were gradually able to piece together some sort of picture of Pictish everyday life, in contrast, historians today still have had to contend with a dearth of primary material. As few writers contemporary with the Picts had anything good to say about them, it is easy to see how some later historians could also form a derogatory viewpoint. The task of denigrating them is crucially made all the easier by damning descriptions by Dark Age histories written by the Welsh-speaking monks Gildas and Nennius in the post-Roman period. These chroniclers depicted the Picts as nothing more than raiders and barbarians, and it is unsurprising that many people today remain ignorant of the cultural achievements of these poorly understood people. The historical record referring to the Picts is therefore extremely one-sided, and its validity must be treated with scepticism when attempting to gain insight into their society, culture, or place in the wider European context. Relying on these ancient snippets brings us no closer to understanding the Picts; if anything the historical record reflects more on the other nations who encountered the Picts, and on their own world view. It is certainly a possibility that important native documents may well have been written within Pictland by Picts, but simply failed to survive the vagaries of time. This lack of written material would ensure that later historians could effectively marginalise the Picts, or even lazily dismiss them as illiterate barbarians.

The lack of written material may possibly reflect a willingness by the Picts to place their trust in a culturally entrenched oral tradition for the transmission of information from one generation to the next. A society's preference for embedding key information in an oral tradition may be difficult for us to grasp in the twenty-first century, but if this is based on entrusting important information to especially trained individuals, then reasonably accurate transmission may have been possible over many generations. It is worth considering that in the turbulent times of the second half of the first millennium, paper or parchment may have been viewed as transient and fragile media. In addition, as is evidenced by copies of many early medieval manuscripts, scribal 'corrections' and errors accumulated during the process of copying documents over and over again. These factors may have contributed to a continued reliance on oral transmission. In Celtic society, one group in particular may have been pivotal in maintaining such a tradition – the druids. As well as having religious and legal functions, the druids were renowned for their memories. It is believed these were purposely developed to allow them to memorise large quantities of important information. It is therefore possible that they retained information important to their societies in their heads and were implicitly trusted with that information. It is also possible that other members of society were also encouraged or required to memorise key information that may have been subsequently recalled during, for example, legal disputes or in ceremonial contexts. While this may seem an alien concept to us today, there are still individuals in Scotland who can recite their ancestry back many generations. This oral ancestral lineage is known in Gaelic as the *sloinneadh*, and can be presented as legitimate evidence in hereditary disputes to the ancient heraldic and chivalric court of Scotland, the Lyon Court. It is perfectly feasible that in Pictish society written documents carried little legal weight compared to information carried in the heads of specific trusted individuals. Some apparently indigenously derived written documents, although not in Pictish, have survived in the form of king lists. These may have originally constituted a Pictish royal oral equivalent of a *sloinneadh*, eventually undergoing transcription into manuscript form by Irish monks. Mostly, however, our information on the Picts is derived from, at best, second-hand sources.

Today there is a growing perception that the Picts, and indeed the Celts in general, were much more sophisticated than previously thought. It is now obvious that these indigenous people were capable of producing some quite astonishing works of art. This is evident in Scotland, where Celtic culture flourished among three historically identifiable peoples: the Picts in northern and eastern Scotland, the Welsh in southern Scotland, and the Scots who migrated from Ireland to the west of Scotland around the beginning of the second half of the first millennium. The Celtic heritage of Scotland is impressive and contains influences that ultimately derive from the original Celtic heartlands of Europe and that classic Celtic stylistic source, the so-called La Tene culture. The Scots were almost certainly responsible for treasures such as the *Book of Kells*, probably produced in Iona and its satellite monasteries, for beautifully sculptured high crosses and stunning jewellery. Ancient Scottish Gaelic culture still echoes down the centuries through a continuing tradition of language, music and poetry. The Welsh kingdoms of southern Scotland gave rise to a number of key Welsh poets. Indeed, the oldest surviving Welsh poem is the epic seventh-century *Y gododdin*, set in Dark Age Edinburgh. This incidentally contains the first mention of the archetypical Celtic hero, Arthur, in any narrative source anywhere in the world, centuries before the medieval Arthurian romances. The Picts not only produced beautiful Celtic silver jewellery, but also produced the exquisitely carved 'symbol stones'. They, or rather their ancestors, are also credited with building unique massive stone buildings, the 'brochs', which were shaped rather like the cooling towers of power stations.

The cultural achievements of these three peoples are astounding and are at odds with the casual and derogatory dismissal of these as so-called Dark Age cultures, which was once fashionable. How could 'barbarians' produce such stunning works of art? Art that demonstrates complex ideas and utilises sophisticated manufacturing techniques? Is the phrase 'Dark Ages' actually a misnomer in the context of Celtic culture in the British Isles? If people cared to look at the ancient buildings and monuments peppering the modern Scottish landscape, and the archaeological artefacts in the museums, they would soon realise that the evidence in front of their own eyes suggests that these peoples, including the Picts, should not be viewed as primitive, but rather that their capabilities reflect complex societies and cultures. However, despite the Picts' obvious and still visible cultural achievements, the myth of the naked barbarian Pictish tribesman continues.

A New Approach to an Old Problem

If we want to learn more about the Picts, in the absence of both meaningful indigenous records and any useful traces of language, we must almost solely rely on material artefacts they left behind. However, among these, we do have one possible window into the world of the Picts, one that on closer inspection would seem to place this enigmatic people well within the mainstream of European culture. This window comprises the intricately carved 'symbol stones' and a small quantity of engraved silver jewellery. There are literally hundreds of these symbol stones, located in almost every part of modern Scotland. Some appear to have been far older standing stones that the Picts have reused and some stones that have been carved apparently for the specific purpose of displaying symbols. Others are clearly Christian monuments bearing Christian symbolism alongside the unique Pictish symbols.

The symbols, some seemingly abstract, some of animals or fantastic beasts and some of everyday objects, usually appear in pairs and were used throughout Pictland over at least several centuries (generally believed to be from the sixth century to the tenth century). While up until now there has been no agreement or convincing theory regarding their function, most would agree that they seem to be conveying important information. What this information could be has been a mystery to historians and archaeologists for over two centuries. If the symbols are conveying messages, then the existence of these symbol stones seems to raise more questions than answers. Perhaps, as some suggest, they contain relatively limited information such as clan crests or personal names, or perhaps, as will be suggested in this book, they constitute a much more important source of information that could be key to understanding their society and their place in the world.

In terms of the artistry displayed, the free-flowing lines of the animalistic symbols suggest an artistic culture that had a strong aesthetic sense. Those that represent everyday objects, such as hammers and shears, have a familiarity that reminds us of the continuity of human existence. The strange abstract symbols would seem to be impenetrable to our modern minds and perhaps hint at sacred or secret symbolism. The addition of apparently optional ornamentation in the form of 'rods' cutting through some of the symbols, and the frequent addition of carved mirrors and combs beside the symbols, seem to underline the notion that there is sophistication in the message being conveyed. The apparent complexity of the imagery utilised in the symbols, and the evidence that some symbol pairings seem to have been favoured, while others do not appear at all, hints that the symbols form part of a complicated graphic system, regulated by a set of rules. This possibility not only surprises, but more importantly immediately contradicts the very notion of the Picts as backward barbarians. The prominence given to these symbols, on what were clearly important monuments within the everyday landscape of Pictland, would strongly suggest that the symbolism was of prime importance to Pictish society and culture. Their presence on later Christian monuments not only provides further evidence of their importance but also underlines the likelihood that they must have had a continued fundamental role in Pictish society, one that even the introduction of Christianity and increasing cultural pressures from outside could not apparently undermine. Understanding at least some

1. Aberlemno 1. Example of a Class I Stone (snake and double disc with z-rod symbols). Aberlemno, Angus. (© Iain Forbes)

2. Aberlemno 2. Example of a Class II Stone. Aberlemno, Angus. (© Iain Forbes)

of the underlying ideas behind these symbols would therefore be vital in understanding something more of these long-vanished people and their ancient culture.

The radical theory presented here is that the symbols are actually astrological in nature and relate to specific astronomical events in the night sky. In the context of specific monuments, a symbol pair therefore might be a graphic representation of a specific auspicious alignment of the Sun, Moon, or planets, and effectively proclaiming a divine blessing on whatever endeavour or event was marked by the stone. Therefore it is hoped that, for the first time, the Picts will be revealed as sophisticated astronomers and astrologers, once and for all removing the label of 'barbarian' that has so often preceded their name. Furthermore, there may be the possibility that these potentially sacred symbols were the work of those mysterious shadowy figures and known astrologers, the ancient druids, thus providing a cultural link to wider Celtic beliefs and culture. A further radical theory will also be put forward: this Pictish astrological system was not created in isolation in Scotland, but rather represents the last vestiges of a form of astrology once widespread across Eurasia.

By attempting to understand the Pictish symbols, as well as addressing one of Europe's great archaeological mysteries, we will hopefully increase our knowledge and understanding of the Picts, and so help determine the cultural relationships they had with their Celtic neighbours. The evidence presented here suggests that the Picts themselves were not only a Celtic people but will hopefully also convince the reader that, far from being an isolated, backward culture, the Picts were very much part of a mainstream European tradition and as capable of astounding achievements as their contemporaries throughout the continent. The possibility that they utilised an ancient and once widespread astrological system would also support the notion that the Picts retained key parts of a seemingly sophisticated culture that was once found across Europe and beyond. If we can demonstrate that this premise is correct or at least plausible, then we will not only be able to begin to revise our whole attitude towards the Picts, but we will also have the possibility of revolutionising our understanding of the cultural influences of the peoples of Eurasia.

From our position in the so-called 'Celtic Twilight' we can perhaps, through a greater understanding of the Picts, shine some light on key questions about the relationship between seemingly disparate ancient peoples across continents, but also catch a glimpse of what the Celtic world was like when its 'Sun' was still high in the sky.

CHAPTER 1

PICTISH ORIGINS

The Indo-Europeans

If we are to try to understand who the Picts were, and attempt to place them in a European context, then it would be helpful to have some understanding of the relationships between the various peoples of Europe; their origins, cultures and languages. If we set aside the various controversial and often contradictory genetic studies that aim to plot human migratory patterns, and instead concentrate on language and culture, the most significant advance in understanding these relationships is the realisation that the languages of the vast majority of Europeans share a common origin. Almost all the languages of Europe are actually related, descending from perhaps just one common language, or at least a group of closely related languages. Furthermore, these related modern languages also include others from well beyond Europe's boundaries; from western Asia and northern India. The geographical distribution of these languages has given rise to the term coined by linguists to describe this family of related tongues, 'Indo-European'.

Indo-European can be subdivided into a number of distinct language groups familiar to us all, including, for example, Germanic, Romance, Slavic, Greek, Persian and North Indian languages, and Celtic. It also includes 'extinct' languages such as Hittite and Lepontic. While it is not universally accepted that the Picts spoke an Indo-European language, most linguists not only believe that their language was essentially Indo-European in origin, but that it was part of the Celtic language group, which today includes Irish, Scots Gaelic, Manx, Welsh, Cornish and Breton.

A common origin for so many European and western Asian and Indian languages might suggest there was also originally a wider ancestral Indo-European culture. For example, Celtic, Roman, Greek, and Hindu mythologies exhibit some parallels that might hint at a common origin. Is it possible that various aspects of the social structures, religious beliefs and other fundamental components of society found in different Indo-European cultures can also be traced back in time to a similar common origin? Is it also possible that these seemingly disparate cultural groups, as well as sharing a common linguistic origin, share at least some common ancestry? If this were the case we may be able to hypothesise the existence of an ancestral Indo-European people, as suggested by linguists, migrating from an ancestral home to all the areas where Indo-European languages became established, bringing with them not just language but their culture.

A combination of place-name evidence and the probability that the Picts differed little culturally from the ancient Britons tends to suggest that the Picts may also have spoken an Indo-European language, probably part of the Celtic language group, and most likely related to ancient British, which is itself the ancestor of modern Welsh. Other less convincing theories suggest that Pictish was more akin to another Celtic language, Irish, or even that Pictish was non-Indo-European. If we accept the mainstream view that Pictish was closer to ancient British, and therefore a so-called Brythonic Celtic language, then perhaps we should look at the cultural development and spread of the Celtic branch of the Indo-European family.

The Celts

Prehistory

Around 900 BC, following a period of social upheaval across Europe and the Middle East, a new society emerged in Europe. This culture is referred to by archaeologists as 'Urnfield'. The Urnfield culture was concentrated in central Europe, and is distinguished from the earlier 'Tumulus' culture by a number of key innovations. These include the practice of cremating their dead and placing the remains in urns; a custom that distinguishes their culture from that of their predecessors (hence 'Urnfield'). They also had a strong military focus, producing sophisticated weaponry and building hill forts and similar defences. By about 700 BC iron was beginning to replace the softer metal bronze within the Urnfield area, and this transition from bronze to iron marks the beginning of the Iron Age in central Europe. In the salt mines at Hallstatt in Austria a substantial number of finds from the late Bronze Age and early Iron Age periods were discovered in the mid-nineteenth century. The Bronze Age finds, dating from 1200 BC onwards, are today classified as Hallstatt A and Hallstatt B. However, iron objects were also discovered at the same location which, though later in origin, shows some artistic continuity with finds from the earlier Bronze Age. These finds are referred to as Hallstatt C and Hallstatt D, with Hallstatt C corresponding to a period from about 800 BC to 600 BC and Hallstatt D from 600 BC to 500 BC. The Hallstatt C period was marked not only by an increase in hill fortifications, but also by the appearance of a larger number of burials. These developments reflect an increase in prosperity, and also signal the rise of the elite nobility. It is this period in time, and specifically in relation to Hallstatt, that archaeologists start to use the label 'Celtic'. Graves from this period not only contained numerous items relating to horses but also funerary wagons on which the remains of the dead were laid. These items represent a key element in Celtic society and may relate to the migration of people from the east, who brought with them horsemanship skills.

Other influences were reaching these early Celtic peoples via trade routes from the Mediterranean, notably through the Greek colony at Marseilles (*Massalia*) and northwards up the rivers of southern France. These enabled a flow of sophisticated metal objects, ideas, and other goods such as pottery and wine. This development seems to have been important to the flourishing of an indigenous culture that was able not only to adopt these Mediterranean influences, but crucially to *adapt* them to their own needs. Celtic artisans took Greek art forms and developed these into the so-called Hallstatt style.

By about 500 BC Hallstatt culture was on the decline, perhaps as a result of shifting trading patterns, and new influences began spreading into the Celtic world. These influences included the importation of pottery, metal objects, wine, and other goods from the Etruscans and the Greeks via Alpine routes. It would seem that the Celts valued these objects very highly and not only copied designs and motifs from these sources, as was evident in earlier periods, but adapted them and developed their own distinctive and often complex style. This period of time and the associated Celtic culture is referred to as La Tene, after a site on Lake Neuchatel in Switzerland. After the lake was partially drained in the late nineteenth century, a large number of Iron Age objects, including swords and scabbards, were found. The Iron Age objects appeared to be deposited deliberately in the lake, and are stylistically different from Hallstatt objects, taking the form of what many people today would recognise as typically 'Celtic'. Early La Tene culture, with its Mediterranean influences and its own innovations, was developed in central Europe, notably in the Rhine–Moselle area, but also further east as far as Bohemia. By 200 BC La Tene culture had spread further westwards and eastwards, taking in the whole of modern France, Belgium, the Danube basin, and eventually also Britain, Ireland, the Netherlands, large tracts of Spain, and even northern Italy. The latest phase of the La Tene culture, La Tene III, was eventually extinguished in Gaul following the Roman invasion and similarly in southern Britain in the first century AD. However, La Tene survived in Scotland and Ireland well into the middle of the first millennium AD, and its influence is found in illuminated manuscripts such as the *Book of Kells*, in jewellery and other artefacts and also, crucially for our study, on Pictish monuments.

The Celts in History

The earliest mention of the Celts in written records is in tantalising snippets by predominately Greek writers. Between the eighth and fifth centuries BC, writers, including Homer, refer to *Hyperboreans* and *Cimmerians* far to the north and west of Greece. These tribal names are taken by some to be synonymous with the Celts. The Greeks are extremely vague about the location of these 'Celts', although Western Europe seems to be the likeliest candidate, including modern-day France and parts of the Iberian Peninsula. There are a number of references to Celts in France, perhaps in the Rhone valley or further north, and locating the Celts in this area may relate to the presence of the Greek colony of *Massalia* with its trading links with tribes to the north. By the fifth century BC onwards the Greeks refer directly to the *Keltoi* (or alternatively as *Galatae*) and begin to comment on their 'wild' character. In around 475 BC the classical world itself became directly affected by these Celts, when Celtic tribes crossed the Alps into northern Italy, defeating the Etruscans and settling around the Po valley. The name of one of these Celtic tribes, the *Venetti*, still survives in the name of the city of Venice. The Celts succeeded in pushing the Etruscans and their Roman allies southwards, and established themselves in Tuscany; by 390 BC they had sacked Rome. The fifth century therefore seems to have been marked by remarkable Celtic expansion from their northern European homeland into southern Europe.

The following centuries saw continued expansion; this time into the Balkans and even further afield. By 279 BC Celts had attacked and defeated the Macedonians, had conquered Thrace and attacked Greece, plundering the holy site of Delphi in the process. Celts also around the same time crossed over to Asia Minor and founded Galatia, literally 'the land of the Celts'. Here they became significant players in Asia Minor, consolidating their new territory by defeating the Syrians at the battle of Ephesus. Galatia survived more or less intact until the first century BC before becoming overwhelmed by Rome and its allies. Their name today is preserved in St Paul's *Letter to the Galatians*. This clash between an expanding Rome and the Celtic tribes was to be mirrored elsewhere in Europe with Celtic expansion and domination of large tracts of Europe largely ceasing with the emergence and expansion of the Roman Empire.

In 59 BC, the Romans, under Julius Caesar, invaded Celtic Gaul. By 52 BC Caesar had defeated a united Gaulish force under their leader Vercingetorix at the battle of Alesia, Gaul then becoming a Roman province. Ironically, it is through Julius Caesar's own account of his campaign, *The Gallic Wars*, that we gain much of our knowledge of Celtic society. We are also introduced by Julius Caesar to the druids and their role in everyday life in Gaul. He describes their esteemed place within society, their interest in worship, divination, astronomy, the law, and the arts. Crucially he also draws attention to the druidical links between the Celts of Gaul and of Britain, suggesting that some trainee druids travelled to Britain for their education.

Celts in the British Isles

There is no doubt that Britain and Ireland in the past maintained a number of distinct Celtic-speaking populations. At the time of the Roman conquest of Britain in AD 43, under the emperor Claudius, the population of southern Britain spoke an early form of Welsh (p-Celtic), and appear to have had links to Gaulish tribes. For example, a leader of the *Atrebates* in Gaul, Commius, may also have ruled the *Atrebates* in southern Britain. Other tribal names and links have also been postulated between southern and eastern Britain and the continent at the time of the Roman invasion, including the *Belgae* and the *Catuvellauni*. In the case of the *Belgae*, Caesar specifically mentions their migration to Britain. It is therefore perfectly feasible that other tribal groupings also had strong connections to Celts on the continent; at the very least these may have taken the form of traditional trading links with the possibility of considerable cultural exchange. Other significant tribes in Britain south of the rivers Tyne and Solway included the *Brigantes* in what is now north-west England, the *Parisi* in what is today Yorkshire, the *Iceni* in East Anglia, and the *Trinovantes* who occupied today's Essex. Modern-day Wales was occupied by tribal groups including the *Silures* in the south, the *Demetae* in the south-west, and the *Ordovices* in Gwynedd. North of the Tyne–Solway line, in southern Scotland at the same time, p-Celtic-speaking tribes included the *Selgovae*, the *Votadini*, and the *Dumnonii*.

Both Hallstatt and the later La Tène-influenced art forms were present in pre-Roman Britain, and indeed an insular form of La Tène-influenced art was developed and produced in Britain. Similarly, the large hill fortifications associated with the continental Celts were present, but also show some continuity with the Bronze Age. It is likely that society was organised in a similar way to that of the Celtic-speaking tribes of the continent, dominated by an aristocratic warrior elite, and equally importantly by the druids. The druids not only provided religious guidance, but acted as judges, as astrologers/astronomers, as diviners, had the power to stop warfare, provided advice to the king, carried out animal and human sacrifices and were healers. However, we must exercise a little caution in the use of the word 'druid', as it is not entirely clear how this term was used. Some classical writers referred to druids in an apparently general sense, while others specifically mention three classes of priests in the Celtic world that included *druids* (who specialised in natural and moral philosophy), *vates* (who were soothsayers or prophets), and *bards* (whose main role was that of poet). In this book, to avoid confusion, we will use the more general term 'druid' when referring to the Celtic priestly caste. Druidic training was probably intellectually arduous and required great feats of memory. Roman writers suggested that it could take twenty years for a druid novice to become fully fledged. During this time enormous amounts of knowledge, such as the names of hundreds of stars, of plants and their healing properties, of tribal law and other subjects, would be committed to memory. It is also probable, with their astronomical knowledge, that they calibrated the calendar and decided when important events were to take place based on whether or not a particular day, according to the stars, was auspicious or inauspicious. Although integral to the workings of the tribal society, they apparently transcended tribal boundaries and were able to move freely. The principal centre for druidic learning, not only in Britain but for Gaul as well at the time of Caesar, may have been the Isle of Anglesey. Sacred places were referred to as *nemeton*, and included groves, springs, sites on lakes and rivers, and perhaps also more formal temples. Evidence for modern and ancient place names containing the Celtic word *nemeton* are found in a variety of locations all over 'Celtic' Europe, including Pictland.

In Ireland, there is also some continuity between the Bronze Age and the Iron Age, and, unlike Britain, it would appear that significant Hallstatt artistic influences did not reach the island. However, it is clear that La Tene-influenced art had reached Ireland by about 200 BC. The main flowering of this art form, however, did not occur until the second half of the first millennium, but there is little doubt that through the patronage of the Celtic Church, Irish La Tene-influenced artefacts comprise some of the finest examples of Celtic art found anywhere. The relatively late introduction of Celtic art to Ireland produces something of a conundrum; does this also imply that other aspects of Celtic society, including language, were also latecomers to Ireland? It is probable however that the forerunner of the Irish Gaelic language was already present in Ireland prior to the introduction of La Tene art, and possibly even in the Bronze Age, and it is also worth remembering that some Irish mythological stories contain material which, while undeniably Celtic, also harkens back to Bronze Age society. This evidence underlines the possibility that Celtic society and culture is not necessarily easily defined by specific archaeological artefacts alone, and the absence of Hallstatt art need not imply that other elements of a Celtic cultural 'package' were also absent.

Society was organised along similar lines to that of Celtic Britain, with a warrior elite and a druidic order that commanded enormous respect. Glimpses of this society are visible through the mythological tales that have survived; tales such as those in the Ulster Cycle that evoke a time of heroes, the supernatural and the divine.

Furthermore, Irish law, which survived until the Middle Ages, appears to have been based on an ancient law code steeped in Celtic tradition and society. Druids played, as in Britain and Gaul, a prominent role in Ireland, acting as advisors to kings and even to Christian missionaries such as St Columba. In later Irish and Scottish Highland society, the role of the druid within a Christian context became less relevant, but key druidical activities were continued by particular specialists within these societies. These specialists practised the bardic tradition, the law, played a role in deciding royal succession, and memorised the ancestry of the tribal, or clan, leader. In modern-day Scotland, with its historical and cultural links to Ireland, it has been suggested that the ancient role of the druid in determining claims to clan leadership continues under the guise of the Lord Lyon.

The Picts

Origins

Who were the Picts? This particular question, and variations on it, have been asked many times over the last 150 years or so and it encapsulates how little is known about this 'enigmatic' people. Among scholars there seems to have been little consensus on the origins of the Picts and their linguistic, ethnic and cultural relationship to other European nations, including their nearest neighbours in the British Isles. Were they Celtic, Scandinavian or Germanic, or were they culturally unique, perhaps even the descendants of a much earlier colonisation of the British Isles? Is the answer more complex than that, with many influences contributing to the make-up of the Picts? These questions are at the centre of a debate that has been raging among linguists, archaeologists and historians since the nineteenth century. This lack of agreement on Pictish origins has provided fertile ground for many an academic and amateur alike, and is perhaps one of the most attractive features of Pictish study. Opinions on the origin of the Picts have varied considerably over the centuries, with mythological stories gradually giving way to more careful consideration of the limited evidence. The mythological origin stories are still taken seriously in some quarters even today, with some authors considering that there may be some elements within them that might throw some light on the subject. This may be true, but separating grains of truth from the mythological pile is certainly a daunting task.

The *Pictish Chronicle*, written in Latin, is the nearest we have to a native historical document concerning the origin of the Picts, and lists 'historical' events and characters. The *Pictish Chronicle* actually occurs in a number of different versions, which all vary to some extent from each other. The surviving manuscripts are copies of earlier documents that derive from the tenth and eleventh centuries. In these documents we find an extensive royal list reaching back from known historical figures from the tenth century to what would seem to be Pictish mythological figures, then through biblical figures back eventually to Noah. An origin legend from another early source, the *King List*, describes a story of seven brothers, the sons of a king of the *Cruithne* (the Irish word for a Pict), who each ruled over the seven kingdoms of the Picts. According to the legend, each brother gave their name to their respective kingdom. In other legends from other sources the Picts are portrayed as settling in Scotland after first emigrating from much further afield. Suggestions for this ancient homeland include the territories of Thrace and Scythia. In these accounts, the Picts first of all arrive in Ireland, but are encouraged to settle in Scotland after being given Irish wives by an Irish king. Within these legends lie the seeds of the notion that royal succession in Pictland came via the female line, so-called matrilineal succession. According to this legend the Picts were made to swear on the Sun and the Moon that they would allow such a form of succession. We should view this with caution, as such a story may be have been used as propaganda by the Scottish kings of Dalriada to lay claim to the Pictish throne using Scots/Irish female bloodlines within the Pictish royal genealogies. Pictish matrilineal succession was also suggested by the Venerable Bede, who came from neighbouring Northumbria. Bede as a contemporary of the Picts may have been indicating a genuine feature of their culture, although it is not clear if this was the 'norm' in Pictish succession or an unusual adjunct in certain circumstances.

Towards the end of the nineteenth century the Earl of Southesk, studying Nordic and Pictish carvings, proposed that the symbols were Scandinavian in origin, and by extension that the Picts themselves were of Scandinavian origin, or at least from the same stock. This notion today is not taken seriously, but nonetheless the earl's studies helped generate an increased interest in Pictish origins.

In the twentieth century other writers have proposed even more exotic theories in regard to the origin of the Picts, in particular the suggestion that they were a non-Indo-European people, and of course they can point to other languages, in Europe today, that are non-Indo-European, including Basque, Hungarian, Estonian, and Finnish. The non-Indo-European theory remains popular, based partly on the premise that the Picts were descended from early settlers to Britain, settling prior to the spread of the Indo-European language group. This theory also relies on observations that some tribal names located in Scotland on a Roman map of Britain, attributed to Ptolemy of Alexandria, have been interpreted as having a distinctly non-Indo-European flavour to them. However, we should exercise caution when interpreting place names from this map. Firstly there may have been basic scribal errors produced during the process of making copies of the map. Secondly the place names and tribal names could have gone through a number of changes as a result of being translated or transmuted from Pictish to Latin to Ptolemy's own native Greek, then altered once again to conform to a medieval form of the Latin alphabet. We also do not know for sure if the names listed by Ptolemy bear any resemblance to the names used by the Picts, or rather reflect non-Pictish nicknames or even attempts at translation. Today this is the equivalent of English speakers referring to citizens of Germany as Germans, even though this is not how they refer to themselves. We should be therefore extremely sceptical about claims that tribal names such as *Taezali* constitute real evidence of non-Indo-European speech.

However, the most commonly espoused theory on their origins is that they were essentially a Celtic people, speaking a distinct Celtic tongue that differed both from that spoken by their Celtic contemporaries in southern Britain and in Ireland. We know for example that the Irish monk St Columba, when he was evangelising the Picts, needed an interpreter. Similarly they were also seen very much as a separate entity by their Welsh-speaking neighbours.

Place-name evidence has not been particularly helpful in resolving this debate, at least until recently, as the apparent later domination of Pictland by Gaelic has all but obscured pre-Gaelic native words that could be used to reveal Pictish linguistic origins. However, there are place names that resemble Welsh place names, as well as some that seem to have elements that do not at first glance relate directly to either Welsh or Gaelic. For example, the city of Aberdeen, in the heart of what was 'Pictland', has the prefix 'aber', a Celtic root word meaning 'mouth', and used to describe a river mouth. So does this name have a Pictish origin? Unfortunately, while the word could be Pictish, it could also be Welsh (consider Aberystwyth, and other examples in Wales). This sort of problem arises many times with different place-name equivalents found within Pictland, leaving very few components of place names that could not be confused with Welsh or Gaelic. An example that has long been cited as uniquely Pictish is the very common prefix 'Pit', found across a large swathe of Pictland but apparently nowhere else in the British Isles. The word, often followed up by a Gaelic-derived element within the place name, could mean something equivalent to 'land of'. Use of this prefix often seems to coincide with important sites within agricultural areas, perhaps roughly equating to the modern concept of a mains farm, with satellite small farm holdings clustered around. The prefix 'Pit' also seems to have been interchangeable with the Gaelic prefix 'Bal', suggesting that both terms, for a while at least, were understood perhaps by a bilingual population. Examples of 'Pit' place names are numerous and include Pitlochry, Pittenweem, and Pittodrie.

The notion that 'Pit' is uniquely Pictish is not universally held. Prof. W. F. H. Nicolaisen, in his book *Scottish Place-Names*, discusses the possible origins of the word 'Pit' and its theoretical relationship to similar words in the other Celtic languages. He hypothesises that 'Pit' or rather 'Pett' (the form found in the *Book of Deer* written around the twelfth century) is related to both a Welsh and Cornish word *Peth* meaning 'thing' and the Breton word *Pez* referring to a 'piece'. Furthermore, he sets out the connection between these Celtic words and the Low Latin word *Petia*, which apparently meant a 'piece of land', and is probably in itself a Latinised version of a Gaulish word cognate with the Welsh *Peth*. This Low Latin form developed into the French word *pièce*, and hence the English word 'piece'. If his theory is correct, then the prefix 'Pit' would mean something along the lines of 'the piece [of land] of' and would indicate a strongly Celtic word utilised as a place-name element (almost) uniquely in Pictland. According to Nicolaisen, the Gaulish equivalent of 'Pit' or 'Pett' has also survived in French place names such as *Poitou* and *Poitiers*. These were long thought to be derived from the name of the *Pictavi* or *Pictones* tribe, names that (in a rather neat circle) gave rise to early chroniclers claiming a direct link between the *Pictavi* of Gaul and the Picts of Scotland.

As if the linguistic origins are not complicated and contentious enough, a further possibility exists; when Celtic arrived in Pictland, there was an already established (non-Celtic) Indo-European language spoken there. This theory is also expounded by Professor Nicolaisen, who believes that, as well as a number of clearly Celtic names, there are also non-Celtic names in Pictland that he claims are nonetheless undeniably Indo-European.

Place-name evidence therefore may indicate three possibilities. Firstly, there is possible evidence of non-Indo-European speech in the territory of 'Pictland' in the past. Secondly, there may be indications of a non-Celtic Indo-European influence on place names within Pictland. Thirdly there is evidence of Celtic place-name elements in Pictland, which can be differentiated from the influence of Gaelic.

The first and second points above do not necessarily imply that the Pictish language contained any significant non-Indo-European influences, or indeed any non-Celtic Indo-European influences, but the best we can say is that older place names certainly survived into the Pictish period. Such survival should not surprise us, as there are numerous examples around the world where people live in towns or cities bearing names from languages long forgotten by their residents. In England, large numbers of modern place names have linguistic origins in periods of time prior to the arrival of English. Should we really expect English to be peppered with Welsh words simply because many English place names have Welsh elements? Just because Londoners call their city 'London', a name probably of Celtic origin and subsequently Latinised, does not imply that Londoners understand either Welsh or Latin. However, the use of 'Pit' as a prefix, which was apparently interchangeable with the Gaelic prefix 'Bal', seems to suggest that the meaning of this unusual Celtic element was understood possibly even beyond the Pictish period.

So where does all of this leave us? The rather scant linguistic evidence would seem to suggest that the Picts in the historical 'Pictland', of the later half of the first millennium, spoke a Celtic language (although possibly with older non-Celtic elements). This language was, on balance, probably more closely related to Welsh and Gaulish rather than Gaelic or Irish. We cannot, however, rule out the possibility that 'Picts' in other areas, for example in the west Highlands, and at an earlier period in history spoke a different language or languages. This, for example, may have taken the form of Celtic more closely related to Irish, or perhaps languages influenced more by non-Celtic speech.

The Picts in a Historical Context

The Picts during the Roman occupation of Britain resided in the territory to the north of the Forth–Clyde valley, including the Northern Isles and the Hebrides. There is some evidence that at an earlier stage people also referred to as 'Picts' occupied territory in southern Scotland, and may have held pockets of south-west Scotland beyond the Roman period: the so-called 'Picts of Galloway'. Similarly, there are Irish records that may describe Picts in Ireland, apparently in County Antrim, although the evidence is far from conclusive. What relationship these two possible outlying 'Pictish' populations have to the Picts in 'Pictland' proper is not known, nor is it known whether they shared customs or language.

The most important tribes that later became known as 'Picts' were the Caledonians (hence the Latin name for Scotland: Caledonia) and the *Maeatae*. The *Maeatae* probably occupied the territory immediately to the north of the Forth–Clyde valley, and their name is perhaps preserved in the place names: Dunmyat (hill or fort of the *Maeatae*) and Myothill. The Caledonians occupied the southern Highlands. Their name may be preserved in the cathedral city of Dunkeld (the hill or fort of the Caledonians).

Other tribal names have been elucidated from Ptolemy of Alexandria's map of the British Isles, first drafted around AD 150. These include the *Cornavii* in Caithness, the *Smertae* in Sutherland, the *Lugi* in Rosshire, the *Taezali* in Aberdeenshire, the *Venicones* in Fife and Angus, the *Vacomagi* around the Moray Firth, the *Caerini* and the *Creones* on the west coast, and finally the *Epidii* in Kintyre.

During the Roman period, militarily, the Picts seemed to have caused the Romans considerable problems, forcing them to build two massive coast-to-coast defensive structures across northern Britain. These were Hadrian's Wall, stretching from Cumbria to Newcastle-upon-Tyne, and the lesser-known Antonine Wall, from the village of Bowling on the River Clyde to somewhere around Bo'ness on the River Forth. While both Hadrian's Wall, and the more northerly Antonine Wall, have more recently been regarded by academics as barriers used to control the flow of goods into and out of the empire, there is little doubt these massive structures at times must have served a vital military role. We also know of Roman triumphs over these Caledonians, notably the battle of *Mons Graupius* (more probably *Mons Grampius*) that took place around AD 84, probably in the north-east of Scotland, and as we have seen and according to Tacitus, famously featured the stirring 'speech' of Pictish leader Calgacus prior to the battle. Emperor Septimus Severus's campaign in AD 208 appears to have been something of a disaster for the Romans; while his armies reached far into Pictland, they were unable to engage the enemy in open battle. Instead they were continuously hit by guerrilla raids and seemed to have suffered enormously.

The native population in the Roman period south of Hadrian's Wall consisted of a Romanised Celtic people, who probably spoke Latin in urbanised areas, as well as an early form of Welsh. This population towards the end of the empire would probably be better described as 'Romano-Celtic', thus reflecting the population's Romanisation, at least in the towns. When the legions finally pulled out of southern Britain, a military vacuum appeared, and the region was left vulnerable to attack from a variety of directions, including from Ireland (the raiders being known as the *Scotti* or Scots), Pictland, and from 'barbarian' Germanic tribes on the continent. Internally, Celtic kingdoms began to re-establish themselves, and according to the sixth-century monk Gildas (who may have been from southern Scotland originally) some of these newly established kings turned their backs on the Church, Christianity being well established among the Celts of Roman Britain centuries before St Augustine brought Christianity to the English.

The English as a people emerged following the Roman Empire's demise, and have their cultural roots, including the English language, in Germanic tribes that gained a foothold on the east coast of southern Britain. The English tribes, according to early historical sources, were apparently allowed to settle in Britain at the invitation of the Romano-Celtic leadership of Britain. If these sources are to be trusted, the tribes' intended role was to act as mercenaries in an attempt to defend the vulnerable former Roman province from the Scots and the Picts; however, it appears they soon turned on their hosts. These Germanic tribes were the Angles (hence the terms 'English' and 'Anglo'), the Saxons (a name that gives rise to the Scots Gaelic word sometimes used in Scotland to describe an Englishman, *Sassanach*, literally 'Saxon man'), and the Jutes. What followed is the subject of continuing controversy, but according to Gildas, who was speaking as a Christian Romano-Celt, and who would not look favourably on the pagan Germanic incomers, the English 'takeover' of what is now eastern England was extremely bloody. He describes the surviving native population as fleeing for their lives. Graphically, he paints a gruesome picture of the demise of the Roman towns and their citizens and buildings at the hands of the pagan invaders. What he describes, if he is to be believed, would amount to an attempt at the very least to terrorise the native population, but may have been more akin to 'ethnic cleansing'. Of course it could be argued that Gildas overstated the impact of the Anglo-Saxon invasion on the population, and that the 'takeover' was far less brutal than suggested by Gildas. It may be that pockets of the native population survived in eastern England, gradually absorbed into the new Germanic society, but there is no doubt that previously thriving towns were abandoned and, perhaps most significantly to Gildas, Christianity was abandoned and replaced with pagan Germanic religious practices. Likewise, Latin and Welsh were replaced by the Germanic 'Old English' that absorbed surprisingly few native Celtic words (surprisingly if you accept the view of a more peaceful Anglo-Saxon invasion theory).

These three Germanic tribes, according to early sources, originated from the coastal regions of the European continent, directly opposite what today is eastern England, stretching from Jutland in Denmark to northern Holland. The Angles settled in East Anglia (hence the name), and expanded into the East Midlands (Mercia), Lincolnshire (Lindsey), Yorkshire (Deira), and the North East of England (Bernicia, later Northumbria). The Saxons settled in a large tract of the South East of England: Essex (East Saxons), Middlesex (Middle Saxons), and Sussex (South Saxons), later expanding into the West of England (Wessex – West Saxons). The Jutes' settlement appears to have been confined to Kent (known as Cantware, hence the name of the town of Canterbury). The pattern of settlement described, and the overly neat origins of these tribes may of course may be a gross simplification, so a certain amount of caution needs to be exercised; there may for example have been a significant contingent from parts of Scandinavia.

Gildas, writing his *Ruin of Britain* in around AD 540, dramatically describes the appalling state that the former Roman province found itself in following the withdrawal of Roman forces. As well as describing the apparent brutality of the Anglo-Saxons, he also describes the two other 'enemies' of the Romano-Celtic population, the Scots and the Picts, and provides an explanation as to why the Anglo-Saxon invasion took place: 'Quite ignorant of the ways of war, she [Britain] groaned aghast for many years, trodden under foot first by two exceedingly savage overseas nations, the Scots from the north-west and the Picts from the north.' According to Gildas, the solution to this assault on southern Britain decided by the governing council was that 'the ferocious Saxons (name not to be spoken!), hated by man and god, should be let into the island like wolves into the fold, to beat back the peoples of the north'. Once the English tribes had become established, they now turned on their hosts.

All the major towns were laid low by the repeated battering of enemy rams; laid low, too, were all the inhabitants – church leaders, priests and people alike, as the swords glinted all around and the flames crackled. It was a sad sight. In the middle of the squares the foundation stones of high walls and towers that had been torn from their lofty base, holy altars and fragments of corpses – covered (as it were) with a purple crust of congealed blood – looked as though they had been mixed up in some dreadful wine press.

Gildas goes on to describe how the survivors who escaped from the massacre fled into the mountains, only to be hunted down and slaughtered. Others became slaves, and the many set sail to Brittany, taking with them their native Celtic tongue.

While southern Britain underwent dramatic change during the post-Roman period, the north and the west of Britain experienced raids and the establishment of settlements by the Scots. These raiders probably originated in Ireland, and settled in the west of Scotland and north Wales. While their grip on Gwynedd in Wales was eventually lost, they managed to carve out territory in Argyll and incorporated this into the Irish kingdom of Dalriada, perhaps displacing native Picts in this region. This small kingdom in Argyll, founded by Scots, would later become a key component in the unified kingdom of Alba, known more commonly today as Scotland.

In the post-Roman period, between the two Roman walls, and until their unification with the Scottish kingdom, were a number of Welsh-speaking Celtic kingdoms, including Strathclyde (*Alclut*), *Rheged* (including some territory south of Hadrian's Wall after the Roman pull-out), and *Manau gododdin*, centred round Edinburgh (*Dunedin*).

Further north, beyond the Antonine Wall during this same period of time, a number of Pictish kingdoms emerged, no longer dominating the whole of the mainland north of the Forth–Clyde isthmus. These kingdoms lay in the eastern half of Scotland above the Firth of Forth. In the far north, and including the Northern Isles, was the kingdom of *Cat*, later giving rise to the name of the county of Caithness (the 'ness' or promontory of *Cat*), while the area around Inverness may have formed the kingdom of *Fidach*. Aberdeenshire roughly corresponds to the kingdom of *Ce*. South of *Fidach* and *Ce* lay the kingdom of *Circind*, which was further divided into the kingdoms of *Fotla* (Atholl), *Fib* (Fife, today still referred to as 'the Kingdom of Fife'), and the final portion corresponding to the county of Angus retaining the name *Circind*. The location of the final kingdom, *Fortriu*, is still debated and could either have been in southern Perthshire and parts of Stirlingshire or around Forres in Moray in the north.

By the sixth century the Picts were evidently divided into two large kingdoms: the Northern Picts (located in Aberdeenshire northwards) and the Southern Picts (located in Angus, Perthshire, and Fife). According to Bede, the southern kingdom was converted to Christianity by St Ninian in the fifth century. In the mid-sixth century, St Columba's mission from his monastery on Iona to the Northern Picts brought Christianity to that portion of Pictland.

A number of Pictish kings are recorded in various historical documents that relate to events from the mid-sixth century onwards. Perhaps the best known king is Brude Mac Maelcon, who ruled Pictland from about AD 550 until about AD 585. He is best remembered as the king that St Columba visited on his mission to bring Christianity to the Northern Picts. This event is recounted in *The Life of St Columba* written by St Adamnan, the ninth Abbot of Iona. The site of Brude's palace is not known, but was in the vicinity of the modern city of Inverness and must have been relatively accessible from the island of Iona by boat and foot. St Columba and his companions would have travelled partly by boat, up the Great Glen from Loch Linnhe and then on foot, or by boat, through the series of freshwater lochs culminating in Loch Ness. At the River Ness, St Columba is reported to have banished a water monster, not only demonstrating the power of the Christian god, but perhaps setting in train the myth of the Loch Ness monster. Brude was obviously not entirely impressed and stayed within his locked fortress as Columba approached; St Columba, however, performed a miracle by bursting open the doors of the fortress, this time greatly impressing Brude. The real struggle for the hearts and minds of the Picts began when St Columba took on Brude's druid, Broichan. St Columba saved an ailing Broichan's life by getting the druid to drink water containing a white pebble. White pebbles seemed to have magic healing properties in Celtic Britain and Ireland and have, for example, been found in excavations at Flag Fen in East Anglia, where they had apparently been dropped into water along with other 'offerings'. Later, the two clerics tried to better each other by controlling the weather on Loch Ness. The result of these contests in favour of St Columba was enough to convince King Brude to convert to Christianity. However, this should not be viewed simplistically as a battle between Christianity and druidry, as strangely enough St Columba had his own personal druid.

The seventh century was a period of considerable turmoil for the Picts, with conflict between the four main powers in northern Britain: the Picts, the Scots, the Strathclyde Britons, and the Anglian Northumbrians. By the end of the sixth century, the small Welsh kingdom of *Manau gododdin* based in south-east Scotland, with its likely power base at Edinburgh Castle, had succumbed to Northumbrian conquest, most likely following the battle of *Catraeth*. This event would have led to the expanding Northumbrian Kingdom coming into direct contact with Pictland and Strathclyde.

Although this period saw great enmity between these four peoples, surprisingly it was also a period of intermarriage between their royal houses, presumably as a result of the desire to cement treaties and the resultant short periods of peace. In addition, the influence of the monastery of Iona and its missionaries had by the sixth century brought its own brand of Celtic Christianity to the Scots, Picts and Northumbrians, and had considerable influence through its satellite monastic settlements, including that of Lindisfarne in Northumbria. By around AD 640, the Northumbrians had conquered at least some of southern Pictland, and had even set up a monastic site on the shores of the River Forth at Abercorn under Bishop Trumwine. However, in AD 663 the Celtic Church lost much of its independence at the Synod of Whitby, falling into line with the rest of the Roman Church over key issues, including the manner in which monks wore their hair (tonsure), but more importantly the dating of Easter. Prior to the Synod, Christians, depending on whether they followed the Celtic Church or the mainstream Roman Church, celebrated Easter at different times. This appears to have been a particularly troublesome matter for the Northumbrian court, which had royal connections to the other English kingdoms that followed Roman practice.

In the year 685 the Picts, under the leadership of Brude Mac Bili, moved against the occupying Northumbrians. Following a number of skirmishes with the Northumbrian army under King Ecgfrid further to the south, on 20 May the Anglian army was lured into Angus, where they confronted King Brude's army at *Dunnichen* (known to the English as *Nechtansmere*). The Northumbrian army was thoroughly routed and King

Ecgfrith was killed, thereby removing Northumbrian influence from Pictland. Further success followed in 697 when yet another Brude (Brude Mac Derile) defeated the Northumbrians in the Lothians. Brude's brother and successor Nechton Mac Derile embraced fully the Roman Church in AD 710 and expelled the Ionian monks who had continued to practise the Celtic Church's form of Christianity despite the Synod of Whitby. This move probably marks the deteriorating relationship between the Scottish kingdom of Dalriada and Pictland, culminating in the conquest of Dalriada by the Pictish King Oengus in the 740s. This particular king, allied to the Northumbrians, also attempted to crush Strathclyde but was heavily defeated. Dalriada re-established its independence from the Picts around AD 770.

The ninth century saw concerted attacks by the Vikings against all of the major kingdoms in northern Britain, including that of Pictland. The Northern Isles fell under Norse control and at least part of the mainland portion of *Cat* also succumbed. During this period of great turmoil there emerged a new leader in Dalriada, Kenneth MacAlpine. His father was undoubtedly a Scot of noble birth, but significantly his mother was Pictish. It is this latter fact that has led to the suggestion that through possible matrilineal Pictish succession Kenneth became king of both the Scots and the Picts. The Scottish and Pictish kingdoms were unified around AD 843, therefore creating a new and stronger nation under the Gaelic name of Alba, later to be known as Scotland. The path to obtaining the kingship of a united Scottish–Pictish kingdom, however, was probably not bloodless, but brutal, as suggested in the *Legend of Saint Berchan*, where it is stated that Kenneth achieved his aim by the murder of the Pictish kings at Scone. While the Gaelic language and culture came to dominate this new kingdom, the Picts, their language and customs seem to have vanished without a trace. Likewise, the original 'Welshness' of modern southern Scotland has been totally obliterated.

CHAPTER 2

PICTISH SYMBOL STONES

Classifying the Stones and Symbols

Among the most obvious traces left behind by the Picts on the landscape are their carved stone monuments. These stones have been divided into three categories: Class I, Class II, and Class III. Stones in Class I are comprised of rough or 'undressed' stones, and have incised symbols (the symbols are cut into their surfaces), but have no other decoration. In many cases it would appear that Class I stones were ancient standing stones that the Picts re-utilised for their own purposes. The symbols themselves are usually found in pairs (on unbroken stones), and can also feature the apparently subsidiary symbols of the 'mirror' and 'comb'. There are around 100 of these Class I stones so far identified, and they are found in almost every corner of Scotland from Shetland to Dumfriesshire, from Argyll to the Lothians, but are concentrated primarily in the Pictish 'heartlands' of northern Scotland, the north-east of Scotland, and Fife. These stones and their symbols are generally considered to represent the earliest phase of development of the symbol stones. Dating these is not straightforward. It is complicated by the possible reuse of standing stones that were already thousands of years old when the symbols were carved on them. It is most likely that some pre-date the sixth century AD by a significant margin, although by how much is difficult to say. Symbols have also been found on silver objects, such as the silver plaques from the 'Norrie's Law' horde, and these may also pre-date the sixth century. It is possible that symbol pairs were used on other media prior to being incised on stone, such as wood or animal skins that have consequently rotted away without a trace. Carving on stone may have been an innovation inspired by contact with other peoples, such as the Romans (who erected stone monuments in Scotland as well as elsewhere) and possibly later the Scots and Angles, who also erected stone monuments, or may have been a native innovation that was open to outside influence.

The second category comprises the so-called Class II monuments. Here, in addition to the basic symbols, the monuments are often highly decorated with sophisticated abstract 'Celtic' patterns, and scenes of people and animals. In addition, and crucially, they have been deliberately 'dressed' and the symbols are carved in 'relief' instead of being incised. They often have a Christian context, suggesting again a later date than the Class I stones. These differences may reflect the possibility of the arrival and assimilation of new stone-carving technology from outside Pictland, starting with the arrival of Christian missionaries, and the erection and dedication of churches and other religious sites. The skills employed in creating these monuments are therefore more likely to have been influenced as a result of contact with the Scots and the Angles, who utilised similar carving techniques.

Class III stones are often ornately carved and dressed and like the Class II stones often have a strong Christian context, but unlike the Class II stones do not have any symbols. It is possible that these represent the last Pictish monuments to have been erected, at a time when the symbols had become unfashionable or considered no longer appropriate.

The symbols found on Class I and Class II stones can be quite exquisite in their execution, created with great artistry and free-flowing lines. This is particularly true of the some sixteen or so animalistic symbols that include beautiful representations of lions, deer, wild boar, birds, fish and other creatures. These are usually rendered with detailing reminiscent of the animal figures that appear in the *Book of Kells* and other religious illuminated manuscripts originating from the Celtic Church from the second half of the first millennium, although Class I stones probably pre-date these manuscripts. Parallels have also been drawn with other artefacts featuring animals from the burial site of an Anglo-Saxon king at Sutton Hoo, dating from around AD 650, as well as much earlier examples from Celtic artefacts. However, there has been a tendency in the past to assume that Anglo-Saxon and Irish culture in the Dark Ages was superior to the that of the Picts and therefore it is also assumed that the Picts were not only incapable of artistic innovation but must have imported the artistic style from their more 'sophisticated' neighbours. This is a very large assumption to make and one that has little evidence supporting it. Just as possible, particularly if you accept that Class I stones and the Pictish silver artefacts are pre-sixth century, is that Pictish art was essentially an indigenous phenomenon which developed over a period of time from La Tene art, and was not only open to outside influence, but influenced the art of its neighbours in turn. For example, the *Book of Kells* is thought by many to have been created in the scriptoria of the Abbey of Iona and its satellite monasteries, some within or at least close to Pictish territory. This manuscript, of European significance, was probably later moved along with other treasures to the Ionian satellite monastic site at Kells in Ireland, to keep it safe from Viking raids. Judging by the similarity in style between Pictish symbol stones and the manuscript, it is possible that Pictish artists had a direct influence or even input in the artistic styling evident in the manuscript, particularly that of the representations of animals. In other words, cultural ideas and stylistic innovations may have flowed back and forward between the different cultures and kingdoms in the British Isles, and indeed from much further afield, fuelling a continuing evolution of the La Tene art style with its roots ultimately in pre-Roman Celtic central Europe.

The apparently abstract Pictish symbols, which appear in symbol pairs on hundreds of stones, can be highly sophisticated in design and execution. It is possible that some represent particular objects that would have been recognisable to the population at large in Pictland, such as cauldrons, chariots, or bows, but have been rendered in a two-dimensional manner that makes them difficult to decipher as recognisable objects. In addition there are secondary symbols that are clearly depictions of everyday objects that often appear alongside the principal symbol pairs, usually a hand mirror and comb. More rarely these secondary symbols relate to the art of the blacksmith, including hammers, tongs and perhaps even the blacksmith's anvil.

The symbols predominately appear in a variety of different paired combinations. In addition there are situations where more than two symbols appear within the same context, although this is relatively rare, and it is an occurrence usually not without some degree of ambiguity. Some pairings are more common than others, while some symbols although individually very common across the Pictish monuments, occur rarely in combination. This suggests that certain combinations of symbols might be 'taboo' for some unknown reason, or that specific combinations may convey some sort of specific and repeatable meaning.

The first attempt to properly catalogue the symbols was made by Romilly Allen and Joseph Anderson in the nineteenth century. They produced a list of some fifty symbols, and ascribed a number to each. Not all of the symbols appear in the context of a symbol pair, for example number 32 represents a bull, but is only ever found

3. Examples of some Pictish symbols. From left to right, top to bottom: crescent and v-rod, Pictish beast, snake and z-rod, fish, tuning fork, double disc and z-rod, double disc, flower, triple disc and cross bar (cauldron), notched rectangle with z-rod, flower, mirror case. (© Jane Dormon, Iain Forbes)

4. Strathpeffer stone
(arch and eagle symbols),
Strathpeffer, Easter Ross. (©
Crown Copyright: RCAHMS.
Licensor www.rcahms.gov.uk)

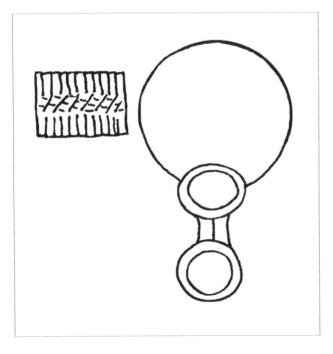

5. Drawing of mirror and
comb. (© Jane Dormon)

6. Abernethy stone (tuning fork and crescent with v-rod symbols), Abernethy, Perthshire. (©
Iain Forbes)

7. Newton House Stone (notched double disc with snake with z-rod symbols), Newton House, Aberdeenshire. (© Crown Copyright: RCAHMS. Licensor www.rcahms.gov.uk)

singularly. Furthermore, some symbols, although appearing alongside symbol pairs, may convey additional information about the pairs, or perhaps add an element of qualification to the principal symbols. The most obvious examples of this are the aforementioned 'mirror' and 'comb' symbols, which occur in a sizeable percentage of stones bearing symbol pairs. What is interesting is that while the mirror symbol appears alone many times, and also in combination with the comb, there are no clear-cut examples of the comb appearing without the mirror.

A number of attempts have been made to modernise and modify Allen and Anderson's basic system. Some symbols have been added to their original list. Other symbols, of similar appearance, have either been reclassified as separate or reconsidered as a single symbol. Anthony Jackson, for example, takes the basic fifty symbols of Allen and Anderson, and counting only symbols that he believes occur in definite pairs, arrives at a list of just twenty-eight symbols, although some of these may be duplications. For example, he classifies the symbol known as the double disc and an obvious variant of this symbol, the double disc with z-rod, as separate. Similarly the crescent, snake, and notched rectangle symbols also have analogous 'rodded' versions that Jackson counts as separate.

In his *Field Guide to Pictish Symbol Stones*, Alastair Mack lists forty-four symbols, but includes a number that are known only to occur singularly. He also lists symbols, not counted by Jackson, that appear to be additional or supplementary. These include the mirror, comb, anvil, hammer, pincers, wheel, and shear symbols. Removing supplementary symbols, as well as counting the rodded and non-rodded versions of a symbol only once, reduces the number to thirty-two. In addition, it can be argued that some of Mack's 'symbols' are not part of a proper symbol pair and therefore cannot be treated as true symbols. These would include, for example, the nine bulls, the bull's head, the horse, and the twin discs. Furthermore, his 'dog's head' symbol and the 'deer's head' symbol may be one and the same. If we were to remove these from Mack's list we would arrive at some twenty-seven symbols. The horse's head symbol is not recognised by Mack as a separate symbol and is therefore not included in this figure; if we were to include this we would therefore have the same number as the Jackson, but without the potential duplication of rodded and non-rodded versions of symbols.

Because of the different criteria by these authors for the definition of a symbol, and also some debate about the classification of similar symbols, there is therefore no definitive list. If we, however, count the rodded symbols as simply variations of their non-rodded equivalents, then a reasonable figure may lie between our revised figure of twenty-three symbols for Anthony Jackson's list (i.e. minus the five rodded duplicates) and the revised figure for Mack of around twenty-eight symbols.

Summary of the Pictish Symbols

The Crescent
The crescent symbol, the most frequently found symbol, occurs eighty-six times in its rodded form and seven times non-rodded (see picture 3). The crescent lies with the horns pointing downwards. The rodded version has an arrow-like shaft forming a 'v' shape and dividing the crescent into three portions.

The Double Disc
This is the second most frequent symbol, appearing in about 40 per cent of the symbol pairs. The non-rodded version appears twenty-one times, the rodded version around fifty-five times (picture 3). The basic symbol consists of two circles joined by a connecting axis. Each circle typically has decoration within it, usually with one or more concentric circles, and sometimes with a 'dot' in the centre. Likewise the 'axis' portion of the symbol can be decorated. This basic symbol actually takes two principal forms; with a z-rod and without. This z-shaped rod bisects the axis between the two, and typically is decorated with spear- or plant-like ends, and small curling motifs emerging from the rod.

Notched Rectangle

This symbol, in common with the double disc, frequently has a z-rod incorporated into the design. An example of this symbol can be found in picture 3. There are ten examples of the notched rectangle known to exist that incorporated a z-rod, and a further six without the rod. The symbol's basic form is a rectangle orientated so that the shorter sides are at the top and bottom. All the examples of this symbol have a notch cut into the base, usually but not always rectangular in form. In addition, on some of the pictographs, a pair of circles or circular notches is cut into the two longer sides of the rectangle; these can be directly or diagonally opposite each other. The z-rods are arranged vertically (therefore resembling a capital letter 'N') rather than the horizontal orientation of the double disc z-rods. Unlike the z-rods of the double disc, the shafts of the z-rods associated with the rectangle are generally plainer, and the ends seem to have more in common with the v-rods of the crescent symbol than the z-rods of the double disc.

Snake

The snake or serpent symbol occurs twenty-three times on stones, nine in the non-rodded form, and fourteen times in a rodded form. As in the case of the double disc and the notched rectangle, the rod takes the form of a 'z'.

Arch

The Pictish arch is another example of a geometric, potentially abstract symbol, and occurs some twenty times (non-rodded) and appears once in a rodded form (see picture 4). The rod utilised by the Pictish artists is of the same variety as that used with the crescent (i.e. a v-rod). Indeed this fact coupled with the vague similarity between a crescent and an arch (and presumably also because the arch's terminals point downwards in the examples so far found, therefore echoing the most common orientation of the crescent) has led some observers to suggest that these two symbols are in fact just variations of the same symbol.

Elephant / Beast

Occurring some fifty-four times, the 'beast' or 'Pictish elephant' symbol is perhaps the most enigmatic of the anamorphic symbols to appear on Pictish stones. Despite representing no known animal, its appearance on different stones across the country is surprisingly consistent. It appears to have a trunk-like snout, a tail, and a crest on its head. Its feet, however, are distinctly odd, ending in almost ethereal spiral structures.

Flower

This is perhaps the most bizarre-looking symbol found on Pictish stone monuments (see picture 3). With eight examples, it usually comprises a triangular base and two bending 'branches' (in one case, three) extending from the upper part of this triangle. In some of the examples, the two branches end in flower like terminals, but apart from this general organic feel to the symbol there is little clue as to what it actually represents.

8. Shandwick stone (double disc and Pictish beast symbols with hunting panel), Shandwick, Easter Ross. (© Crown Copyright: RCAHMS. Licensor www.rcahms.gov.uk)

9. Drawing of the Golspie stone, Golspie, Sutherland. (© Jane Dormon)

Deer's Head / Stag
There are six examples of this symbol.

Horse's Head
This is a similar symbol to the above, but clearly represents a horse's rather than a deer's head.

Salmon / Fish
These fish (fourteen in number) could possibly represent more than one species of fish and are therefore symbols, although they are generally recognised as being salmon (see picture 3).

Eagle and Goose
There are fifteen eagle symbols, depicting the bird of prey standing with wings folded. There are three examples of the goose symbol. The eagle is depicted in picture 4.

Rams
Two small rams appear on the Shandwick stone underneath the Pictish beast symbol. It is therefore debatable if they actually constitute a true symbol or not.

Boar
Only one boar exists in a pairing.

Wolf
There are two examples of this occurring in a symbol pair.

Seahorse / Fish Monster
There are four examples of this symbol which, according to Mack, resembles a seahorse.

The Bow / Helmet
This symbol, only known to appear once, on a stone at Congash in Badenoch, may be an example of a rodded symbol, although the straight rod may simply represent an arrow ready to be fired.

Triple Disc and Cross Bar
This symbol, which occurs fourteen times, has been interpreted as a cauldron or even a chariot. A chariot would seem the less likely candidate given the circular form of the central disc.

Tuning Fork
This symbol occurs eight times, and represents no known object from the period. This symbol appears in pictures 3 and 6.

10. Aberlemno 2 (notched rectangle with z-rod and triple disc and cross bar symbols with battle scene), Aberlemno, Angus. (© Iain Forbes)

Triple-Oval
This symbol occurs five times.

Miscellaneous Symbols
These include the 'ogee' (a ribbon-like design), the 'double-crescent' (two crescents back to back with a small circle and dot in the centre), the 'step', the 'rectangle' (picture 9), the 'disc' and the 'mirror case' (picture 3).

Symbol Pairing

The Pictish symbols usually appear in pairs, but can we be sure that a particular pairing is genuine? For example, many stones are damaged and fragmentary, and although in many cases two symbols or the remains of two symbols may appear to be paired on a fragment, this may not be the case; the two symbols may originally have been paired with other symbols on other parts of the stone now lost. Bearing that in mind, the most frequent pairings include the rodded crescent and beast symbols, rodded double disc and rodded crescent, and the arch and beast. There are apparent anomalous situations where both symbols appear relatively frequently on symbol stones but rarely appear in a pair together; for example, the beast and the snake symbols. Pairings of two identical symbols are relatively rare, despite the relatively high frequency of some of the symbols. For example, there are no authenticated occurrences of two beast symbols in a pairing. Similarly, despite the rodded crescent being the most frequently found symbol, there are no clear-cut examples of a pairing of two rodded crescents. In some situations, the order of the symbols within the pair may be important. There are, for example, five occurrences of the beast symbol being paired with the arch; however, in all of these cases, the arch symbol is first.

Due to the small number of symbols involved, it is very difficult to say whether all of the above anomalies are significant or not. It is possible that these hint at some sort of structure, or set of rules, determining pairings, with some sort of complicated hierarchy being demonstrated, with certain symbols combining well with some and not with others.

Previous Interpretations of the Pictish Symbols

Previous attempts at understanding the Pictish symbols can be roughly divided into two categories. Firstly, there have been investigations into the artistic and cultural influences that may have contributed to the design of the symbols. Secondly, there are the attempts to understand the meaning (both generally and specifically) of the symbols. These two approaches are of course not mutually exclusive, and different authors have used both to differing degrees.

In the *Origins of Pictish Symbolism*, written in 1893 by the Earl of Southesk, a possible connection between Scandinavian and Pictish symbolism is explored. Each Pictish symbol was compared to symbolism associated with the Nordic gods, with the hope that this would provide some understanding of what the individual symbols might mean. Some of the 'matches' seem at best vague, with only a few symbols resembling their potential Scandinavian counterparts. The interpretations discussed by the author are not only based on Scandinavian imagery, but also delve into possible influences from across Europe and Asia. While seeming a little dated now, due to his bias towards a Scandinavian origin for the Picts and their symbols, Southesk's book nonetheless contains a great deal of insight and thought about the subject. If viewed from a less Nordic-centric viewpoint, perhaps what the book reveals is not a convincing argument for a Scandinavian origin for the symbols, but rather points to parallels between Pictish symbolism and a wider ancient European or even Eurasian influence.

R. B. K. Stevenson, in his chapter in *The Problem of the Picts*, examined the influence of contemporary Irish and Anglo-Saxon art on the symbols and Pictish art in general, in the process finding parallels. Inga Gilbert's book *The Symbolism of the Pictish Stones in Scotland* explores Pictish art in a wider Indo-European context. By linking the artistic style and form of the symbols, she suggests that there are ancient Indo-European connections between the Picts and a number of ancient peoples across Eurasia, including the Sumerians, Scythians, and Hittites. Perhaps, as in the case of Southesk, Inga Gilbert's fascinating and illuminating work has received less attention than it deserves, but once again points to possible commonality across cultures that are seemingly separated by great distances in time and space.

Perhaps the most common theories involve interpreting the symbols as representing names (personal or clan) or heraldic crests. Depending on the theory, these could be utilised as integral to grave markers or other similar commemorative monuments, or perhaps as territorial boundary markers. In regard to the former, it would be imagined that the first symbol represented a deceased person's name, commemorated by a second individual represented by the second symbol. These various theories are dealt with in more detail in Elizabeth Sutherland's book *In Search of the Picts*. These interpretations are by and large based on little evidence or meaningful analysis, and crucially largely fail to address or explain the various anomalous situations, including the presence of additional symbols. In his book *The Symbol Stones of Scotland*, Anthony Jackson describes a number of much more complex hypotheses, combining well-developed ideas on social anthropology with a methodical analysis of the frequency of the symbols. From these analyses he sets out a theory that proposes that the symbols represent individual Pictish lineages. In his system, the function of the pairings would be to represent alliances, including marriages, between key lineages. His theories on a potential Pictish matrilineal society and the resulting potentially complex marriage patterns between different lineages are fascinating, as is his 'association of the Pictish symbols with mystical powers'. Perhaps most importantly, Jackson has stimulated debate on the meaning of the symbols, and shown that much can be gained from time spent analysing the symbols and utilising techniques from other academic disciplines.

CHAPTER 3

THE SHANDWICK STONE

In Search of a Pictish 'Rosetta Stone'

Prior to 1822, Egyptian hieroglyphics were unintelligible. In that year Jean-Francois Champollion announced, to a largely sceptical scientific community, that he had deciphered part of the inscription of an ancient Egyptian stone found at el-Rashid some twenty-three years earlier. The stone, better known to us as the 'Rosetta Stone', was inscribed in three different scripts: hieroglyphics, Demotic (an Egyptian cursive writing system), and Greek. Champollion's breakthrough was not just to decipher the Egyptian names 'Ptolemy' and 'Cleopatra' on the stone, but by using both the Greek and Coptic languages (Coptic he theorised had the same root as ancient Egyptian) he was able to understand the basic construction of the hieroglyphics. He also showed that certain hieroglyphs represented particular sounds. Using this crucial information gleaned from the Rosetta Stone, he deciphered a cartouche containing four 'glyphs' from an illustration of the ruins of the temple at Abu Simbal. The initial symbol consisted of a circle with a dot in the middle. Champollion inspirationally guessed that this was the Sun. He consulted his books on the Coptic language, and found that the Coptic word for the Sun was *Ra*. The second symbol resembled our modern letter 'm' and the two following identical symbols he guessed from their shape that they represented the letter 's'. The cartouche therefore read *Ra-m-s-s*, which he interpreted as the name of the famous Pharaoh 'Ramasees'. This simple breakthrough led to the eventual deciphering of all the hieroglyphs, and opened the door on the ancient Egyptian world. With the deciphering of the Egyptian hieroglyphs came not only a greater understanding of ancient Egyptian life, from the spiritual to the mundane, but a stirring of the imagination of the public at large to everything Egyptian.

Is it possible that deciphering the Pictish symbols might also lead to a greater understanding of their culture? In a comparison between the hieroglyphs of ancient Egypt and the symbols of Pictland, the contrasts could not be starker. There is no obvious equivalent of the Rosetta Stone, no long inscriptions that might conceivably constitute any sort of narrative, and indeed Pictish symbols normally seem to occur in pairs rather than as part of anything that might conceivably be a coherent written message. Egyptian hieroglyphics are not in short supply and literally cover the surfaces of many important archaeological sites; Pictish symbols by comparison are rare. Furthermore, written Pictish is virtually non-existent, being limited to few inscriptions principally in the Irish script *Ogham*. The simplest view is that the information encoded in Pictish symbols, if they are communicating information at all, is very limited indeed. Apart from the possibility that they represent names, they may not be communicating language at all, but imparting some other information. The Rosetta Stone also has the advantage of carrying two other scripts that allowed scholars to piece together the meaning and phonetics of hieroglyphs. Unfortunately no such stone has so far been found in Scotland, and it is highly unlikely that one ever will be. However, given that the symbols appear in pairs, and that there appear to be only a limited number of symbols used in the context of the pairings, the task of deciphering or at least deducing some meaning from these may not be an impossible task.

The potential rewards in deciphering the Pictish symbols, in terms of our knowledge of this enigmatic culture, should not be underestimated. From the vantage point of the early twenty-first century, we know little about the Picts and any significant new information about them would therefore be welcome. Even the most basic questions about their language and culture have yet to be answered with any degree of certainty. Were they Celtic, or do they represent the survivors of an earlier indigenous race? Were they Indo-European or non-Indo-European? Does the answer to their ethnicity or cultural origins lie in a complex mixture of these possibilities? While the information encoded within the symbol pairs may well be limited, it is worth remembering that the Picts carved them prominently on prestigious and public monuments, and so therefore regarded their meaning as highly significant. Even a basic understanding of the type of information the symbols encoded would therefore provide important clues about their society. In the absence of an obvious 'Rosetta stone', we must examine the existing material and hope that sufficient clues are found to begin a systematic deciphering of the symbol pairs.

The Shandwick Stone

In the northern Scottish county of Easter Ross, beside the Moray Firth, and protected from the elements by a modern glass structure, stands the Shandwick stone. For over a thousand years this Class II cross slab had largely survived the elements when it was blown down in a gale in 1846. The stone unfortunately broke into two pieces and was subsequently repaired. Despite the damage incurred, this 9-foot-high stone may well represent one of the most significant Dark Age monuments in North West Europe. While the information chiselled on this stone does not at first glance look promising, it may well provide the first clues that will allow the deciphering of the symbols and ultimately the clues to the origins and culture of the Picts.

The front of the Shandwick stone reveals the high art of the Pictish craftsmen in its intricate cross. The style of the cross shows similarities and therefore a relationship to the high crosses of Ireland and western Scotland, as well as the monumental sculpture of the other neighbours of the Picts, the Anglian kingdom of Northumbria. Beasts, angels and knotwork crowd the cross, and the unswerving Christian faith of the patron of this cross slab is proclaimed for all in the community to see. The other side, delivered with the same artistic style, is however very surprising.

The back of the Shandwick stone is divided into eight panels, and was well described by J. Romilly Allen and Joseph Anderson in their two-volume work, published in

Above: 11. Shandwick stone (with shelter), Shandwick, Easter Ross. (© Iain Forbes)

Right: 12. Shandwick stone (cross side), Shandwick, Easter Ross. (© Crown Copyright: RCAHMS. Licensor www.rcahms.gov. uk)

1903, *Early Christian Monuments in Scotland*. Within these panels are incised strange beasts, hunters, birds and a host of other animals. The largest figure is that of the bizarre and supernatural-looking 'Pictish beast', which dominates the top panel. This classic symbol, found on many other stones throughout Scotland, dwarfs three smaller symbols within the same panel: two rams and an unidentifiable four-legged animal.

The Shandwick Stone Hunting Panel

The panel immediately below the Pictish beast symbol displays a bizarre collection of animal, human, and fantastical figures seemingly arranged in a jumble. There is, however, some hint of structure, with almost all of these figures facing towards the right-hand side of the stone. This strange composition has in the past been interpreted as both a divine hunt and ritual hunt. Adding to the evidence that this may be a hunting scene are depictions of various woodland animals, including the wild boar, and two deer. A possible pine marten, a hare, and a bird of prey are also present, although their relevance to a hunting scene is less clear. The two carvings of deer, in tandem with other examples of more orthodox hunting elements, might well indeed lead some to identify the composition as an early example of the medieval divine hunt, with the deer perhaps representing human souls. It has also been proposed that the order from left to right represents the motion of the Sun from east to west, perhaps an analogy of the passage of mankind from birth to death.

However, there are a number of curiosities as well as inconsistencies contained within the Shandwick stone's hunting scene that warrant further investigation. Firstly,

13. Shandwick stone (hunting panel), Shandwick, Easter Ross. (© Iain Forbes)

what is the significance of the figures that are not facing to the right? Secondly, some of the figures simply would not be expected to be found in a Pictish forest or, come to that, any forest. What role would a goat-rider, a lion, an oversized eagle, bulls, and a calf play in such a hunt? Furthermore, we have the incongruity of fighting figures in the bottom left-hand side and, at odds with the chase, a kneeling horseless hunter is firing his bow at a deer on the bottom right-hand side. There is clearly much more to the imagery than meets the eye. As mentioned above, we must also square the obvious Christian imagery of this stone with a proposed divine hunt and the presence of such a strange menagerie.

The seemingly peculiar composition depicted on the monument at Shandwick may hold clues that would allow us, at least partly, to understand the context of the stone. It may also be possible in understanding the context, to begin to understand the other elements of the neighbouring panels, principally the elusive Pictish symbols immediately above the 'hunting scene'. A thorough re-examination of the Shandwick 'hunt' may therefore reveal a much more complex message than has so far been imagined, one that might explain some of the eccentricities of this curious panel, and may also have the potential to provide a starting point in an attempt to understand the symbols. A new understanding of the panel might also shine a little more light on the culture and beliefs of the Picts.

Could the seemingly complex and strange mixture of creatures actually represent a more structured picture than we have so far imagined? As mentioned previously, the tableau does appear to have some partial structure, in terms of a general left to right procession or orientation of the figures. The 'odd' characters involved in the 'hunt' may also have significance. At first glance the overall picture is therefore extremely confused, and a more detailed examination is certainly required.

There are a number of human figures depicted on the panel, with three on horseback, one tall figure on foot, two figures that appear to be in combat with each other and a seventh kneeling figure, who is apparently aiming a bow and arrow at a stag. The kneeling hunter seems to be wearing a deerskin costume and antlers and is similar to other figures found in Pictish monumental art. The two warriors, who occupy the bottom left-hand side of the panel, are also vaguely reminiscent of other figures found on Pictish stones. The tall unmounted figure in the top centre appears to be rather odd. Unfortunately much of the detail of the head area and the object carried in front of the figure are obscured by wear and by damage to the stone, but the figure nonetheless – along with the warriors, the bowman, and stag – visually dominates the scene. The three horsemen, taken as a group, seem to be pursuing the large figure of a stag in the right-hand corner of the panel.

Taken as a whole, the 'human' characters on the stone seem peculiarly mismatched. If they are all participating in a hunting party, then this must surely be the most chaotic and unlikely sport. The kneeling hunter requires stealth, a steady hand, a lack of scent and above all quiet and calm. He would certainly not be able to get close to his quarry while another stag is being hunted down by horsemen. The bowman must surely be operating in an unrelated scene, a forest far from the din and fear of the upper portion of the panel. The bowman's world must also be far distant from that of the duelling figures that appear only to be interested in each other and are oblivious to all around them. The tall central figure is enigmatic; little clue is given as to what the figure is doing among all this chaos. Despite the figure's position in the midst of the riders, it lends little confidence to the notion that it is involved in the vigorous pursuit going on around; again the impression given is that these groups of figures may occupy the same panel, but do not occupy the same scene.

There is another figure that at first glance might qualify as a human. This is the curious carving on the right-hand edge of the panel, between the two stags. This character appears to be riding a goat, and is carrying an object in each hand. The objects are hard to discern, but once again it is clear that this is no ordinary participant in a hunt, and the relationship with the stag above is at best distant. If you examine the area around the antlers of the stag at the bottom right of the panel, an area where we would expect to find the goat rider's legs, it becomes clear that there are no legs. The goat and rider therefore is more likely to represent a hybrid or chimera-like beast, not dissimilar to the concept of a centaur (examples of which appear on other Pictish stones). There are numerous animals within the 'hunting' scene. The three largest animals include the stag in the top right-hand corner, an eagle and what, surprisingly, may well be a lion situated between the warriors and the tall centre-top figure. Two animals face to the left and therefore are not in keeping with the largely overall right- facing aspect of the scene: the stag 'at bay' which is looking back at the hunter, and one of a pair of bulls at the centre-bottom of the scene which appears to be confronting the other bull. A cow, or perhaps a calf, takes up a curious position between the warriors, which suggests that perhaps this animal is involved in a dispute between the figures.

In terms of the birds present on the panel, it has been suggested that as well as the obvious eagle, the small bird in close proximity to the bowman could represent a woodpecker (presumably because of the stance of the animal), and the long-necked bird beside the tall central figure could be a crane.

A Celestial Hunt

If we consider the typical composition of scenes found on Pictish stone monuments, one point that some observers have raised, is the way in which the Picts seemed to think little of mixing people, animals, mythological creatures, objects and sometimes abstract objects within the same picture. The symbol pairs also seem to follow a similar mix, with recognisable animals, imagined animals, identifiable and abstract designs. Until now there has been no real attempt to address this peculiarity of Pictish art and no coherent explanation as to why there is such a mixture. What is proposed here is that there is a very simple and straightforward explanation for this seemingly peculiar situation, one that is startling and has major consequences as to how we should view the Picts and their achievements. The range of figures displayed on the Shandwick monument, and other similar Pictish carved scenes elsewhere, is similar to the range of figures imagined forming the constellations of the night sky and that are presented in star atlases. For example, the northern night sky has constellations represented by human figures, woodland beasts, birds, exotic creatures, mythical creatures and inanimate objects. There are bears (the Great Bear and a Little Bear), hunting dogs, human-like figures (including hunters), and horses or horse-like animals (Pegasus and Equuleus). There are even paired figures such as Gemini (representing twins) and Pisces (depicting two fish). There are also inanimate objects, such as a lyre (Lyra) and weighing scales (Libra). Indeed it could be said in relation to the figures and symbols found on Pictish stones, and carefully catalogued by other authors, where else but in the night sky would you find a similar mix of symbolism?

A constellation, of course, is a group of stars that appear to our eyes to be close together in the sky and form a recognisable shape, although in reality the constituent stars may be many light years apart. We can divide the constellations into two broad categories. The first category consists of those that do not appear to rise or set but are present every night in the sky. These are the so-called circumpolar constellations. Perhaps the most recognisable of these is the Great Bear, sometimes referred to as the Plough. The second category consists of constellations that rise and set in the same way as the Sun, Moon and planets and would include, for example, the zodiacal constellations such as Aquarius and Cancer. These constellations would only be visible in the night sky at certain times of the year. Facing southwards therefore, such a constellation would rise above the horizon to your left in the east, and set on your right to the west. If we accept the possibility that the hunting scene on the Shandwick stone is actually a depiction of the heavens, or at least a portion of the heavens, then could this explain the left to right orientation of the tableau? On the stone the majority of the figures face right, and this could suggest the rising of the constellations, their procession across the sky, and their eventual western setting.

Testing the Astronomical Hypothesis

The first task in testing this novel hypothesis is to try and identify imagery relating to astronomy on the hunting panel. The most obvious place to start is to attempt to match some of the figures carved on the panel with other descriptions and depictions of constellations found in other cultural traditions, preferably those of neighbouring Celtic peoples. Unfortunately very little has survived of early Celtic notions of the heavens, so little that it could not be usefully utilised in an analysis of a potential Pictish cosmology. The Pictish nations also bordered for many hundreds of years with territory controlled by a people with another celestial tradition: the Romans. It is certainly not without the bounds of possibility that Graeco-Roman ideas on the heavens could have been known to the Picts.

The Graeco-Roman version of the night sky forms a major component of modern star maps, providing us with the names and connected mythology of the majority of constellations visible in the sky of the northern hemisphere. In contrast the southern hemisphere constellations are fairly modern, many being named as European explorers ventured into the southern hemisphere. The Graeco-Roman view of the night sky, and the constellations they saw adorning it, was not immutable, with constellations from time to time being redrawn and renamed. This process also continued well beyond the Roman era, with astronomers up until the eighteenth century constantly reviewing the constellations they drew in star atlases. The constellations that have undergone less change, and appear to include some of oldest constellations, are those of the zodiac, and it is these we shall consider first in our exploration of a potential Pictish cosmology on the Shandwick stone.

The zodiacal signs, the twelve constellations that lie on or close to the Sun's path (ecliptic), were well established by the classical period, and even influenced Egyptian representations of the heavens (for example, the Egyptian 'Denderah' zodiac painted on a tomb ceiling). These classical zodiac signs, however, are ultimately thought to have their origins in ancient Babylon, and it is within this early civilisation that much of our understanding of astronomy, and the relationship between the motion of the Sun, Moon and planets against the background of 'fixed stars' seems to have originated. The Babylonian contribution to astronomy and the calendar is astounding, and they are usually accredited with the initial development of Western astrology and astronomy, as well as having a strong influence on Eastern astrology.

Given the antiquity and considerable influence the Babylonian solar zodiacal signs had on the other civilisations around them, it would seem logical to try and identify candidate figures within the Shandwick panel as potential representations of signs of the zodiac. We could also hypothesise that the Picts may have recognised some or all of the zodiacal signs familiar to the Romans and other ancient civilisations. If we can find evidence of a number of possible zodiacal constellations on the panel, then we may be able to examine the spatial relationship between these candidates to ascertain whether this corresponds in any way with the night sky. We therefore may be able to provide some evidence to support a cosmological hypothesis for the composition.

Most people regard the zodiacal constellations as 'star signs' relating to their birth dates and are familiar with the astrological columns found in magazines and tabloid newspapers. The relationship between modern star signs and the sky is nowadays obscure, but originally your star sign was the constellation of the zodiac (each of which take up one-twelfth of the ecliptic, or 30 degrees) in which the Sun was positioned at the time of your birth. Due to the slow natural 'wobble' in the Earth's axis (precession) and changes in the Western calendar, the dates of the star signs, however, no longer correspond to events in the night sky.

Constellations of the Zodiac

Aries is generally regarded as the first constellation or sign of the zodiac, and holds this position in view of the fact that in Roman times the Sun moved into this sign at around the spring equinox. The sign for this constellation is of course a ram.

Taurus, the bull, is a spectacular constellation. It encompasses two wonderful star clusters, the Pleiades (or Seven Sisters) and the Hyades. It is easily identifiable in the sky partly because of the beautiful Pleiades, and because the horns of the bull are easily discernable below the Seven Sisters. The constellation's brightest star (alpha star), Aldebaran, forms part of the lower horn and stands out from the rest, not just in terms of magnitude or brightness, but also in terms of its brilliant reddish-brown colour. To astronomers, the colour emitted by Aldebaran identifies it as a relatively cool red giant star, a name that also reveals its enormous size in relation to our own Sun. As red giants are not particularly bright, Aldebaran's magnitude demonstrates its close proximity (relatively speaking, at least in galactic terms) to our own solar system.

The next constellation the Sun 'enters', Gemini (the twins), gets its name from two bright stars that appear to lie close together, and at first glance appear identical in colour and magnitude to the naked eye. These stars are known as Castor and Pollux and are often depicted as twin boys.

Cancer is an indistinct constellation, and it is difficult to make out a crab shape from the collection of stars making up this particular asterism. It is more likely that our view of this zodiacal constellation comes from the fact that, in astrology, this 'house' was thought to be ruled by the Moon. The Moon's most obvious effect on our planet is its role in creating tides in the oceans, and so a creature that exists in the intertidal zone, and whose life is therefore controlled by the Moon, makes a perfect animal representation for this portion of the zodiac.

The next sign, Leo, is the most regal of all the signs in the zodiac, and is not only represented by the kingly lion, but is said by astrologers to be ruled by the Sun itself, the most powerful influence in the sky.

Virgo is thought to be one of the most ancient constellations in the heavens, with its origins perhaps even before the Babylonians. It is one of the 'human-like' constellations and represents a female figure. It may originate from the time when our ancestors were making the transition from a life of hunting and gathering to that of farming. This sign, sometimes called 'The Maiden', is usually shown as a young woman carrying a wheat or corn spike (representing the star Spica), and has obvious connections to fertility and is a symbol of the harvest. In the ancient world, the Sun would have been in this 'house' at harvest time in September.

Libra is seen traditionally as a pair of weighing scales. It is therefore the only sign of the zodiac depicted as an inanimate object. The constellation is principally made up of three bright stars, sitting in the form of an isosceles triangle, almost perfectly balanced, and straddling the ecliptic.

The eighth zodiacal sign is represented by an animal more at home in southern Europe, or the Middle East, and would have little resonance with the peoples of northern Europe in the Dark Ages. Scorpio or the Scorpion when viewed from southern latitudes appears in its entirety, with pincers and a sting. Its most prominent star, Antares, is often referred to as the 'heart of the Scorpion', and is extremely bright. In northern latitudes, in the first millennium, this constellation would never have been seen in its entirety.

Following Scorpio, there is the zodiacal constellation of Sagittarius (the Archer). Today this figure is seen as a centaur wielding a bow and arrow, but previously it was seen as a human hunter with a bow. Further back in time it is thought that the constellation may simply have been visualised as a bow and arrow.

The next three constellations reside in a portion of the heavens traditionally associated with a celestial watery realm.

The first of these signs is Capricorn. Modern depictions tend to rather lazily imply that Capricorn is a goat. However, it should be properly referred to as a 'sea goat', and is described as a creature with a goat's head, a body with only the front legs present, and a mermaid-like tail.

The second sign found in this strange watery region of the sky is Aquarius. This sign is of course known as the 'water bearer', and is traditionally shown as a human figure pouring water from a large pot. The water from this vessel provides the imaginary aquatic environment for the zodiacal Capricorn and Pisces, as well as for the non-zodiacal constellations of Cetus the whale and the southern fish. The Babylonians probably saw a less complex version of this constellation in the sky, seeing just the pot and water, with the human figure being added by later civilisations.

The final constellation in our modern zodiac is Pisces, the third 'watery' sign. It is a fairly nondescript constellation, represented by a pair of fish.

Is There a Shandwick Zodiac?

Is it therefore possible to identify some of the figures shown on the panel on the Shandwick stone as figures from the zodiac? It is clear from the outset that there are certain zodiac-like candidates missing. There are, for example, no fish, crabs, scorpions, nor are there any weighing scales. However, there are a number of figures that have at least a little resonance with some of the zodiacal constellations.

Taurus Candidate

On the stone there are not one but two bulls. These two near-identical figures are presented facing each other, strongly suggesting that they are interacting. If one or both of these bulls represented Taurus, then we would have to explain the presence of more than one figure. It is also worth pointing out that there are other bovine-like figures nearby, which would seem to be cow- or calf-like, and this grouping may hold some significance.

Leo Candidate

There is also a lion-like animal in the centre left of the scene, which could just possibly correspond to the constellation Leo. This figure, above and to the right of the warriors, has in the past been likened to a lynx, presumably on the very basis that a lion would be considerably out of place in a Pictish hunt. However, the European lynx could not be more different from the large cat figure depicted. The lynx's proportions are considerably different from both the domestic cat and the lion, its legs are very long for its size, and its head looks almost ridiculously small. In addition it has characteristically pointed ears, tufted at the top. This description is undeniably a long way from the cat on the Shandwick stone, and on this basis alone may be ruled out as the carving actually sports a very large head, and stout short legs. The other obvious Pictish animal candidate would be the wild cat. This animal is similar in proportion to the domestic cat although a little larger, but again the proportions of the Shandwick cat, although closer, do not suggest a wild cat. This figure is undoubtedly a member of the big cat family and, particularly because of the head shape, the best fit is the lion.

Gemini Candidate

If we now turn to the human-like figures found in the zodiac, moving round from the first sign of the zodiac, Aries, in a counter-clockwise direction across the night sky, the first 'human' asterism is that of Gemini, the twins. The closest match to this constellation is that of the two fighting figures on the bottom left-hand side of the panel. The two figures certainly seem to be very similar to one another, with the same swords and unusually shaped shields. They also seem to have adopted a similar or even identical (and opposite) stance. Both are naked and their hair, as best as can be discerned from the worn stone, is also similar. If this is a depiction of the constellation Gemini, then it is a long way from our modern idea of this zodiacal sign, often depicted in newspapers or magazines as two cherubic boys. Surprisingly, however, two adult brothers in conflict are typical of how a number of cultures have viewed this constellation. The two principal stars of Gemini, Castor and Pollux, are typically seen as equals but opposites, representing such fundamental and related concepts of light and darkness, good and evil, mortality and immortality. Even the Greeks saw these twin stars as two adult heroes, seemingly identical, but one mortal and the other immortal. These concepts underlie much of our religious thought even today and emerge in various ways culturally, for example as the Chinese 'yin and yang' and in the Old Testament as the brothers Cain and Abel. Castor is usually thought of as representing light and Pollux darkness. In other words it is eminently possible that Gemini could have been viewed by the Pictish artist in a more complex way than we would view the constellation today, with twin heroes representing a balance between dark and light, perhaps even good and evil, in eternal conflict, but at the same time inextricably linked.

Sagittarius Candidate
Another possible choice for a zodiacal figure is the hunter with the bow in the bottom right-hand side of the Shandwick tableau. As has already been pointed out above, Sagittarius was depicted in the distant past not as a centaur but as a less complicated human figure with a bow and arrow. Could this figure be a Pictish version of the constellation Sagittarius? In the context of a hunting scene, it does not seem particularly odd that an archer is present, but it has already been pointed out that this bowman and his hunting technique do not fit well with the other events around him. What of his quarry? There is no constellation today in the night sky which fits with the figure of the deer. Furthermore, it would be only logical to assume that any constellation representing a deer or stag would have to be in close proximity to our putative Sagittarian hunter. We shall return to the problem of the deer later on.

Virgo Candidate
The figure in the top centre of the panel is very difficult to discern, partly because of the damage to the stone. The first pertinent question about this figure is to ask what sex it represents. It is almost always regarded as a male, presumably because it is in the middle of what people generally regard is a hunting scene and clearly such an event is viewed as a male domain. As we have already seen, however, this is no ordinary hunt. There is no reason why we should not challenge the assumption that this figure is indisputably male. The figure is very slender and quite graceful; could this therefore be a representation of a female? Could the clothing be female? Depictions of Pictish males on various stones seem to suggest that their clothing reached down to just above or just below the knee. The female horse rider depicted on the magnificent 'Hilton of

Cadboll' stone is wearing clothes that seem to reach to the ankle. In contrast, on the same monument the legs of the male riders and trumpeters are discernible, suggesting bare legs or leggings from the knee downwards. The Shandwick figure appears to be wearing long clothing a reasonable distance below the knee, although not quite reaching the ankles. The head area is very indistinct, due to the damage to the stone, and the hint of long hair does not help identify whether or not this is female, as both Pictish men and woman seem to have sported long hair. The figure is holding out an object in front of it; again damage to the stone makes it very difficult to identify what this might be. Could this figure resemble any of the zodiacal signs? If the figure is regarded as male, then the answer is no. If the figure is seen as female, then there arises a fascinating possibility: the figure's stance is very reminiscent of depictions of Virgo, the maiden. Could the object being held out in front of the figure actually be the Spica or wheat sheaf? If it is, then this would be a classic image of the Virgin with her symbol of harvest.

Spatial Relationships between the Zodiac Candidates

While the possibility may seem for the moment still relatively remote that these are actually meant to represent constellations of the zodiac, the fact is that such an unlikely mixture of characters makes more sense as a collection of constellations than as a hunting scene. If the figures do indeed represent the zodiac and other constellations, then we should also be looking at the structure of the scene and the spatial relationships between the figures to see if this in any way resembles the night sky. The lion's position, for example, may be significant. It occupies the space to the right and slightly above the twin warriors. If we let our eyes travel diagonally upwards and to the right from the twins, through the lion, we come to our postulated Virgo figure. This order of the figures may hold some significance. It also should not escape our notice that in order to pass through our other possible zodiac signs, our eyes then would travel diagonally downwards and to the right, passing through the 'wild boar' to reach our Sagittarius. Our potential zodiac signs therefore may follow the line of an arc, one that significantly could correspond to the arc of the ecliptic (Sun's path) in modern star maps. This pathway passes through the signs of the zodiac.

Furthermore, we can examine the sequence of these possible zodiac figures, and look for correspondence with the night sky. Following this possible arc from the bottom left to the middle top, and then on to the bottom right of the panel, the sequence of our possible Pictish zodiac figures starting with the twins might therefore be Gemini/Taurus, Leo, Virgo, and Sagittarius. In addition, a wild boar figure sits between the potential Virgo and Sagittarius figures. In reality, each month the Sun progresses through the following zodiac signs in this order: Taurus, Gemini, Cancer, Leo, Virgo, Libra, Scorpio and Sagittarius. While the figures that have so far been tentatively identified as zodiac figures are approximately in the correct order, we would seem to have signs of the zodiac missing from the panel and the addition of a boar to the sequence. We clearly need to explain the absence of Cancer, Libra, and Scorpio, and the substitution of either one or both of these last two with a wild boar.

The simplest explanation for Cancer's absence is that the crab is an aquatic animal, and even the artist's bizarre hunting scene could not stretch to the incorporation of a crab, or any other aquatic animal. Another explanation, turning again to the heavens, is that unlike the other constellations in this sequence, Cancer is a relatively inconsequential constellation to the naked-eye observer, being made up of only faint stars. Perhaps the sculptor was interested only in constellations that are easily discernible or contained particularly bright stars.

The credibility of the hunting scene is already stretched by the presence of some of the figures present and a case could be put forward that, in addition to Cancer, neither Libra nor Scorpio would fit particularly well within such a scene. It is also possible that these last two significant constellations may well be represented on the stone not as a pair of scales or a scorpion but as a Pictish equivalent, for example the wild boar or stag figures. This idea would of course challenge the very notion that our modern zodiac was the universal Western convention at the time of the Picts, and if proven right could even provide a clue to the possibility of the existence of an alternative astronomical tradition in Pictland. This tradition might be uniquely Pictish or perhaps have once been more widely spread in Europe, with some similarities to the Graeco-Roman model, but crucially with a number of key differences.

Some of the figures on the Shandwick monument, according to this initial analysis, therefore may well hint at a cosmological meaning imbedded within the hunting scene, one that would explain the strange composition of the panel. Furthermore, this could be the first evidence that the Picts were not only interested in the night sky, but had their own interpretation of the constellations. If further evidence could be produced to support this possibility, then this would represent a startling breakthrough in how we view these so-called barbarian people.

CHAPTER 4

AN ALTERNATIVE ASTRONOMICAL TRADITION?

Pictish Cosmology: Distant Influences

The possibility that the Shandwick stone might represent a Pictish view of the night sky, if proven, could provide a valuable and fascinating insight into a people about whom we have known very little until now. At the very least we would have the first evidence that the Picts were interested in the night sky. Furthermore, the apparent characterisation of constellations as figures present on the Shandwick stone might also suggest that the Picts may have attached mythological meaning to the constellations, in much the same way as the Greeks and Romans. For the moment it is worth looking at these possibilities in more depth, before turning our attention later to the enigmatic Pictish symbols.

If we were to accept the hypothesis presented here, which suggests that the Shandwick panel does not simply represent a 'hunt' but rather some sort of astral map, then we would also have to accept that many of the figures depicted do not correspond to our modern constellations with which we are familiar. We are therefore forced to construct a hypothesis that the Picts, in the later half of the first millennium, had their own indigenous version of the northern sky. While this has some parallels with our own modern view, we would hypothesise that it also showed significant differences in the interpretation of key constellations. In this situation, there are two possibilities to explain the possible origin of a Pictish version of night sky. Firstly, they may have developed, at least in part, their own unique astronomy and cosmological mythology independently of other traditions, while incorporating some outside influences. This might explain the incorporation of a few key zodiacal asterisms. The second possibility is that a Pictish view of the night sky reflected another independent or semi-independent viewpoint, which at one time was widespread: for example, across northern Europe or even beyond, a night sky with some commonality with the 'traditional' Graeco-Roman sky but crucially with some key differences. In this second scenario, we might envisage this alternative tradition as having become gradually extinct in other areas, as Mediterranean influences intruded. Perhaps because of the Picts' geographical isolation and their position outside the Roman Empire, this alternative night sky survived at least until the creation of the Shandwick stone in Scotland, while becoming subsumed by Roman ideas elsewhere. If this was the case then it is possible that other cultures in other parts of Europe carry echoes of these alternative constellations. It is also possible that earlier cultures also retained elements of a tradition of an archaic night sky, prior to the establishment of our now familiar constellations. If we could find such evidence and were able to confirm the existence of alternative constellations matching the figures on the Shandwick stone, then this would have dramatic consequences, not only for how we view the Picts, but also for our knowledge on the development of astronomy in Europe.

Greek Mythology and Archaic Constellations

The science of archaeology has given us many fascinating insights into the lives of our ancestors and has helped us to gain something of an understanding of the everyday lives of ordinary people from the distant past. In the case of civilisations that have left us written records, contemporary authors have helped to flesh out an image of what it must have been like to live in these different eras and as a result we have some inkling of how specific societies functioned at many different levels. However, many societies unfortunately left very little or no written evidence behind, and in these cases we are forced to rely more on archaeology, as well as the often dubious opinion of contemporary writers from other lands, to glimpse how these societies functioned. Without indigenous and contemporary records, peoples such as the Picts seem particularly distant and mysterious.

However, there are potential alternative sources that may offer a tantalising glimpse into the seemingly lost worlds of the past: the folk tales and mythology of a culture. While superficially they may be interpreted as nothing more than children's tales, they can provide real insight into ancient beliefs. There are many examples of stories or myths that have come down to us in the present day and which appear to have their origin in distant times, having been passed from generation to generation by oral transmission, eventually being written down with the introduction of literacy. So, for example, elements of the myths of ancient Greece pre-date authors such as Homer and hint at an even more archaic Greek world. Aspects of Irish and Welsh mythology likewise reveal their millennia-old origins, despite not being written down until medieval times. Many of these ancient stories from around the world seem to invoke ideas on the origin of the world, the deities involved in the origin, and their supposed interaction with the first people. These stories therefore provide that vital glimpse into how everyday people saw their place in the world, their religious and other belief systems, and their societies. We still must exercise some caution, however, and remind ourselves that stories transmitted orally are vulnerable to change. It is perhaps helpful to compare and contrast similarly themed stories from different origins and to look for commonality. In the European tradition, many of these myths concerning the gods seem to reflect a cosmological (or cosmogonical) aspect, with stars and planets being related to deities and particular events.

Many of us are familiar with the names of constellations in the night sky, and are also aware that there are often stories relating to each major northern constellation. The stories we are familiar with in the west are almost all Greek in origin, are very ancient, and form a significant part of Greek and Roman mythology. Stories such as the tale of Andromeda, the maiden bound to a rock at the mercy of a sea monster, with the associated characters of her mother Cassiopeia, her father Cepheus, the hero

Perseus and the winged horse Pegasus, are all reflected in the names of constellations in one particular area of sky. Similarly, the constellation Orion (the giant hunter) and his dogs can be seen in the night sky harrying Taurus the bull, while Scorpio, Orion's nemesis, nips at his ankle. So it is across much of the northern sky, with ancient and fabulous stories being told down the centuries explaining how the stars and constellations came into being.

Hercules

Perhaps the best-known Greek tales, which are thought to have a particularly ancient provenance, are those known as the Twelve Labours of Hercules. In this tale, the character of Hercules (more correctly *Heracles*) kills his own wife and sons, and is given twelve seemingly impossible tasks to carry out as penance by Eurystheus. Some of these tasks clearly seem to relate in some way to specific constellations, with some of these more obviously signs of the zodiac. Recently a number of writers have gone as far as suggesting that most if not all of the tasks have a cosmological origin or function, with the number of labours corresponding to the number of zodiacal signs. The relevance for us and our investigation of the Shandwick stone is that this would require the possibility that the story of Hercules reflects an alternative cosmos from our modern view, which ironically we normally consider as largely Greek in origin. One possible explanation for this apparent anomaly would be that the Twelve Labours of Hercules is archaic in origin, with some of its associated constellations pre-dating the more familiar Graeco-Roman versions. This would of course imply a change in the ancient Greeks' view of the zodiac at some point in their history, or that the tale of Hercules was originally a non-native myth. If we accept at the very least that some of the tasks or labours have cosmological meaning, then it would be relevant to establish whether or not there are parallels within these stories to some of the figures within the Shandwick hunt. As with all mythology potentially relating to the sky, it is impossible to say whether the Twelve Labours might have been invented in order to explain objects and events in the night sky, or whether stars and constellations were later used to embellish and illustrate the tales.

Let us examine the tasks in more detail and look at their possible suggested cosmological meanings. The first task set for Hercules reveals a classic and indisputable Greek star myth at the outset of his labours. Hercules was asked to kill the Nemean lion and bring back its skin. He duly sets out to kill the lion, but he is unable to achieve this with any of his weapons; he eventually succeeds by strangling the lion with his bare hands. Depictions of Hercules usually show him with the skin of the Nemean lion over his shoulder. After presenting the body of the Nemean lion to Eurystheus, he then nails it to the sky. This thereby explains the presence of constellation Leo in the night sky.

The second task set is for Hercules to kill a guardian of the underworld, the ferocious multi-headed Lernaean hydra. To make matters worse, the goddess Hera sends a crab to nip Hercules in the heels as he attempts to kill the beast. The hydra is represented in the sky by a long convoluted constellation of the same name, found just below the ecliptic. Of course the zodiacal constellation incorporated neatly into the story is Cancer the crab, the faint constellation just above the head of Hydra. That the principal role is given to the hydra in the story, rather than Cancer, emphasises the fact that the principal star of Hydra (Alphard) easily outshines any of the stars of nearby Cancer.

The third task, of great interest to us in connection with the Shandwick panel, involves the capture of the Ceryneian hind (or alternatively the Arcadian stag). The problem was that the hind (which interestingly possessed antlers that glinted) could run incredibly fast, and Hercules was forced to chase after the hind for a full year. The chase could therefore be interpreted as representing a complete cycle of the Sun through the zodiac. The hind has not so far been satisfactorily identified with any constellation, although there is some evidence that the Greeks thought of the constellation Hercules itself as the hind when the Sun was in the zodiacal constellation of Scorpio.

The next task, also of interest to us, is the capture of the Erymanthian boar. It was during this episode that Hercules encountered the centaurs. No satisfactory celestial equivalent has been found to be identified with the boar. However, the constellation Centaurus, located below Libra and Scorpio, is directly linked to this particular task.

The fifth task was to clean out the Augean stables in a single day. Hercules achieved what was thought to be the impossible, by diverting the course of two rivers through the stables. The constellation Capricorn was referred to as the Augean stables by the Greeks, and the rivers might well refer to that great celestial river, the Milky Way, which runs through the constellation, and also to the celestial waters pouring from the pot of neighbouring Aquarius.

The sixth task was to get rid of the Stymphalian birds. These were hideous creatures with claws and feathers of metal. Hercules achieves this by frightening them with a huge pair of metal clappers, then shooting them with his bow and arrow. The arrow in this case is identified with the constellation Sagitta, which lies close to the constellation Aquila (the eagle). The two other birds, which occupy the same area of the night sky as Aquila, have been identified as Cygnus, the swan, and Lyra. Lyra is viewed nowadays as the ancient musical instrument the lyre, but to the Greeks it represented a vulture. The arrow is fired from the constellation Sagittarius the hunter, therefore suggesting that Hercules takes on some aspect of the constellation Sagittarius. These three avian constellations rise one by one with the Sun as it moves into Sagittarius.

The seventh labour required Hercules to travel to Crete and the court of King Minos. On Crete a ferocious bull had been devastating the island. Hercules captured the bull and rode it back. It has been suggested that Taurus is the most likely constellation to be linked with the Cretan bull.

Task number eight involved catching the horses of the Thracian Diomedes. These were four man-eating horses, and this rather bloodthirsty task ends up with Hercules feeding Diomedes to his own horses, thus calming them and making their capture straightforward. It has been suggested that the four horses may well be represented by the four bright and prominent stars making up the square of Pegasus (the winged horse). Pegasus is a large constellation just above the ecliptic and rises with the zodiacal sign of Aquarius.

The ninth labour was to acquire the girdle of Hippolyte, the Queen of the Amazons. There is no obvious reference to links with any constellations, although it possibly refers to either the constellations of Virgo or Andromeda. The constellation Andromeda has a 'belt' or 'girdle' comprising three stars.

The tenth task was to steal the cattle of Geryon, a three-headed warrior giant often interpreted as the constellation Orion, who owned a two-headed watch dog, Orthrus. This character is associated with Canis Major and the star Sirius, the 'dog star'. Hercules kills both Orthrus and Geryon, and runs off with the cattle. However, the goddess Hera scatters the cattle, and in another calendar association it takes a whole year for Hercules to capture them again. A link between the story of Geryon and a zodiacal sign is found within another Greek tale, that of Castor and Polydeuces (Pollux). In this tale the twins also raid Geryon's herd of cattle with their cousins, Idas and Lynceus, but fall out with their fellow rustlers. Idas kills the mortal twin Castor, but the immortal Pollux is so grief-stricken that Zeus agrees to reunite them by placing them in the sky as the constellation Gemini. The Greeks believed that the stars in the Milky Way were cows surrounded by spilt milk. Gemini sits on one side of the Milky Way above the ecliptic while Orion, just below Gemini, and Sirius sit on the other side of the band of the Milky Way, below the Sun's path.

The eleventh labour was to acquire the apples of the Hesperides. The garden of the Hesperides was said to be on the slopes of Mount Atlas, one of the two mountains that Atlas stood on while supporting the heavens on his shoulders. Atlas was the father of numerous daughters; two groups of these are commemorated by the two most famous star clusters in the sky, the Pleiades (just above Taurus) and the Hyades (also part of Taurus). The seven Hesperides sisters (daughters of Atlas) may have been represented in the sky by the seven stars of what is now called the Little Bear (Ursa Minor).

The final task for Hercules, and his most difficult, was to bring back the three-headed dog Cerberos from the underworld. Not only does he have to find his way in and out of the underworld, but he has to get past Charon, as well as deal with the god of the underworld, Hades. His other major difficulty of course is how to get in alive and to escape alive. He achieves this, while also managing to rescue his friend Theseus. There are no obvious connections to known constellations for this particular labour.

Perhaps the first comment to make about the Hercules story is that while there seem to be some parallels between some of the signs of the zodiac (as we understand them) and certain tasks, some of the tasks seem to relate to non-zodiacal constellations, and some are difficult to relate to anything obvious in the night sky. However, this does not rule out the possibility that within this myth are traces of an older version of the zodiac and some of its associated constellations. The most straightforward associations between the zodiac and the twelve labours are found in task one (the lion, Leo), task two (the hydra and therefore Cancer), and task seven (the bull, Taurus). Then we have a number of tasks with some association with specific zodiacal signs. These are task three, where the hind or stag has associations with the constellation Scorpio; task five, where the stables have associations with Capricorn; task six, where the Stymphalian birds are associated with Sagittarius; and task ten, with Geryon's associations with Gemini. In a number of cases, the relationship between the mythological creatures in a particular task relates to their spatial proximity in the night sky, so for example the Stymphalian birds are depicted in the sky close to Sagitta and Sagittarius. Similarly,

Cancer the crab, sent by Hera to nip Hercules on the ankle, is immediately above the constellation Hydra. If this is also the case with the remaining tasks, then we might hazard a guess that the appearance of the centaur in task four (the Erymanthian boar) might suggest that a zodiacal 'boar' constellation might be found close to Centaurus. In other words, the boar could be in the vicinity of Libra or Scorpio.

Hercules and the Shandwick Stone

Could the alternative zodiac, suggested by the Hercules myths, bear more resemblance to the figures on this Pictish monument than our more familiar traditional zodiac? There would certainly appear to be some similarities. It is therefore pertinent to eliminate the possibility that the Shandwick stone is actually a depiction of the Twelve Labours of Hercules, rather than echoing an ancient and shared view of the night sky. If this was the case then we might expect substantial similarities between them. It would certainly not be beyond the realms of possibility that the Picts would be aware of the tale, as it must be remembered that they were close neighbours of the Romans for several hundred years, and must have had substantial contact with them. The Romans were enthusiastic about Hercules and his story, and it is perfectly feasible such tales could have made their way into Pictland during the Roman period in Britain. However, although there seem to be figures in common between the story and the stone, there are also many differences that cannot easily be explained. For example, there are the hunters in the top of the panel, the duelling twins in the bottom left-hand side, and several animals, all of which seem to have no direct part in the tales of Hercules. The hunter with the bow is trying to shoot the stag, not capture it and a second stag appears in the top right-hand side. It is difficult to know how to interpret the role of the tall central figure in the stone, within the context of the Hercules myth, although if it was a female figure it could conceivably represent the Amazon. Crucially, in relation to characters from the Hercules myths far more is missing from the Shandwick panel than is present. So we have no hydra, or crab, nothing that seems to relate to the Augean stables, nor the Thracian horses, Geryon, or Orthrus. There are no apples, nor the three-headed dog. Furthermore, the order of the figures that appear in the both the story and the stone do not coincide. On the Shandwick stone there is the possibility of order, which may relate to the order of the zodiac. The zodiacal order in the Hercules tales is more chaotic, and it could well be that later Greek versions of the myths and indeed Roman versions were unaware or perhaps simply unconcerned about the order the stories were told in, preferring dramatic effect to astronomical accuracy. If we are to believe that the Shandwick stone is a Herculean tableau, then we would have to postulate that the Picts had access to a version that is no longer extant and varies dramatically from the more familiar version. This in itself would be astonishing. We therefore have the fascinating possibility that the Shandwick stone has figures that appear in the Twelve Labours of Hercules but not in the classical zodiac, but also has figures that are zodiacal but do not appear in the Hercules myths.

What sort of relationship could there be between the Pictish carving and Hercules? The most obvious solution, as originally suggested, is that the myths of Hercules represents an ancient cosmology with references to an alternative zodiac that differs in a number of ways from the more familiar traditional zodiac that was introduced to

Greece from the East. We would also then have to postulate that the Picts version of the zodiac originated, at least in part, from the same source as the Greek alternative. On the Shandwick stone we looked at the possibility of a zodiacal arc from the bottom left to the bottom right of the panel. Some of the figures in this arc, it was suggested, might correspond to Gemini, Leo, Virgo and Sagittarius, but with no figures corresponding to Cancer, Libra or Scorpio. Bearing in mind the story of the twelve labours, if we take cognisance of the stag, in the bottom right-hand side adjacent to the hunter, as well as the presence of the wild boar on the path of our hypothesised arc, then these elements in the panel could well represent the zodiacal figures of Libra (corresponding to the boar), and Scorpio (corresponding to the stag) if we were to accept an alternative 'Herculean' zodiac. To this we could add the possibility that the bulls in the bottom left-hand side might represent Taurus. We should also note the close proximity that the eagle (also one of the Stymphalian birds in Hercules) on the panel has to the arc, and its relationship to the hunter figure, our potential Sagittarius.

Perhaps this potential commonality between Hercules and Shandwick does indeed offer a glimpse of an ancient European cosmology, complete with its own set of constellations. This may have been eclipsed in Greece by newer ideas from the East, and later elsewhere in Europe by the influences from the Roman Empire, but was one that doggedly persisted in both the tale of Hercules in Greek culture and also at the very north-west edge of Europe, beyond the Roman Empire, in Pictland.

Other civilisations throughout the world also have their own mythologies that are linked to specific constellation or stars, and the universal nature of these stories, whether from Australia, Peru, ancient Egypt, West Africa, China, India or Greece, suggests something fundamental about the link between the human psyche and the night sky. New discoveries and new interpretations of Neolithic and Bronze Age monuments and artefacts in Europe, for example Stonehenge in England, Newgrange in Ireland, the Nebra Disc found in Germany, and the strange conical Bronze Age 'wizard hats' emblazoned with the Moon and stars found in several European countries, all suggest that the movement of the heavens was just as fundamental and important to Europeans living in northern Europe as it has been to other peoples and civilisations. Scotland is dotted with stone circles, in large numbers (in what previously formed Pictland), including the great complex of circles at Callanish in Lewis, which is widely believed to be aligned to the lunar cycle. It might not therefore be too surprising, given our growing understanding of the role of astronomy in Stone Age and Bronze Age Europe, that the Picts could have retained an interest in astronomy and had their own versions of constellations in the night sky with perhaps even their own cosmology to explain it all. While some of the elements of Pictish astronomy and cosmology may have differed from other cultures in northern Europe, it is also likely that there may have been some commonality between their own ideas of the cosmos and those of other Indo-European cultures, including the ancient Greeks and other northern Europeans, particularly their other Celtic neighbours.

CHAPTER 5

CELTIC MYTHICAL CHARACTERS AND THE SHANDWICK HUNTING PANEL

Celtic Cosmology

It is possible that we may find within Celtic mythology, as with Greek mythology, that there are references to ancient constellations. These references could take the form of heroes, monsters or other fabulous creatures. Although there is no surviving Pictish mythology, it is possible that it may have borne some relationship to that of Ireland and Wales. It is known that there are many close parallels between the legends of these two countries and it is eminently possible, if we accept that the Picts were indeed Celtic, that Pictish mythology also contained elements and characters common to the other Celtic traditions. If the hypothesis is correct, which suggests that the figures taking part in the hunt on the Shandwick stone relate to constellations, then the form each figure takes and their relationship to the others around it may provide a basis for comparison with Celtic mythological tales. It may therefore even be possible to tentatively identify some of these figures. A comparative analysis between Celtic myths and the hunting panel could also perhaps find further evidence for 'wild boar' and 'stag' constellations, and provide clues about some of the other characters that appear on the stone. Clearly, a successful outcome to this analysis might suggest greater cultural commonality between the Celts of Ireland and Wales and the Picts than previously suspected, and therefore help considerably in determining whether or not the Picts were themselves essentially a Celtic people. In addition, we may be able to understand something more of the context of the Shandwick stone, and our ultimate goal of understanding the meaning and purpose of the symbols.

Searching for the Hunter: The Tale of 'Culhwch and Olwen'

On the Shandwick stone, on the right-hand side of the hunting panel, is a depiction of a wild boar. This is not an animal found as a constellation in the night sky we are familiar with, but it is an animal that not only seemed to have held a special mystical place in the minds of the peoples of northern Europe, but, as we have seen, also features, in the guise of the Erymanthian boar, in one of ancient Greece's most famous cosmological myths. Its presence on the Shandwick stone, among other figures with possible zodiacal connotations, could therefore provide the very real possibility that the Picts recognised, as the Greeks appear to have done, a constellation representing this creature in the sky.

Outside the classical world of Greece and Rome, there are of course other European mythological traditions; however, it is the stories of the Celts which are for many perhaps the most interesting and evocative. Stories passed down orally from generation to generation reveal glimpses of another world, one very much like that described in Greek mythology: a world of heroes, monsters, gods and goddesses. In the second half of the first millennium many of these stories, or at least fragments of them, were written down by monks. However, within these surviving sources can be glimpsed motifs and references that seem to be much older and may originate, like many of the Greek myths, in the Bronze Age. As with Greek mythology, some of these stories may indirectly refer to cosmology. It is known that the Welsh recognised the constellation of Ursa Major (the Great Bear) as relating to their hero, Arthur.

One Welsh mythological tale, in which Arthur is a relatively minor character, may well provide evidence of not only a Celtic wild boar constellation, but also of other constellations linked to elements of the story. This is the tale of 'Culhwch and Olwen', which forms part of the famous collection of ancient stories, the *Mabinogion*. The hero of the story is Culhwch (Arthur's cousin), who falls in love with Olwen, the daughter of Ysbaddaden the giant. As in most Celtic stories, however, the route to true love is never easy and, in a curious and distant parallel to the Twelve Labours of Hercules, Ysbaddaden sets Culhwch forty impossible tasks before he can gain Olwen. It is the penultimate challenge faced by the hero that is perhaps most interesting from our point of view.

The challenge set for Culhwch is to obtain three magical objects found between the ears of the giant wild boar, the Twrch Trwyth. This animal was really an evil king who had been transformed into a boar, and just like the Erymanthian boar was unbelievably strong and ferocious. Two of the objects Culhwch had to recover have interestingly enough a familiar Pictish symbolic flavour to them: a comb and a pair of shears. The third object that needed recovering was a razor. Culhwch gathered around him a most impressive hunting party, which consisted of no less a figure than Arthur plus many of Arthur's own men, including Cei, Bedwyr, and Gwalchmei. These three characters were transformed in later Arthurian tales into Sir Kay, Sir Bedevere, and Sir Gawain. He also required the help of Mabon ap Modron, who has been identified with the Celtic god Maponus, the hunter. Before the services of Mabon can be obtained, he must first be freed from his prison and unfortunately, prior to this, his prison must also be found.

An interpreter (Gwrhyr) is sent to ask some of the most ancient creatures in the world if they know the whereabouts of Mabon. Among the creatures asked are a wise bird, 'the ousel'; the 'stag of Redynvre'; the 'owl of Cwm Cawlwyd'; and the 'eagle of Gwernabwy'. The eagle tells Gwrhyr, 'I have been here for a great space of time, and that I first came hither there was a rock here, from the top of which I pecked at the stars every evening; and now it is not so much as a span high.' Finally, the eagle redirects Gwrhyr to the salmon (the Celtic repository of all knowledge), which identifies Mabon's prison, from which he is eventually freed. Following his escape from captivity, Mabon joins the hunt for the great wild boar, the Twrch Trwyth. This supernatural creature lived in Ireland with his seven piglets. Early attempts to remove the three treasures were unsuccessful. Irish heroes on the first day of the hunt failed to make any ground on the boar. The following day it was the turn of the Welsh; however, Arthur's companions also tried and failed. Even Arthur, who fought with the boar for nine days and nine nights, failed to make headway. Gwrhyr, the interpreter, tried to parley with the Twrch Trwyth, but the boar was so incensed with his treatment he promised to go to Britain and cause chaos there. This he did, crossing to Britain with his piglets, and was subsequently chased by Arthur and his band, who had crossed the sea in his ship *Prydwen*. The chase was long and difficult, with many of Arthur's warriors falling as they criss-crossed the Welsh countryside. Likewise, one by one the piglets were slain. The boar was eventually driven into the Severn estuary. Only here, where the boar was at a disadvantage, did he eventually yield up the shears and the razor. The boar then headed for Cornwall, still in possession of the comb. The final struggle is described as even worse than that which had gone before. The comb was ultimately retrieved, and the boar was driven into the deep ocean pursued by two magical hounds.

Is this a cosmological tale? It is tempting to suggest that the ancient other-worldly creatures which converse with the interpreter, mentioned in 'Culhwch and Olwen', may actually refer to constellations, reinforced by the description of the eagle's pecking at the stars. Gwrhyr's conversation with the animals might suggest a procession of constellations, preceding the arrival of Mabon, who may therefore be personified by a particular star, planet, or constellation. In this scenario Mabon's prison could be viewed as an analogy of a constellation, or celestial body, which has remained below the horizon for an extended period. Mabon's 'release' therefore might represent the first rising of this constellation, or heavenly body, at a particular time of year. The final imagery of the boar plunging into the sea could be seen as a graceful and poetic way of describing the path of a constellation as it sets in the west, the setting in some way relating to the rising of another constellation or planet. From the perspective of western Britain, the setting of a boar constellation would take place in the Atlantic Ocean, with the celestial figure seemingly disappearing beneath the waves on the horizon. Perhaps the hounds also refer to constellations or stars, setting either immediately after a boar constellation, or perhaps rising simultaneously in the east as the boar sinks in the west, therefore appearing to chase their quarry across the night sky. The imagery of the story certainly would seem to hint that it could well be cosmological in origin.

Heliacal Risings and the 'Twrch Trwyth'

While stars and their constellations travel nightly across the sky, many rising one after the other, each individual star rises at a slightly different time each progressive evening. A star that on one particular day rises at sunset, over a period of months, will rise later and later. Eventually it will rise just before sunrise. Therefore during the course of a year each rising star will on just one day rise simultaneously with the Sun. This is referred to as a 'heliacal rising'. The star will also set on just one day with the Sun, and this is the so-called 'heliacal setting'. For the brighter stars, these events could take on major significance in the minds of observers; for example, the heliacal rising of the spectacularly bright Sirius in ancient Egypt was thought by the Egyptians to trigger the Nile floods, thereby ensuring the fertility of the fields of the Nile valley. This celestial event was therefore believed to be vital to the survival of the country. In the story found within 'Culhwch and Olwen' we have a character, 'Gwrhyr', who converses with a series of animals, one after the other. If a cosmological interpretation is correct then we might imagine several possible scenarios. Firstly, we might perhaps postulate that this character represents a planet, the Sun, or the Moon. His conversation with each animal therefore could be analogous to the journey of these bodies across the star background, passing near, or even through, different constellations. A second possibility is that each animal might represent neighbouring constellations surrounding a specific star or constellation linked to Gwrhyr, with the interpreter speaking to each animal in turn. A third possibility is that the order in which he speaks to each animal may be a reference to the successive heliacal risings of different constellations.

If we list the animals in the order in which Gwrhyr spoke to them, we produce the following list: the wise bird, the stag, the owl, the eagle and the salmon. By examining possible candidate constellations we could try to determine whether or not there is a relationship between these candidates and the order of the animals in the story. Since the only animal within the story that apparently exists as a modern constellation is the eagle, we could make a start in unravelling this tale if we assume for the moment that the eagle is cognate with the modern constellation of Aquila the eagle. The principal star of this constellation is Altair, which is the twelfth brightest star in the night sky. Aquila is of course not a zodiacal sign but is very close to the zodiac, being positioned just above Capricorn and Sagittarius in the sky. Its physical relationship to Sagittarius is therefore, interestingly enough, mirrored in the spatial relationship between the eagle and the bowman on the Shandwick stone.

Using astronomical software it is actually possible to simulate the night sky over the British Isles in the latter half of the first millennium. With this technique we can determine the date of the heliacal rising of the star Altair in the constellation of Aquila, as well as other prominent stars that rise around the same time. If we ignore the stars and constellations representing human characters or inanimate objects leading up to the rising of Sagittarius (the hunter), and concentrate on those representing animals, then we can produce a list of principal stars from constellations that rose with the Sun.

A few days prior to the heliacal rising of the brilliant star Spica in AD 700, the constellation Corvus, the crow, rose in the dawn sky. Corvus is a classical constellation representing a crow, a bird renowned (like all members of the crow family generally) for its intelligence. The next major constellation representing an animal to rise was Cygnus, the swan. Alongside Cygnus in the sky is the constellation Lyra (the lyre). We have already seen that there was once a Greek constellation representing a vulture, with its magnificently bright star, Vega. Unfortunately the star and its associated constellation are circumpolar and do not heliacally rise at all, although like some of the other brighter stars of Cygnus it brushes the horizon due north in the autumn at sunrise. After Cygnus the stars of Scorpio start their heliacal ascent with its principal star, Antares (the Scorpion's red heart). Following Scorpio is the eagle constellation, or Aquila. The next constellation to heliacally rise is Delphinus, the dolphin. According to Richard Hinckley Allen, the constellation, seen principally by classical astronomers as a dolphin, was also known in Greek as the 'sacred fish'. Finally Sagittarius, the hunter, rises with the Sun just prior to the midwinter solstice.

The constellations representing animals listed above are therefore in the following order: Corvus, Cygnus, Scorpio, Aquila and Delphinus, all leading up to the appearance of Sagittarius the hunter. We therefore have two birds, a scorpion, an

Table 1.

Star Name	Constellation	Heliacal Rising Date
Gienah Corvi	Corvus	23 September
Albireo	Cygnus	25 October
Antares	Scorpio	16 November
Altair	Altair	21 November
Alpha Delphinus	Delphinus	24 November
Nunki	Sagittarius	20 December

Heliacal rising dates for principal stars of animal constellations, September to December 700 AD.

eagle and a dolphin. For the purposes of identification we could also substitute the dolphin for the alternative Greek notion of this constellation as a sacred fish, noting that the Celts revered the salmon. In general terms, if we are not too worried about the specific species of bird, we have then at least some similarity in mix and some similarity in order for the animals that Gwrhyr the interpreter spoke to in his quest to find Mabon the hunter. In the 'classical' sky the heliacal risings occur in the following order: a crow, swan, scorpion, eagle, sacred fish, and Sagittarius the hunter. In this Welsh tale the order in which each animal is approached is as follows: the wise bird, stag, owl, eagle, salmon, and Mabon the hunter. The similarity could be improved further if we could prove, in the context of the night sky, that the scorpion and stag were interchangeable. A working hypothesis might therefore be that the wise bird corresponds to Corvus the crow, the owl to Cygnus, the eagle to Aquila, the salmon to Delphinus, and Mabon to Sagittarius. This would leave us with the stag from the tale and Scorpio in the list of heliacal risings. We know, via the tale of Hercules, that the ancient Greeks connected the Ceryneian hind or Arcadian stag to the constellation Scorpio. Could the Celtic tale of 'Culhwch and Olwen' also be hinting at such a connection? Does the 'stag of Redynvre' actually represent an alternative interpretation of the constellation Scorpio?

Another simpler approach, when looking at the list of possible candidate stars and our Welsh list of animals, is not to view the specific order as wholly important (although it may well be highly significant), but rather to notice that the candidate constellations occupy a discrete area of the night sky. This area approximates to a rectangular portion of the sky stretching along the ecliptic from Libra to Sagittarius, then northwards (i.e. above the ecliptic) towards Cepheus and Draco. The constellations within this area are Libra, Scorpio, Sagittarius, Ophiuchus, Aquila, Scutum, Delphinus, Vulpecula, Cygnus, Lyra, Sagitta, and Hercules. The position of Ophiuchus is interesting within this group of constellations, as it borders Hercules, Lyra, Aquila, Sagittarius, Scorpio and Libra. Perhaps Ophiuchus in this 'Welsh' cosmos represents the interpreter Gwrhyr.

In our list of stars above, the sequence in which they rise culminates in the rising of the bright star Nunki. This star is in the constellation of Sagittarius the hunter, and would therefore fit very well with the appearance of Mabon the hunter in the 'Twrch Trwyth'. Perhaps the rising of Nunki originally marked the turning point of the year, and represented the god Maponus or Mabon. We still have as yet no firm match for the stag, but if the hypothesis that the story of the 'Twrch Trwyth' represents events surrounding the nightly course of specific stars, or constellations, then it could be possible that the Welsh recognised the constellation Scorpio as a stag. We will return to this possibility later on.

On the hunting scene from the Shandwick stone we have three birds, two stags, a wild boar, and a hunter. The wild boar occupies the space between the possible Virgo figure and the kneeling hunter, our candidate Sagittarius. If this reflects how the Picts perceived the constellations in the night sky, then the spatial relationships of the figures would imply they envisaged a wild boar in close proximity to a hunter, stags and birds. This would seem to echo, at least in part, both the Hercules myths and 'Culhwch and Olwen'. It might even be the case that Libra, or a constellation close to Libra, to the Welsh actually represented the wild boar, the Twrch Trwyth itself, right in the midst of the action. In the Greek tale of the Twelve Labours of Hercules, we know that one of his tasks involved capturing the Erymanthian boar, but despite many of the tasks seeming to be associated with specific zodiacal signs, no satisfactory match has been found for this creature. It would seem, however, that Libra makes a reasonable candidate for a wild boar constellation, especially if we remember that the story of the Erymanthian boar involved a centaur. This is represented in the sky by the neighbouring constellation of Centaurus. Such a possibility would seem to fit well with both the story of 'Culhwch and Olwen', and also with the figures on the hunting panel of the Shandwick stone.

Celtic Cosmology and the Fighting Warriors

For those familiar with Celtic mythology, the two warriors, apparently in combat with each other in the bottom left-hand side of the Shandwick hunting panel, should bring to mind the central theme of the Irish epic story *Táin Bó Cúailnge* (or *The Cattle Raid of Cooley*). This tale is thought to be ancient in origin, and has been compared, justifiably, to the Greek Homeric tradition. The principal character in this story is the hero Cuchulain, a figure also comparable with the best Greek heroes. The story concerns the outbreak of war between the Irish provinces of Ulster and Connaught, and has arisen essentially because of an argument between Maeve, the queen of Connaught, and her husband King Ailil. Each boasts that they are wealthier than the other but here in ancient Ireland, as in other ancient societies, wealth is measured in cattle. While they can match each other on the number of fine cattle they own, Queen Maeve's fortune falls short of her husband's, due to his ownership of a magnificent white bull. Not to be outdone, Maeve casts her jealous eye to the neighbouring kingdom of Ulster, and to the finest bull in all Ireland, the Brown Bull of Cooley. Maeve, unable to obtain the bull by legitimate means, soon appropriates the bull by means of a cattle raid into Ulster. In response, the king of Ulster quickly gathers an army of the finest warriors to retrieve his prize bull and seek revenge, but his warriors unfortunately fall into a magical deep sleep, which of course prevents them from marching on Connaught. However, one warrior is immune to the magic due to his divine parentage, Cuchulain. This supreme warrior is alone but not at all intimidated. He goes out to meet Maeve's considerable army, challenging her warriors one by one to single-handed combat. In true Celtic heroic tradition he despatches everyone thrown against him. Finally, Maeve sends in the Connaught champion, Ferdiad. This hero is the equal of Cuchulain but more importantly is his old friend and blood brother. Despite their closeness, after a truly epic struggle lasting three days, Ferdiad, much to Cuchulain's anguish, is slain. However, the Ulster champion in this titanic contest has also been mortally wounded and he too dies. Maeve claims victory, but this is short-lived, as the white and brown bulls also engage in a fight to the death. The great conflict rages back and forward all over Ireland. Eventually, the brown bull manages to kill the white, and escapes back to Ulster. Like Cuchulain, this fight has taken an enormous toll on the brown bull and on his return to Ulster his heart bursts.

Could this story also contain elements of sky mythology? Peter Beresford Ellis certainly thinks that the *Táin Bó Cúailnge* contains such imagery, pointing out that that King Ailil's palace is described as being circular, with twenty-seven windows. From these he can observe his twenty-seven 'star wives'. This number is the approximate number of days that the Moon takes to complete one orbit of the earth. Beresford Ellis also pointed out that this number corresponds to the number of lunar mansions, or *nakshatras*, used in ancient Indian Vedic astrology (which can be twenty-seven or twenty-eight). A lunar mansion is a portion of sky around the ecliptic corresponding to the Moon's progression over twenty-four hours. Each mansion is identified by a key prominent star. In Hindi mythology the *nakshatras* are clearly seen as female, with each star identified as a wife of the Moon god 'Chandra'. Beresford Ellis therefore suggests that King Ailil's 'wives' might therefore be identified as the principal star in each mansion, and Ailil could therefore be the Celtic personification of the Moon.

In the story, Cuchulain is clearly no ordinary mortal man, nor is his 'brother' and near equal, Ferdiad. The Ulster hero is thought to be none other than the son of the god of light, Lugh. Ferdiad is the son of the goddess of the underworld, and it is not beyond the imagination to see this clash as a classic battle between light and dark, epitomised in many cultures by fighting brothers or twins. Similarly the clash between the two bulls, one white and one brown, may also represent the eternal struggle between light and dark. We therefore seem to have some parallels with the classical image of the Gemini twins, Castor and Pollux, who of course are not just to be viewed as characters from mythology, but as important stars in the night sky.

The possibility that Cuchulain and Ferdiad represent the eternal struggle between light and dark emerges in some of the descriptions of the two combatants. The physical description of Cuchulain, in particular his red and gold hair, is reminiscent of the Sun; when he bathes his hair turns dark red. This is a clear allusion to the Sun setting into the western ocean. Ferdiad likewise, at times, has a non-human appearance. During the battle with Cuchulain, he momentarily takes on a dark and other-worldly aspect.

Perhaps these two warriors were represented in the night sky by the two stars of Gemini, and the tale has a distant relationship to the story of Castor and Pollux.

The other principal element to the story of the *Táin Bó Cúailnge*, and as important as the struggle between Cuchulain and Ferdiad, are the two bulls: the white bull of Connaught and the brown bull of Cooley. If the two warriors might possibly be matched to the principal stars of Gemini, then it is also possible that the bulls represent stars that are in some way related to this constellation. A possible identification of candidate stars is surprisingly straightforward, lying within the neighbouring constellation of Taurus, the bull. This constellation is made particularly distinctive by two clear 'horns' which form a very obvious 'v' shape extending towards Gemini. Between these two constellations lies the Milky Way. Today, Taurus rises well before the stars of Gemini, but over a thousand years ago this was not the case. Taurus would have risen, in both Ireland and Scotland, alongside Castor and Pollux. It can therefore be readily demonstrated that there was a clear relationship between these two constellations, at the very least in terms of rising. Gemini would have risen slightly further to the north than Taurus, and therefore the twins would appear to the left of the horns of Taurus. Each horn is dominated by a very bright star, the lower by the reddish-brown Aldebaran, and the upper by El Nath, a brilliant white star. Could these two stars have represented the white bull and the brown bull? Intriguingly, the key to the celestial origins of the *Táin Bó Cúailnge*, and specifically the warriors and the bulls, may lie in a fragment of Irish cosmology; the Milky Way, which separates Gemini and Taurus, is known in Irish as the *Bóthar na Bó Finne* or 'the path of the white cow'. This seems to have some strong parallels with the ancient Greek notion of the Milky Way representing a herd of cattle, Geryon's cattle. The cattle represent discrete but recognisable stars within the band, while the 'milky' component of the band supposedly represent the cow's spilt milk. Our candidate for the white bull of Connaught, the star El Nath, actually lies in the band of the Milky Way, perhaps reinforcing the relationships between bulls and the celestial cattle. Close by, the brilliant star Capella, part of the classical constellation of Auriga, lies on the Milky Way, and could also form part of a 'white bull' asterism.

On the Shandwick stone, the presence of the two warriors facing each other with two bulls immediately to their right, also confronting one another, seems not only to fit with the configuration of the rising constellations of Gemini and Taurus, but with the ancient Irish story of the cattle raid on Cooley. This part of the panel may well represent a story relating and explaining the rising of these two constellations, a story that at least in part resembles some of the components of the *Táin Bó Cúailnge*. Furthermore, the calf lying between the warriors seems to indicate that their struggle is over cattle, and in the context of both the story of Castor and Pollux, and the *Táin Bó Cúailnge*, it could conceivably be a fight over a celestial herd representing the Milky Way.

In Welsh mythological tradition there is a tale that would seem to have some characteristics that may also fit a wider tradition of warrior opposites. This story may help to illustrate that this concept not only existed in Ireland, but may also have played an important role in the folklore and traditions of Celts residing in Britain. Once again, rather than quaint cherubic boys we have, within the Welsh tradition, two warriors opposing each other, both literally and metaphorically. The significance of this to the Shandwick stone is that the tale's existence demonstrates that within Dark Age Celtic Britain there was a tradition with echoes of Cuchulain and Ferdiad, and it again raises the notion of opposing but intertwined forces fighting each other, a sort of Celtic 'yin and yang'. If we consider that the Picts, as well as being in close proximity to Ireland, neighboured Welsh-speaking kingdoms to the south, then the possibility that the Picts also recognised such concepts is increased markedly. This Welsh story, which once again centres on a dispute over cattle, is full of imagery which is undoubtedly stellar. This story concerns two sons of the god Beli and the goddess Don; these are Nynniaw and his brother Peibaw. As in the *Táin Bó Cúailnge*, they boast to one another about who owns more cattle. This argument soon ends in conflict. Charles Squire recounted the story in his book *Celtic Myth and Legend*:

> The tale, put into writing at a time when all the gods were being transfigured into simple mortals, tells us that they were two kings of Britain, brothers. One starlight night they were walking together. 'See,' said Nynniaw to Peibaw, 'what a fine wide-spreading field I have.' 'Where is it?' asked Peibaw. 'There,' replied Nynniaw; 'the whole stretch of the sky, as far as the eye reaches.' 'Look then,' returned Peibaw, 'what a number of cattle I have grazing on your field.' 'Where are they?' asked Nynniaw. 'All the stars that you can see,' replied Peibaw, 'every one of them of fiery-coloured gold, with the Moon for a shepherd over them.' 'They shall not feed on my field' cried Nynniaw. 'They shall,' exclaimed Peibaw. 'They shall not' cried Nynniaw. 'They shall' said Peibaw. 'They shall not,' Nynniaw answered; and so they went on, from contradiction to quarrel, and from private quarrel to civil war, until the two authors of the evil were turned by god into oxen for their sins.

In this story we can recognise a number of common themes that are found in the both the myth of Castor and Pollux and also in the *Táin Bó Cúailnge*: two divine or semi-divine 'brothers' in conflict – either between themselves or with others – over early society's most treasured possession, cattle. What is interesting about this particular Welsh story is the unambiguous link to the stars, which is also reflected in the story of Castor and Pollux. This celestial connection is now seemingly less clear in the story featuring Cuchulain and Ferdiad, although we should remind ourselves that even here there are allusions to the Sun and 'star wives'. The cattle in question in this particular story, in a parallel with those featuring in Castor and Pollux, would seem to be stars, although Peibaw's cattle are not specifically mentioned as stars of the Milky Way. In another version of the same story a giant becomes involved in the conflict, claiming the stars and the sky for himself. This again parallels the story of Castor and Pollux, who are involved in raiding the cattle of Geryon, a giant linked to the constellation of Orion who, as we have seen, is in turn linked to Hercules. The Welsh giant in question is Rhitta, the king of Wales, who like Geryon is warrior-like. In Rhitta's case, he commands an army and attacks the brothers for the destruction they have brought on the people and countryside of Wales. The punishment for their crime, once Rhitta defeats them, is that the brothers are to be banished and, rather bizarrely, have their beards cut off. The remaining twenty-six of the twenty-eight kings of Britain rise up against Rhitta, for what they see as a tremendous slight, and war breaks out. Unfortunately they also lose and have their beard cut off by the giant, who consequently adds further to his 'extensive field'. Kings from outside Britain then became involved and also have their beards cut, the hair now being used to make a mantle for the giant. Now only one person stands between the giant's claim on all the stars in night sky: Arthur. This legendary figure has a rival claim on the firmament and defeats Rhitta, cutting off his beard in the process, thus winning the whole of the night sky.

If Geryon is linked to the constellation Orion, which lies close by but on the other side of the Milky Way from the constellation representing Gemini, then is it possible that the Welsh mythological characters of Nynniaw, Peibaw and the giant Rhitta are equivalents of the Greek mythological characters that we know are associated with these particular constellations? We will return to this possibility later on. It is also interesting that there are twenty-eight kings mentioned, and perhaps like the twenty-seven star wives of King Ailil, these might suggest the twenty-seven or twenty-eight days of the lunar cycle. Could each king, including Nynniaw and Peibaw, represent stars on the Moon's monthly path? If Nynniaw and Peibaw represent the twin stars of Gemini, and if we count this as one lunar mansion, then we would arrive at a total of twenty-seven potential Welsh lunar mansions. For the second time, therefore, we may have a reference in a Celtic tale, concerning a conflict between warriors over cattle, to potential lunar mansions. Does this then hint at a Celtic astrological system based on the cycle of the Moon? If this really is a Welsh star myth then the whole story may reflect the winter dominance of the constellation Orion, that is Rhitta, who eventually gives way to the summer stars, suggesting that Arthur may have been represented in the sky by a summer constellation or perhaps even by the Sun itself.

We can now also see that the imagery in the bottom left-hand side of the Shandwick stone, with the two warriors and the two bulls, as well as fitting with key motifs in *Táin Bó Cúailnge*, has imagery that also fits well with the story of Nynniaw and Peibaw. In this case, we not only have the two brothers facing each other, but also the two bulls facing each other which may represent the two brothers transformed into oxen. We could therefore have the possibility that the Picts had a star myth, reflected in this portion of the stone, with at least some of the common elements found in the story of the Cuchulain and Ferdiad conflict, and in the story of Nynniaw and Peibaw. We therefore can now reconstruct the bare bones of this hypothetical Pictish myth. The basic elements of such a story could be that the two divine brothers, representing the stars Castor and Pollux, become involved in conflict with each other over cattle. Two bulls, representing the stars El Nath and Aldebaran, struggle in a parallel conflict over the same cattle, and are therefore intrinsically connected to the brothers, perhaps even to the two men transformed. Both men and bulls are engaged in a celestial and eternal struggle. The tales of both Castor and Pollux and the *Táin Bó Cúailnge* may reflect a Bronze Age cultural emphasis on wealth measured by head of cattle. Similarly the Welsh story of the brothers and the imagery on this Pictish stone may hint at the same common Bronze Age heritage.

Finally there is a tale from Wales, found in the *Mabinogion*, which also echoes some of the themes found in the *Táin Bó Cúailnge*. The two characters in the story, with roots that lie in Dark Age Welsh oral tradition, do not seem to be twins or even brothers, but as in the story of Cuchulain the basic theme of light and dark is very clear. Further analysis of the tale also suggests that it may reflect an astronomical origin. The story concerns two rivals in pursuit of the same woman. The first suitor is Gwyn ap Nudd, and his rival is Gwyrthur ap Greidawl. The object of their desire is Creurdylad, daughter of the Welsh sea-god Llyr. Creurdylad will be better known to readers as Shakespeare's Cordelia, daughter of King Lear, as the characters in his play originated from within the Welsh mythological tradition. Drawing once again on Charles Squire's book *Celtic Myth and Legend*,

> Gwyn has a rival a deity called Gwyrthur ap Greidawl, that is 'Victor, son of Scorcher'. These two waged perpetual war on Creurdilad, or Creudylad, each in turn stealing her from the other, until the matter was referred to Arthur, who decided that Creudylad should be sent back to her father, and that Gwyn and Gwyrthur 'should fight for her every first of May, from henceforth until the day of doom, and that whichever of them should then be conqueror should have the maiden'. […] In Gwyn, god of death and the underworld, and in the solar deity, Gwyrthur, we may see the powers of darkness and Sunshine, of winter and summer, in contest, each alternatively winning and losing a bride who may seem to represent the spring with its grain and flowers.

The case for the identification of the characters Gwyn and Gwyrthur as representing the forces of light and darkness is strengthened when we consider the curious circumstances concerning Gwyn's and Gwyrthur's fate. Firstly, the concept of them being forced to fight on the same day annually 'until the day of doom' reminds us of a calendar event, events that are governed by the motion of the heavenly bodies, by the cycles of the stars and planets. The never-ending nature of the punishment could also suggest the eternal cycle of these bodies in the night sky. It is possible that the two adversaries in this story represent summer (the time of light) and winter (the time of darkness), with 1 May in the story signifying a turning point in the year and the return of the Sun. It may also be significant that an examination of astronomical events around the date given (1 May), using computer software, reveals another possible explanation for the story. Dependent on latitude during May, in the early medieval period, and if we chose AD 700 as an arbitrary date, Castor would rise with the Sun. Likewise, about two weeks later, Pollux rises with the Sun. These heliacal risings, as we have already discussed, were seen as highly significant, forming the basis of a number of astrological systems and even governing festivals. The heliacal rising of Castor in Scotland in AD 700 occurred on 1 May. It should be noted that the Welsh kingdom of Strathclyde, centred near Glasgow, had strong connections with three of the four prominent ancient Welsh bards, and could also have had connections to a significant portion of ancient Welsh literature. Significantly, 1 May happens to be the date of the one of the most important Celtic festivals, *Beltane*. It is therefore possible that this tale is describing the rising of the first of the twin stars of Gemini, which marked a major turning point of the year and therefore was the actual signal for the start of this ancient festival. Due to the Earth's slow processional motion, the stars of Gemini no longer rise on 1 May.

In the *Táin Bó Cúailnge* we have seen how the fraternal adversaries, Cuchulain and Ferdiad, are interlinked with cattle ownership and raiding, and hypothesised that the story itself relates to the constellations Gemini and Taurus. Could this story also be linked to the marking of *Beltane*? Curiously enough, in both Scotland and Ireland, fires were traditionally lit at *Beltane*. The young men of the community would leap across these fires to show their bravery and athleticism. Later when there was little but embers left, the community's cattle would be driven across the remains of this *Beltane* fire. Perhaps there is some long-lost celestial symbolism found within these traditions, which mirrored the rise around May Day in the dawn sky of the two warriors alongside the rise of the rival bulls. Rising with the two constellations on May Day was the Sun; perhaps this was represented by the *Beltane* fire.

Could the warrior pair on the Shandwick stone also relate to the heliacal rising of Castor and Pollux, and could the positioning of these twins also relate to *Beltane*?

Celtic Mythology and the Virgin

If there is a possibility that the Shandwick stone figures relate to constellations, then can we find evidence from Celtic mythology which might help identify our notional Virgo figure? If we once again turn to Welsh myth, the female figure of Virgo has a number of possible parallels with characters in these stories; in particular there is very strange story from the *Mabinogion*, which just might help, involving the god Math. This story is entitled 'The Legend of Math and Goewin'. Math is the brother of the goddess Don, one of the principal figures in the Celtic pantheon of gods and goddesses. Don also features in Irish mythology as Danu, and in the name of the mythological Irish race the *Tuatha Dé Danaan*. Her name has also been linked to river names, including the rivers Don in Aberdeenshire and Yorkshire, and also to the Danube in central Europe. Math is considered to be a great warrior. He has, however, like many other mythological heroes, a major weakness. In a curious parallel to the Greek Achilles, he is practically invincible, but has one potentially fatal flaw; his feet are the only part of him vulnerable to attack and therefore could potentially lead to his demise. Unlike Achilles, however, his weakness is not exposed as a result of a fortuitous blow in battle, but rather it is expressed when he is not fighting. When not at war, he will die without having his feet placed on the lap of a virgin. This bizarre tale is not easily explained and seems to make little sense. If we hypothesise that some characters within the *Mabinogion* actually refer to stars, then we may be able to explain this conundrum. If we assume that Math's maiden, Goewin, might represent a Celtic Virgo, then can we examine a star map to identify Math and explain the story? The constellation Virgo lies on and parallel to the ecliptic, the Sun's path. Her 'lap' roughly corresponds to a line drawn between the brightest star in Virgo, Spica, and another, Zeta Virgini. If we extend this line outwards away from the ecliptic, northwards in the sky, it hits the neighbouring constellation of Bootes and in particular is in very good alignment with Bootes' brightest star, Arcturus. This star is the second brightest in northern sky. Bootes itself represents the figure of a man and lies at right angles to Virgo. What is perhaps most significant is that his legs reach down and almost touch Virgo's lap. If we remember that Virgo represents a fertility symbol, it makes perfect sense to view the legend of Math placing his 'feet' in her 'lap' as a thinly disguised sexual reference. The relationship between Spica and Arcturus could also relate to the concept of the Virgin becoming fertilised, eventually 'bearing fruit' at harvest time. It is therefore possible that the heliacal rising of Arcturus, and then Spica, may have had some significance in marking the harvest. This is further emphasised when it is remembered that the star Spica represents a ripe wheat sheaf. Furthermore, Bootes is regarded as a constellation with its origins in the transition from a hunter-gatherer society in Europe to a farming society. His hunting persona is therefore in keeping with the possibility that Math is his Celtic counterpart, and with Math's close relationship with the maiden.

If we again turn to a computer simulation of the night sky and examine the heliacal risings of the two stars Arcturus and Spica, we find that in AD 700 Spica rose heliacally across Europe on 27 September. Going back to AD 1, the heliacal rising would have occurred on 22 September. Spica would therefore be intrinsically involved with marking the end of the harvest all over Europe, and its heliacal rising significantly would also have occurred shortly after the autumn equinox, thus marking the change in seasons. Arcturus, because of its greater distance from the ecliptic, would show more variation with latitude than Spica, but its heliacal rising would allow a countdown in days to take place prior to Spica's appearance. Therefore we can see a possible role for Arcturus as a royal herald for the arrival of Spica. In the Welsh kingdom of Strathclyde, Bootes would rise with the Sun on 3 September, in north Wales on 5 September, and in Rome on 15 September.

If Welsh legend hints at a possible harvest couple, corresponding to Virgo and Bootes in the story of Math and the Virgin's lap, then does the Shandwick stone also have a candidate for Math or Bootes? There would appear to be two candidates for this role on the panel. The Virgo figure has male riders on both sides, and either of these might be identified as a possible Math. There does not, however, appear to be any connection between the feet of either figure and the maiden's lap, although the right-hand figure may be extending a spear shaft back towards our possible Virgo figure.

The Celtic God of Light and the Lion

Previously we looked at the possibility that the lion figure on the Shandwick stone might represent the constellation of Leo. Can we therefore identify within Celtic mythology allusions to the constellation of Leo?

Besides the characters mentioned above, other fascinating characters appear in the Welsh mythological tradition, and some of these also seem to have connections to the stars. For example, there are Gwydion, the druid of the gods, and Gwydion's wife, Arianrod, who is bizarrely also his sister. Arianrod's name, according to Charles Squire, means 'silver circle', and this has been widely interpreted as a celestial reference. Two possibilities exist to identify Arianrod; firstly, the 'silver circle' could represent the silvery band of the Milky Way, or secondly it could represent the silvery Moon. That Arianrod is connected to the night sky in some way is further confirmed by the name of one of the few constellations that has kept a Celtic version of its name. This is the constellation we know today by its Greek name of Corona Borealis. We know that this was referred to by the Welsh as Arianrod's Palace.

Arianrod and Gwydion had two sons, and once again we find within them the recurring theme of opposites. One son, Dylan, is associated with darkness or night, the other, Lleu, with light or day. Dylan's plunge into the sea as soon as he was born should also remind us of the Twrch Trwyth and its disappearance into the western ocean. Does Dylan, like Arianrod his mother, also represent a star or a planet, and if so which? Lleu is a god of light, a solar deity, and indeed his name has in the past been thought to relate to a root Indo-European word meaning light, although there is some dispute currently over this. The words 'lux' and our own word in English 'light', it has been suggested, may be cognate with the same root. His full name is Lleu Llaw Gyffes, which has been translated as 'light of the long hand' or sometimes as 'lion of the steady hand'. Lleu has an Irish counterpart in Lugh, who is also Cuchulain's father, who we have already seen features prominently in Irish legend. The story of how Lleu got his name sounds a little whimsical and contrived. As a test of his marksmanship, Lleu took aim with his bow at a wren's leg. He managed to pierce the bird's leg, and Arianrod, with obvious pleasure, remarked, 'Truly the lion aimed at it with a steady hand' therefore giving rise to his name. As Charles Squire observed about the origins of Lleu's name,

> This name of the Sun-god is a good example of how obsolete the ancient pagan tradition had become before it was put into writing. The old word Lleu, meaning 'light', had passed out of use, and the scribe substituted for a name that was unintelligible to him one like it which he knew, namely Llew, meaning 'lion'. The word Gyffes seems also to have suffered change, and to have meant originally not 'steady', but 'long'.

While Squire makes an interesting point in regard to the possibility of a scribal error, it may not have been a mistake. Is it possible that the supposed confusion between 'Lleu' and 'Llew' is actually a deliberate pun? A pun perhaps in common currency at the time of transcription and deliberately intended to elevate the god to an even more exulted status? If Lleu was associated strongly not just with the Sun, but also a divine or celestial lion, then there would be a strong temptation to deliberately pun his name. More recently, some linguists have cast doubt on the relationship between the god's name rendered in the various Celtic forms (Lug, Lugh, or Lleu) and the theoretical proto-Indo-European word for light (*leuk*). These doubts relate to theories on the necessary linguistic steps required for *leuk* to evolve into the Celtic forms of the god's name, although there are other scholars who have put forward possible explanations as to why this still may be reasonable. In addition, there are some scholars who have proposed that perhaps 'Lugh' may actually be a more specific term indicating the light from lightening bolts or flashes. The Gaulish version of Lugh or Lleu, 'Lugus', seems to have been roughly equivalent to the Irish and Welsh versions in terms of character and attributes. However, there is some confusion as to how the Romans interpreted Lugus. Caesar hints that he, without specifically naming the god, was the equivalent of the god Mercury and was Gaul's most popular deity. Mercury in the Roman pantheon is a relatively minor figure. Mercury and the Irish Lugh, however, do seem to share some attributes, particularly their mastery of 'all arts'. However, the god Apollo seems to be closer to Lugh in terms of solar symbolism, and clearly Lugh is not a humble messenger but a warrior with flaming red hair and a fiery spear. We therefore must be very careful when assuming that the Romans were correct in associating particular

Gaulish gods with their supposed Roman equivalents, and they may have chosen to see similarities for reasons of expediency. Similarly, the etymological study of Indo-European words is still it appears very much in its infancy, and this is reflected in the confusing array of suggestions for the origin of 'Lugus'.

Continuing with the hypothesis regarding the possible pun of Lleu's name, if a god of light had an association with a celestial lion, can we identify which star or constellation might have represented such a lion? Apart from the regal association with the figure of the lion, we can go a long way to answering these questions if we hypothesise that Lleu was associated with one of the most important constellations in the sky, Leo. The answer, therefore, to the translation of Lleu Llaw Gyffes as 'lion of the steady hand' may lie in the status of Leo within the zodiac.

In astrology, each star sign has been traditionally associated with a ruling planet. According to the traditions of astrology you were particularly blessed if you were born while your zodiacal Sun sign had its ruling planet residing within its confines. In other words, it was believed that the influence of a particular constellation was substantially enhanced when its ruling planet resided within it. Present-day astrology distributes the eight planets, excluding our own planet Earth, but including the recently expelled Pluto, plus the Moon and the Sun, among the twelve signs of the zodiac. Prior to the discovery of Neptune, Uranus and Pluto, in the eighteenth, nineteenth and twentieth centuries respectively, each real planet ruled two signs each, with the Moon and the Sun ruling the remaining two. Saturn, the slowest traveller across the sky, and outermost of the original known planets, ruled the constellations of Aquarius and Capricorn. The imagery here is striking; these two wintry signs were ruled by the very symbol of senescence and time – the ancient Saturn. Jupiter ruled the signs on either side of Saturn's two signs, Pisces and Sagittarius. Mars ruled Scorpio and Aries, Venus ruled Taurus and Libra, and the innermost planet, Mercury, ruled Gemini and Virgo. The Moon ruled the zodiacal constellation Cancer, which is followed by the constellation of Leo Major, which in turn was ruled by the Sun. Leo and Cancer are also directly opposite in the heavens, and, in the calendar, to Saturn's two winter zodiac signs.

Leo therefore, like Lleu, is strongly associated with the Sun, a fact that might help explain the potential scribal pun on his name. Another clue that this solar deity was associated with Leo is the alpha star Regulus. The name of this star, one of the brightest in the sky, simply means 'ruler', and is a diminutive of the word *rex* or king. While we are familiar with the notion of the lion as a king, there are other reasons why Regulus may have a much more prominent role as a stellar ruler. According to Richard Hinckley Allen, it was called this 'because of the belief that it ruled the affairs of the heavens' and he also states, 'Thus as Sarru, the king, it marked the 15th ecliptic constellation of Babylonia.' Another probable reason is that Regulus lies very close to the Sun's path, the closest of all the principal bright stars. It is so close to the ecliptic that the Sun almost eclipses the star every year in August. This makes it almost unique, and emphasises its relationship to the Sun.

The theory that there is an association between the Celtic god Lleu and the constellation Leo may be further enhanced when we consider the phenomenon of precession and the traditional date of Lleu or Lugh's festival. Lleu's name is thought to be commemorated in a number of place names in both Britain and Europe, including

Lyon (*Lugodunon*) in France, Leyden in Holland and perhaps even London. The timing of the festivals dedicated to this Celtic god is significant. Lyon, in the Roman period, hosted a festival on 1 August, probably rededicated by the emperor Augustus Caesar from Lug to Apollo. In Ireland and Scotland, Lugh's festival is known as *Lughnasa*, and is also associated with 1 August. Similarly, Wales has the 'August Feast' or *Gwyl Awst* associated with Lleu. The Celtic festival of *Lughnasa* (Lammas), on 1 August, is one of the four principal points in the Celtic calendar, which also includes *Beltane* (May Day), *Samhain* (Halloween), and *Imbolc* (St Bridget's Day).

Can we link the date of the festival associated with Lleu, or Lugh, in his various forms with Leo's alpha star, Regulus? If we could, it would indicate a likely relationship. If we use our standard date of AD 700 in a simulation of the night sky, we find that the heliacal rising of the Regulus with the Sun would have occurred exactly on 1 August, the date of the major Celtic festival of *Lughnasa*. The heliacal rising of Regulus today occurs around 22 August. The association of a specific Celtic festival date with a significant celestial event is astounding. This event would have occurred during the very time when the Irish and Welsh mythological tales were becoming fixed, when scribes started to write down oral stories. The phenomenon of precession would have created a gradual drift away from this date for the heliacal rising of Regulus to later in August as the centuries progressed. Likewise, going back in time from AD 700, we would find that this astronomical event would occur at the very end of July in 1 AD. This event would be latitude-insensitive due to the proximity of Regulus to the ecliptic.

Would we not expect then the modern date for the celebration of *Lughnasa* to be significantly later in August, as precession moved the Sun's apparent position against the stellar background? If the date was set according to a perceived association between the star and the Sun, we would expect it to be shifted, but only if there were people capable of and willing to make the complicated observations required to adjust the festival calendar. This possible 'freezing' of the *Lughnasa* date during the last few centuries of the first millennium, most likely at around the beginning of the eighth century, could even indicate when Christianity in Ireland had finally subdued the remnants of an organised druidic tradition. By AD 750 the heliacal rising of Regulus would have been occurring on 2 August. Assuming *Lughnasa* was not a fixed festival, but was dependent on celestial events, then we must reach the rather startling conclusion, for those who today recognise and mark *Lughnasa* (and indeed the other Celtic festivals), that we should celebrate these some twenty-two days later than we do at the moment. As previously discussed, the twin warriors on the Shandwick stone may represent the beginning of May, specifically May Day, and the lion's position therefore may correspond to 1 August or *Lughnasa*.

It is also possible that specific star risings were used to determine the timing of all four of the major religious Celtic festivals. This would imply that there were individuals who were tasked with observing the movements of the heavens. Given the religious significance of the festivals, it is likely that the observers would have been from the druidic orders, and one is reminded of Caesar's observation that Gaulish druids could name 360 stars, one for every day of the Celtic year. This might suggest that they saw significance each day in a particular rising star, but presumably the most important events were marked by the most important stars.

CHAPTER 6

An Ancient European Cosmology

Ancient Skies

So far we have found parallels between the Pictish imagery on the Shandwick stone and Greek and Celtic mythology. This has allowed us to tentatively suggest that a number of characters from Celtic mythology were represented as constellations in the night sky; furthermore, figures on the Shandwick stone may actually depict these or very similar celestial characters. We have also explored the possibility that the wild boar on the stone represents a long lost constellation in the vicinity of Libra, perhaps even Libra itself. Its presence on the stone might not only be emphasising the astronomical significance of the animal, but also echoing the mythological and cosmological connections found within ancient Greek and Celtic stories. A similar case can be made for the stag figure that appears on the bottom right of the hunting panel, and indeed the bowman who appears to be hunting the stag. The stag and the bowman may well be Celtic equivalents of Scorpio and Sagittarius, two constellations that sit side by side in the night sky. The boar and stag feature in the story 'Culhwch and Olwen', along with a salmon and two birds, and it is possible that these are also represented in the same area of the night sky as the hunter Sagittarius. The two birds might correspond to Aquila (the eagle) and Corvus (the crow). The salmon in the story (although not on the stone) may correspond to Delphinus. The two warriors on the monument could relate to both Irish and Welsh mythological stories regarding brothers who fight over cattle, or bulls, and also to the Greek mythological Gemini twins. Beside the two warrior figures on the Shandwick stone are two bulls that are also facing each other, and these might be explained in this same context. The cattle motif is further enhanced by the presence of the calf between the warriors, suggesting to the viewer that the fight is indeed over cattle. The warriors and the bulls may have been linked to the festival of *Beltane*. It was also suggested in the previous chapter that the Celts envisaged a Virgo-like character as a constellation. Finally we explored the possibility that there may have been a connection between the constellation Leo and the Celtic god known as Lugh, Llew or Lugus. This suggested that the Celts also recognised Leo, the lion, in the night sky and it was used to mark the date of one of the key Celtic festivals dedicated to Lugh (*Lughnasa*).

The God Cernunnos, the Stag and the Boar

We will now further investigate the possibility that seemingly long-forgotten 'boar' and 'stag' constellations occupied a portion of the night sky in the neighbourhood of Ophiuchus, Scorpio and Libra, and indeed may have corresponded to two of these classical constellations. This region may well have included long-forgotten constellations, with only echoes of their existence surviving in Greek and Celtic mythology. The hunting panel on the Shandwick stone may well be the means to confirm this exciting possibility. A casual examination of the constellation of Ophiuchus, however, gives us no obvious clues to there being any stag or wild boar connection. This classical constellation is large and represents a celestial human figure normally depicted holding two snakes. The snakes are sometimes classed as the separate constellation of Serpens, and this can be further divided into a right and left portion. Ophiuchus has in the past been associated with Aesculapius, the surgeon on Jason's ship the *Argo*. A clue, however, from one of Europe's finest archaeological treasures may provide a link between the stag, the boar and the constellation Ophiuchus. This Greek mythological figure with his serpents is, strangely enough, reminiscent of a figure that apparently featured in Celtic religious belief. This god, known as 'Cernunnos', whose name according to Miranda Green in her *Dictionary of Celtic Myth and Legend* means 'horned or peaked one', is depicted usually with antlers on his head, and sometimes with the ears of a stag. He often holds a snake or ram-horned snake. He is seated in a lotus or cross-legged pose reminiscent of the gods from the Indian subcontinent. His most famous image is the one that appears on the Gundestrup cauldron found in Denmark. This cauldron is generally thought to be Celtic (although may have been custom manufactured in Thrace) and probably dates from the first century BC. Cernunnos is shown holding in his left hand a large snake, and in his right hand a torc. He has a large pair of antlers on his head and is surrounded by beasts with, significantly for us, a stag to his right and an animal that is usually interpreted as a boar to his left. As pointed out by Gregory Coulter in *The Lost Zodiac of the Druids*, the snake-holding Ophiuchus seems therefore to have some parallels with the various images of Cernunnos, and it would be tempting to speculate on whether the two figures have long-forgotten connections or perhaps a common origin. Cernunnos' identification as a human figure with stag-like physical features, and a strong association with animals, fits well with the concept that in Celtic tradition there are frequently found gods or heroes who can 'shape-shift'. As Miranda Green states in the context of Cernunnos and his stag association, 'perhaps one of those beings … underwent transmogrification or shape-shifting from human to animal form'. Furthermore, Cernunnos would seem to make a reasonable candidate for the animal interpreter, from the story of 'Culhwch and Olwen', Gwrhyr. If it could also be argued that the constellation Ophiuchus and the god Cernunnos do have associations, then we should note the close proximity that Ophiuchus has to the animal constellations, which we proposed as corresponding to the creatures that Gwrhyr conversed with. Indeed, who better to talk to the animals than a Cernunnos/Ophiuchus character?

In *The Lost Zodiac of the Druids*, Gregory Clouter investigated the complex imagery of the Gundestrup cauldron, theorising that the figures are cosmological. One of his conclusions was that the figure of Cernunnos is indeed the constellation Ophiuchus in the night sky. He also interprets the animal to the right of Cernunnos as a hound and equates this to the constellation Libra. The evidence presented here, however, would tend to suggest that Libra is one of the candidates for a wild boar and this is the more common interpretation of the animal figure that appears beside Cernunnos on the cauldron.

However imaginatively we view the asterism corresponding to Ophiuchus, and try to match this to Cernunnos, the evidence so far presented is still relatively weak for a positive identification of this constellation as the stag, or wild boar, that features in the *Mabinogion*. If the god Cernunnos could be associated with the constellation Ophiuchus, then another possibility is that a Celtic 'Cernunnos' constellation might have been formed by combining the constellations Ophiuchus and its smaller close neighbour, Scorpio. In this scenario the much larger constellation would represent the god, but at the same time half of the constellation could also be seen as having some of the attributes of a stag. This might provide an explanation for the god's shape-shifting abilities and also explain the symbolism of Cernunnos on the Gundestrup cauldron. As Ophiuchus lies to the north of the ecliptic and Scorpio predominately to the south of the ecliptic, this possible split zodiacal sign would be important when considering the paths of the Moon and planets through this region of the sky. The Moon in particular wanders considerably from the ecliptic and would therefore sometimes pass through Scorpio (i.e. below the ecliptic), perhaps emphasising a cervine aspect, while at other times passing through Ophiuchus (i.e. above the ecliptic), emphasising a more human-like aspect. It is also worth noting that Ophiuchus is one of the thirteen zodiacal constellations, but is the only one which is not recognised as an astrological sign. Indeed, the Sun spends a longer time traversing Ophiuchus than it does neighbouring Scorpio.

Turning now to Scorpio, how likely are we to find associations with stags or deer? Scorpio, according to classical legend, is the creature that slew the giant Orion, but was itself in fear of the arrow of Sagittarius. Using an arrow to kill a scorpion would seem to be a little strange, but might just hint at the possibility that Sagittarius may not have always been aiming at a diminutive scorpion. Perhaps the constellation once represented a larger creature, one more suitable for a hunter. The month of October, traditionally the month associated in the classical world with Scorpio, is known in Scots Gaelic as *Damhair*, derived from the word *damh* meaning 'stag'. Generally, it is thought that the name relates to the stag rut that occurs in the Highlands in the autumn, but it is not beyond the realms of possibility that the name is in some way connected with an alternative cervine Scorpio. Even if there is not a connection between *Damhair* and an ancient European view of the constellation Scorpio, the Gaelic name for the month provides some potential reasons as to why northern Europeans may have seen Scorpio as a stag. The October stag rut is of course the time when the animal is at his most potent and magnificent. This in itself could have inspired the notion of a stag constellation exulted by the Sun in autumn. If there is evidence that the Picts included a stag within their own zodiac, it would be tempting to suggest that the Gaelic month of *Damhair* in some way reflects this. It is worth noting that in the closely related Irish language the name for October is different. For now there is simply not enough evidence to connect the Gaelic name for October with an ancient version of the constellation Scorpio, which would also necessitate evidence of continuity from the Picts to the later Gaelic-speaking population of the Highlands. It is also the case that rare white stags are seen as a symbol of good luck in Scotland and are viewed as 'other-worldly', hence it is considered almost taboo to hunt them. Could the white stag be linked to the concept of a celestial deer constellation? According to the *Oxford Dictionary of Mythology*, a stag enticed people into the 'otherworld', an idea that was later Christianised, with the animal being thought of as guiding souls to heaven. Perhaps this also suggests that the stag was seen in a celestial or cosmological role, acting as an intermediary between earth and heaven.

Another important reason why northern Europeans may not have recognised Scorpio as a Scorpion is that the stars of Scorpio, even at their zenith, rise very little above the northern horizon. Indeed, the Scorpion's tale and sting are simply not visible at northern latitudes. This second point would have a natural effect on the overall impression the asterism would have on the eye. It seems reasonable therefore that northern Europeans may have viewed this particular constellation as something else, with the possibility of a stag substituting for the scorpion.

Turning to a map of the night sky, it is worthwhile considering the shape of the northern, visible portion, of the constellation Scorpio. This portion, and indeed the whole of the constellation, is dominated by the red giant Antares. This is viewed traditionally as the scorpion's heart. Above this is a small group of bright stars that define the scorpion's head. Extending further northwards from these are the scorpion's claws. If northern Europeans really envisaged Scorpio as a stag, then does such an interpretation make sense in terms of the shape of the constellation? Assuming that the stag was seen as upright, as these figures usually are, then the obvious first characteristic to look for is the stag's antlers. It is not at all difficult to imagine the pincers of the scorpion being viewed by northern Europeans as the antlers of the more familiar stag. The head of the scorpion would also fit well with the shape of the stag's head. The red star Antares may therefore have been viewed not as the scorpion's heart, but rather as that of a stag.

Recapping our reconstruction of a Welsh mythological view of this portion of the sky, derived from the story of 'Culhwch and Olwen', our search for a stag constellation has so far produced two candidates. Firstly, the constellation Ophiuchus, which shows some interesting parallels to Cernunnos the antlered god. Secondly, we should not forget Hercules' third task, that of the Ceryneian hind, and the strong Greek association of the hind or stag with the constellation Scorpio. We therefore have evidence that the neighbouring constellation Scorpio might have been viewed by at least some Europeans as a 'stag' or at least a stag constellation existed in this area of the sky. We should also take cognisance of the figure of Mabon and the possible identification of this hunter as a Welsh Sagittarius.

If we turn our attention at this point to our potential 'Rosetta stone', the monument at Shandwick, the panel on its reverse side shows a hunter, complete with deerskin and antlers, taking aim at a stag. The stag seems to be fully aware of the presence of the hunter and is arching back his neck, thereby facing his assailant. If we turn to our star map, the resemblance of this composition to the constellations of Sagittarius and the northern portion of Scorpio could not be closer. The bow of Sagittarius points directly at Scorpio, likewise the Shandwick hunter's bow at the stag. The putative stellar pincers are arrayed to the right which suggests that if these were the antlers of a stag then its head would be pointing back towards Sagittarius, and on the stone the Pictish stag looks back at the hunter. The stag's springing front legs can be made out in the sky, and are mirrored by the Shandwick deer. Finally, a closer inspection of the Pictish hunter's antlered headgear reveals some resemblance to the triangular group of stars positioned at the top left of Sagittarius. It seems reasonable at this point to suggest that the Pictish hunter is none other than Sagittarius, or a Mabon-like figure, and his quarry is a stag representing a northern European viewpoint on the constellations of Sagittarius and Scorpio.

There is a potential flaw in this hypothesis, and specifically in our interpretation of the bottom right-hand corner of the Shandwick panel. This flaw is that in the zodiac Sagittarius follows Scorpio and not the other way round as shown in the panel. Following our diagonal from our possible Virgo, running through the figure of the wild boar, we seem to hit Sagittarius first and this is therefore not in the correct zodiacal order. However, if we take the very reasonable stance that in the minds of the Picts, the hunter and the stag are inextricably linked, it would make perfect sense to depict them properly interacting, rather than one being placed above the other. Furthermore, while Scorpio may well be the zodiac sign preceding Sagittarius, in fact in the sky these constellations rise almost together, with the constellation Sagittarius rising to the north (left) of Scorpio. Therefore the particular spatial relationship in the sky is actually well represented on the Shandwick stone. This is an almost identical situation to the one that arose with Gemini and Taurus, and with the positioning of the warriors and the two bulls on the stone.

The Stag and the Boar in Other Indo-European Traditions

There is further evidence for Scorpio being seen originally as a stag beyond the Mediterranean basin, this time surprisingly in the ancient Indian astrological Vedic system. In this eastern zodiac, with its twenty-seven lunar zodiac signs or *nakshatras*, the constellation Scorpio is divided into three of these lunar mansions. These are *Vishakha*, *Anuradha*, and *Jyeshta*. *Anuradha* is symbolised principally by a lotus flower, but has as its 'animal symbol' a female deer, the *Mgira*. Furthermore, *Jyeshta*, with its principal star Antares (the alpha star of Scorpio), has as its animal symbol the stag. Perhaps this also tantalisingly hints at a long-lost stag constellation, although this time not in Europe but in India. It may at first seem unlikely that there could be a cultural connection between northern Europe and India, but it is important to remember that the languages of North India, and those of Europe, are thought to have the common linguistic ancestor proto-Indo-European. It is therefore perfectly possible that there are other ancient cultural connections.

There is also a fragment of fascinating evidence from a traditional German folk rhyme. There is little information as to how old this poem is or anything else on its origins, but it apparently describes an alternative zodiac or at least a sequence of stars or constellations associated with the changing seasons:

Eber, Riese, Himmelskuh zählen wir dem Winter zu.
Hase, Wolf und Menschenpaar stellen uns den Frühling dar.
In Hahn und Hengst und Ährenfrau die Sommersonne steht genau.
Schwalbe, Hirsch und Bogenschütz sind des Herbstes feste Stütz.

This has been translated into English as:

> Boar, giant, and celestial cow we count to the winter.
> Hare, wolf and human pair represent the spring.
> At rooster, stallion and corn-ear-woman is summer solstice.
> Swallow, deer (stag) and archer are the frame of autumn.

From the above text, which is clearly referring to the night sky, only the human pair (Gemini), the corn-ear-woman (Virgo), and the archer (Sagittarius) are obviously discernible, although the celestial cow may represent Taurus. But noticeably within the sequence we have the appearance of a stag and a wild boar. The stag is associated with the autumn, as is Scorpio, while the boar is associated with the winter. In addition, the stag appears in the poem alongside the archer. This perhaps may hint at alternative northern European constellations including a stag and a wild boar. Some of these may even be zodiacal.

Outside Pictland but within the British Isles there is another possible example of an alternative northern European view of this same area of the night sky, and specifically the area around Ophiuchus. The so-called 'Parwich tympanum' is a pre-Norman, Anglo-Saxon stone carved arch from the church in the village of Parwich in Derbyshire. This is thought to have been carved in the eleventh century or perhaps much earlier. While there are clearly elements of Christian symbolism within the scene depicted on the stone arch, the mix of animals seems puzzling. Interestingly in the scene there is a deer or stag with a wild boar placed above it. In addition there is a pair of serpents, a rather indeterminate bird that sports talons, what appears to be a horse carrying a cross and is therefore usually interpreted as 'the lamb of god', and a beast that has been interpreted as a wolf. Examining the area of the night sky around Scorpio, our candidate Pictish stag constellation, we have the adjacent constellations of Ophiuchus and Libra, which represent our principal candidate for a wild boar constellation. Ophiuchus is of course in Greek mythology the serpent holder, and as mentioned previously, there is the possibility that this constellation may have been visualised by Celts as Cernunnos, the shape-shifting stag god. In the same area of sky, close to Ophiuchus' serpent, we have Aquila the eagle. Sitting directly below Scorpio is the constellation Lupus. This has been interpreted by different cultures as a wolf or other beast such as a lioness or leopard. Finally to the east of Aquila we have two horses: firstly the small constellation of Equuleus, the foal, seen by some classical authors as a horse head, and secondly, further east, Pegasus the flying horse. The mix on the Parwich tympanum would seem to a reasonably good match for the area around Ophiuchus, but once again the match is dependent on accepting the presence of a wild boar and a stag in that region of the sky. Why the 'lamb of god' would have been depicted as a horse or foal is unclear, but might be explained if Church authorities had attempted to Christianise pagan constellations. In this case they may have tried to persuade people to view Equuleus, the foal, as the 'lamb of god', with the sculptor compromising on this new interpretation by carving a partly traditional version.

Further echoes from ancient cultures in Europe and Asia may also have resonance with the Shandwick stone. Many cultures, including for example Hungarian and

Persian, have similar stories describing a hunter, sometimes twin hunters, or brothers perpetually chasing after a stag in much the same way as Hercules. This stag is no ordinary stag, but is white and holds the Sun in his antlers (the 'Legend of the White Stag'). This chase story might have arisen as a result of the relationship in the night sky between Gemini and Scorpio. At the autumnal equinox, the Sun is in Scorpio, between the pincers or, in our theoretical alternative version, the antlers. As the Sun sets in Scorpio due west, Gemini rises in the east and is present in the sky until the dawn. Therefore the two constellations, in effect, are on opposite sides of the sky and appear to chase each other, with neither ever being able to catch up with the other. The Shandwick stone, whether intentionally or not shows this exact same relationship, with Gemini in the bottom left-hand corner and a stag in the bottom right-hand corner.

It would therefore seem that there are various strands of evidence coming together from Europe and Asia that collectively suggest that there was once a 'stag' constellation, in the vicinity of the classical constellation of Scorpio. This is most likely to correspond to Scorpio itself. What is astonishing is that from several very disparate sources – various European traditions, a Pictish stone, Welsh mythology, Vedic astrology, Greek mythology, a German poem and an Anglo-Saxon carved arch – we find the same pattern repeating itself.

The Ancient Night Sky of Europe

In this chapter we have explored the possibility that Europeans, in the past, had a different view of some of the constellations in the northern sky, compared with the classical version of the stars. For example, there is the very real possibility that the constellation of Scorpio may have been seen as a stag by a number of different peoples in Europe, and maybe even beyond. Similarly, there are indications that a wild boar constellation was also recognised in the night sky by different cultures in Europe in the same area of sky as a stag. We have also seen that Greek and Celtic mythologies would seem to suggest that the stag and the boar were once seen in the night sky. In terms of physical evidence, significantly, the Pictish Shandwick stone, perhaps the Celtic Gundestrup cauldron and the Saxon Parwich tympanum, depict the presence of a stag and a boar in the context of other figures that may relate to constellations in the region around Scorpio and Sagittarius. The case presented here would suggest that the Europeans, and perhaps other cultures including ancient Persia and India, recognised a separate and distinctive interpretation of the constellations of the night sky. The imagery on the Shandwick stone would therefore suggest that the Picts were not only well acquainted with this version of the heavens, but had retained this view for much longer than their counterparts elsewhere.

Chapter 7

The Shandwick Stars and Constellations

Expanding Pictish Cosmology

It would appear from the evidence so far collected that, in the past, Europeans saw the sky very differently. Their night sky may have included some constellations that are familiar to us today, but also some that are completely unfamiliar. Echoes of this version of the cosmos may well still exist in number of cultures scattered across Europe, and perhaps even as far as India. Surprisingly, the Pictish stone at Shandwick not only fits well with the notion of this alternative night sky, but provides a reasonably detailed pictographic description of both 'conventional' constellations, in addition to a large number of figures that may well represent previously unknown constellations. Recognisable, or at least partially recognisable, constellations include Gemini, Taurus, Leo, Sagittarius and possibly Virgo. Radically different constellations would include a wild boar (perhaps Libra) and a stag (perhaps Scorpio).

So far we have mainly concentrated our efforts largely on the possible zodiacal figures carved in the stone, but what of the others? Can we identify some of the less obvious figures on the Shandwick stone? If we can achieve this goal, then it may be possible to fathom out why this seemingly bizarre 'hunting scene' appears on a Christian monument, alongside apparently unintelligible Pictish symbols.

There is some evidence in the form of different ancient cosmological stories that some of the figures (the warriors and the bulls, as well as the hunter and the stag) form distinct groupings. The two warriors sit very well together with the two bulls, which are positioned to their right, reflecting their actual spatial relationship as they rose at the time of the Shandwick stone's creation. In addition, the calf or cow sitting between the two swordsmen resonates well with stories from both Celtic Ireland and ancient Greece. Similarly the kneeling hunter and the stag at bay seem to go naturally together and their spatial relationship resonates with the actual configuration of Sagittarius and Scorpio in the sky. Furthermore some of the surrounding figures have resonance with stories from Wales. The approximate order from left to right on the panel could therefore be expressed as Gemini-Taurus, Leo, Virgo, Libra and Sagittarius-Scorpio. This fits reasonably well, but not perfectly with the actual zodiacal order, which is Taurus, Gemini, Cancer, Leo, Virgo, Libra, Scorpio, and Sagittarius. However, taking into account the pairing of Gemini-Taurus and Sagittarius-Scorpio and their actual relationship in the sky, the order is encouraging and identification of other figures on the stone as 'constellations' may add further evidential weight to the idea that the Shandwick panel is cosmological, as well as help further confirm the identity of the 'zodiacal' figures. In addition, if there really is structure to the panel, then there is the potential to relate each figure's position on the tableau to the appearance of the corresponding constellation or star in the night sky. If we assume that each figure's position should approximately match the heliacal rising of their corresponding star, then it should be possible to construct a timeline running from left to right for all the figures.

If we think about the Shandwick panel as representing the order in which a series of heliacal risings occurred, starting with the stars of Gemini and Taurus and finishing with the stars of Scorpio and Sagittarius, then the panel itself can be explained as an astronomical calendar rather than a straightforward map of the sky. In effect, this means that figures would be expected to approximately mirror the night sky. It is also possible that rather than recording a progression of key heliacal risings, the panel records the sequential rising of prominent stars on a particular night, starting at sunset and continuing until dawn.

Heliacal risings, as we have seen, are generally specific for time and place, and as such ideally we must take into account Shandwick's latitude, and the year the stone was carved. Unfortunately for the time being we have to settle for an estimate of the stone's creation, which reasonably could be AD 700, give or take 100 years. If we set our time clock to our arbitrary AD 700, and our latitude to that of Shandwick (58 degrees north), we can make a list of the heliacal rising dates for the most prominent stars. We should also be aware that although we can model the moment of a star's rise along with the Sun, in practice the star will only become visible in the dawn sky several days later. The star, depending on its magnitude, will appear only briefly before its light is drowned out by the rising Sun. Each progressive day, the star would rise approximately four minutes earlier, moving gradually away from the dawn back into the night sky.

We must also consider the definition of a constellation in relation to the phenomenon of a helically rising star. Clearly the heliacal event refers to a single, prominent or important star, not to a sprawling constellation. It is therefore possible that a large constellation may incorporate more than one such star. In the case of Taurus, for example, the constellation not only has a number of bright stars, including the brilliant red giant Aldebaran, but also contains two famous star clusters, the Pleiades and the Hyades. It may therefore be possible that bovine figures on the left-hand side of the panel could represent some of these prominent Taurean features, rather than a number of different constellations. Figures may be positioned on the stone in relation to a specific star within a given constellation. So for example, the lion's location could be determined by the date of the helical rising of Regulus, the eagle by Altair, and so on.

The Left-Hand Side of the Panel

Determining the Time Frame

Assuming the tall central figure at the top of the panel is Virgo we can then use this constellation's principal star, Spica, as a marker. We might therefore assume that the figures to the left of our putative 'Virgo' must represent stars or constellations that in Pictish times rose heliacally prior to 27 September, but after the rising of Castor in Gemini and the Pleiades in Taurus around 25 March. Clearly there are far too many unmatched constellations to take account of the remaining figures on the left-hand side of the panel. In addition, there are some constellations that although technically do not rise heliacally, nevertheless appear to brush the horizon in the north. So for example, Lyra, the lyre or vulture, reaches its nadir (or lowest point) just 5 degrees above the horizon, and starts to climb again on 20 September. Such a bright star, descending almost to the horizon, may appear to an observer as subsequently rising heliacally.

Although there appear to be differences between a possible Pictish zodiac and the classical zodiac, there is also some general agreement. It would appear that our possible Pictish night sky had a significant degree of commonality with the Graeco-Roman sky. If this was the case then the constellations above the ecliptic would have an overwhelmingly terrestrial flavour to them, comprising of human-like figures, animals and birds, while a significant proportion of constellations below the ecliptic may well represented characters that inhabited an aquatic world. If this was the case then this might suggest that we largely concentrate on classical constellations from above the ecliptic, which fit well with a hunting scene and ignore those that are clearly sub-ecliptic and aquatic.

The first of these stars to heliacally rise at the end of March and the beginning of April in the Pictish period are in Taurus and Gemini. Other prominent stars rising would include those of Orion, rising between the end of June and mid-July. Leo started to rise at the beginning of July. Other constellations rising during this period include Auriga, Canis Minor, Lepus, Canis Major, Corona, Bootes, Virgo, Corvus, and Hercules. We should also note that Orion, Canis Major, Canis Minor, Lepus, and Corvus are all from below the ecliptic.

Returning to the overall organisation of the hunting scene, and considering the arc of zodiacal figures starting with the warriors and bulls, passing through the lion, the maiden and boar and finishing with bowman and stag, we might hypothesise that the figures lying below these might well represent constellations or stars below the ecliptic, while those above the arc may represent constellations or stars above the ecliptic. In terms of the left-hand side of the panel there would therefore be no figures represented below the ecliptic, therefore ruling out Orion, Canis Minor, Canis Major and Lepus. Corvus could still feasibly appear on the right-hand side. This leaves us with Gemini, Taurus, Auriga (sharing El Nath with Taurus), Leo, Corona, Bootes, Lyra, Hercules and Virgo.

If the maiden figure in the centre of the panel corresponds to the rising of the star Spica, can we also find a date corresponding to the far left of the panel – the starting point for the calendar? If the two warriors do represent Gemini, then the left-hand figure would correspond to the star Castor. An observer in the north of Scotland would note that Castor just brushed the horizon, due north, at the end of March. From the perspective of Shandwick in Pictland in the eighth century, Pollux would have heliacally risen much later than Castor, on 30 May.

The Calf or Cow

If we estimate Castor's heliacal nadir at around the end of March, and establish Pollux's heliacal rising to have taken place around 30 May, there is the implication that the calf lying between them might represent a constellation or specific star that rises between these two points in time. At this northern latitude, surprisingly, there is a candidate that does exactly that; the constellation of Taurus. This constellation also rises slowly and ponderously, star by star, over a similar time frame to Gemini – from 25 March to the end of May. If the kneeling calf figure represents the object of conflict between the two swordsmen, then it is more likely that this creature represents a cow rather than a calf. Specifically, it may well represent the celestial herd of cattle over which there is a disagreement about ownership. With the band of the Milky Way running between Gemini on one side and Taurus and Orion on the other, and bearing in mind both the ancient Greek and Irish interpretation of the Milky Way as having a connection to celestial cattle, it would make sense if the calf figure represented a bright star in the Milky Way band. El Nath makes a reasonable potential candidate.

Horned Animal

Moving on, the next northern constellation that rose is Leo with Algieba on 21 July. The alpha star, Regulus, rose on 1 August. Corona was the next northern constellation to rise, with its brightest star Alphekka, towards the end of August. Perhaps the best match for this star and semicircular constellation would be the horned animal above and to the right of the warriors.

Two Horsemen

From their position on the stone the two horsemen, which feature on the left-hand side of the panel, could represent the rising of two of the three following possibilities: Auriga on 18 April, the incredibly bright Arcturus in Bootes rising on the 30 August, or the rising of Kornephoros in Hercules on 24 September. All three of these classical constellations represent human-like figures.

The Heron

The last figure to consider on the left-hand side of the panel would be the heron. This figure occupies the space immediately to the left of our Virgo figure. The best fit for this figure would be the constellation Lyra, which skims the northern horizon in late September, with the star Sulafat rising on 23 September, but also the spectacular Vega, rising from its almost horizon-touching nadir on 20 September. The constellation Lyra, as mentioned before, was seen as a vulture in ancient Greece. There were of course no vultures in Pictland, so perhaps a heron with its similar long serpent-like neck actually makes quite a neat substitution.

The Right-Hand Side of the Panel

Turning to the right-hand side of the panel, we have the zodiacal arc running from the possible Virgo figure through the wild boar to the hunter and the stag. If these figures do indeed represent zodiacal constellations, then the figures below these may be depicting Pictish constellations below the ecliptic. The non-zodiacal figures above our imagined ecliptic line consist of a man on horseback, an eagle (already provisionally identified as Aquila), a large rightward-facing stag, two small difficult-to-identify mammals and the goat man. If we list the heliacal rising of stars associated with constellations above the actual ecliptic, from the rising of Spica up until the rising of the stars of Sagittarius and Scorpio (possibly the hunter and stag at bay), then we get the following list; Serpens, Hercules, Ophiuchus, Cygnus, Aquila, Pegasus and Andromeda. Therefore we have seven potential candidates for five figures. If we accept Aquila's identification with the eagle, let us now consider possible candidates for each figure and the dates of appropriate heliacal rising stars.

Right-Hand-Side Horseman

Given the need to be heliacal and above the ecliptic, the only reasonable candidates for the horseman that appears on the right-hand side are Hercules and Ophiuchus. The stars of Hercules, as already mentioned, can be either heliacal or circumpolar with respect to the latitude and time frame of the Shandwick stone. The heliacal stars of Hercules rose between 17 September (prior to Virgo's alpha star Spica) and 13 October (after Spica). Its position in relation to Spica would therefore be dependent on which of the two prominent heliacal stars the Picts saw as more important. Furthermore, since a great deal of the constellation is not heliacal at all, it is also possible that it was not considered suitable for inclusion in the tableau.

In an earlier section in this book, we drew parallels between the cosmology of Ophiuchus and the Celtic deity Cernunnos – a god associated with deer and often depicted as a hunter, but not on horseback. Rasalhague, brightest star of Ophiuchus, would have risen on 19 October in AD 700.

The Eagle

It would make sense if the eagle carving on the stone was identified with the classical constellation of Aquila. However, does the eagle's position on the panel actually tally with the heliacal rising of the constellation? The prediction from the sequence on the stone would be that the star or constellation representing the Pictish eagle would be above the ecliptic and rise after constellations represented by a wild boar. As the order of the hunter and stag may be deliberately reversed on the stone in order to retain their relationship in the night sky, we might also expect that any star representing this Pictish eagle to rise after Scorpio, but prior to Sagittarius. Aquila is certainly above the ecliptic, with its physical location in the sky between Ophiuchus and Pegasus, approximately 'above' Sagittarius and Capricorn. Altair, Aquila's principal star, is extremely bright (magnitude 0.8) and rose on 18 November in AD 700. It therefore rose after Ophiuchus and after Libra, as predicted (with Libra as our candidate wild boar). Furthermore, also as predicted, the sequence is indeed reversed in respect to its rising relative to Sagittarius and Scorpio, therefore retaining the combined image of the hunter shooting his prey. It is therefore very reasonable to argue that Aquila and its alpha star Altair make an excellent match for the Pictish eagle, and its identification as Aquila helps to add further comfort to the notion that the panel is cosmological.

The Hare

A hare-like animal is found below the legs of the right-hand horseman and above the eagle. Its position, assuming that this is an accurate reflection of its position in an order of appearance, might suggest that its major star rises sometime between Rasalhague and Altair, and possibly after the stars of Libra. This would give us a time frame from about 10 October to 18 November AD 700. In addition, the diminutive size of figure could also give us a clue about the size or brightness of the constellation being suggested. The two main Libran stars, Zubeneschamali and Zubenelgenubi, rose around 16 October. Remembering the switching of position of the bowman and the stag on the panel, if we take the Pictish bowman's position as an approximate guide to represent the rising of Scorpio and note that the archer is roughly in line with the hare, then we might assume that the hare constellation rose around 3 November. It is unlikely that it may have risen prior to 16 October or later than 18 November. This suggests that there are three potential candidates. Vulpecula, the fox, rose around 27 October. Sagitta, the arrow, rose around 7 November. Finally, Serpens Cauda rose around 11 November. The closest date is therefore that of Sagitta, but either of the other two may have an equally valid claim.

Small Mammal

There is a small mammal, between the eagle and the archer and stag, which is very difficult to identify. It could represent a young carnivore, for example a puppy or young wolf, or could even depict a lamb. If we once again try to construct a time frame we see that the figure is roughly in line with the eagle, perhaps slightly to the left, which might suggest a heliacal rising date of some time from around 17 November up to approximately midwinter. As in the case of the hare, and in contrast to the oversized eagle, the small size of this figure may indicate that the constellation we are looking for is relatively small and insignificant compared to Aquila. There are three possible candidates for the young mammal. Delphinus, the dolphin, rose on 19 November. Scutum, the shield, also rose on the same day. Equuleus, the foal, rose on or about 8 December AD 700. The first candidate, Delphinus, is located in the sky to the left of Aquila and relatively distant from Sagittarius and Scorpio. In a previous section we discussed the Twrch Trwyth story and the appearance of a salmon in relation to the search for Mabon, and related this fish to the constellation Delphinus. Given this relationship and the aquatic nature of this constellation in most astronomical traditions, including apparently now the Welsh tradition, we could well reject Delphinus as the match for a young mammal. The third candidate mentioned above is Equuleus. This 'foal' is so called because of its proximity to Pegasus, the winged horse, and is a faint constellation with its brightest star having a magnitude of 3.9. It is much closer to Aquarius than even Capricorn and as far from Scorpio and Sagittarius as Delphinus. Its physical position does not therefore seem to tally well with the position of our figure. The second candidate, perhaps more promising, is the constellation Scutum. This is again a faint constellation with its brightest star attaining a magnitude of just 3.9. In contrast to the other two candidates, both its heliacal position and its physical position match well with the position of the figure, the brightest star heliacally rising two days after Altair, and its physical location directly above Sagittarius.

Large Stag

A large Stag dominates the top right-hand side of the panel and is the largest animal figure on the tableau, exceeding both the eagle and the lion. If we use this simple fact as a guide, then it would imply that we are looking for an exceptional constellation. As usual, we are also assuming that the constellation we are searching for is heliacal, or at least has a prominent heliacal rising star, and is above the ecliptic. Furthermore, its position at the extreme right-hand side of the picture suggests that we are looking for a constellation rising through December AD 700.

There is only one constellation that fits the bill – Pegasus. This constellation will be familiar to many readers as the mythical beast whose body is represented by the distinctive 'square of Pegasus'. This group of four very bright stars dominates the region of the night sky above Pisces. The second brightest of these stars is Scheat, magnitude 2.4, and it is this star that marks the top right-hand corner of the 'square' and rose first. At Shandwick this event would have occurred on 2 December, after Aquila had risen above the horizon and as the first stars of Sagittarius were beginning to rise with the Sun. The next star of the 'square' to rise is Alpharatz, and is the brightest of the four stars. This star (magnitude 2.0) rose on 13 December. These four stars seem therefore to fit well with the position of the large stag. One other, less likely, possibility is that the stag represents the Plough or the Great Bear (Ursa Major); this constellation lies above Virgo and Bootes, but never rises or sets.

Goat Man

Perhaps the strangest figure in this bizarre hunting scene is the figure that appears to be part-man and part-goat. Following previous logic, we should be looking for a late rising star in a constellation that is not enormous in size, but not particularly small either, with a rising star perhaps after Altair in Aquila, and Scheat or Alpheratz in Pegasus. Therefore the star would probably have risen after 30 November and certainly before 8 January. The first bright star to have risen after Scheat is in fact Mirach. This star has a magnitude of 2.1 and therefore rivals Alpheratz in luminosity. It is located in the neighbouring constellation of Andromeda and rises on 5 December. This could therefore be a possibility, although it is quite distant in the sky from Scorpio and Sagittarius.

A further possibility, which strangely enough encompasses at least part of the notion of a goat man, is that this figure represents Capricorn. This constellation represents the 'goat fish' and sits in the classical heavens in the region known as 'the water', swimming in the river flowing from Aquarius, alongside Pisces, Piscis Austrinus, and Cetus. Could this chimerical Pictish figure be a non-aquatic parallel of the classical water monster? Certainly, the rise of one of its brightest stars would fit neatly with the position of the goat man with Dabih rising on 23 December, but the lack of an aquatic element to the figure, and the inclusion of the human head and torso, would seem far too distant to have any real possibility of a relationship to Capricorn.

Another potential match for the goat man hinges on the notion that it might be a Pictish equivalent of a centaur. This half-man half-horse is represented in the traditional view of the heavens by two constellations: Sagittarius and the neighbouring Centaurus. Most of Centaurus is invisible in Scotland, sitting too far to the south. The only bright star of any importance is Menkent (magnitude 2.1), and this rose heliacally on 7 November. This is an unlikely candidate for the goat man for several reasons. Firstly, only a fraction of the constellation would be visible to the

Picts, therefore any reference to Centaurus would have to come from astronomical traditions much further south. It would therefore be unlikely that the centaur would take on a peculiarly Pictish slant. Further, there are examples of centaurs carved on other Pictish stones, and these appear very much as you would expect, with no hint of a 'goat' flavour to them. Finally, Centaurus is below the ecliptic, while the position of the goat man is above the zodiacal figures on the panel. Furthermore, we also see that the heliacal rising date of 7 November seems to fit badly with the time frame we have constructed. The identity of this figure would therefore seem something of a mystery.

The Woodpecker
The woodpecker on the stone is one of two animals that are below our hypothetical ecliptic line on the right-hand side of the Shandwick panel. The bird appears to be close to the back of the hunter and its orientation has led to its identification as a woodpecker. In terms of our time frame, the bird is roughly in line with the right-hand rider, and the boar, which would give a date of approximately mid-October. It would also appear to have risen after Spica, meaning after 27 September, but prior to Altair on 18 November. The likeliest candidate for this bird, within the context of the classical heavens, would be Corvus, the crow. This compact constellation lies close to Virgo, but its brightest star, Gienah (magnitude 2.6), rose about four days prior to Spica. This would seem to place it a little early within the time frame of the tableau, but Gienah is only marginally brighter than three more of Corvus' stars, Algorab, Minkar, and Kraz, the last of these rising on 2 October. Therefore, the positioning of the woodpecker may not be far out in relation to the Virgo figure.

Another problem is its apparent physical proximity to the hunter figure on the stone, rather than the expected relationship with its sky-neighbour Virgo. This may simply be a question of the space available on the panel to the sculptor, but it is peculiar that the fox-like creature that occupies a similar time slot to the bird is positioned closer to the Pictish Virgo.

The Pine Marten
There is one figure still to be considered and this animal at first seems hard to identify. However, anyone familiar with the fauna of the Highland forests would recognise this creature as the pine marten. The position of this figure on the stone would suggest, firstly that the candidate constellation lies below the ecliptic, and secondly the constellation or its stars rose fairly soon after Spica. There is no obvious classical equivalent to this figure, so it is possible that this will remain unidentifiable. It is also possible that stars from other constellations may have been seen as part of a 'marten' constellation. Candidates might include stars from the extreme end of Hydra, or from parts of Ophiuchus.

The Overall Picture

The framework that we have gradually put together for the Shandwick panel could give us a possible range of dates representing the heliacal rising of stars from around the end of March, with the rising of Taurus, to 23 December, with the heliacal appearance of Dabih in Capricorn. Alternatively we could view the figures on the panel as representing a progression of stars or constellations over a particular night, with the first stars to rise recorded on the left-hand side and the last on the right-hand side.

If we consider the heliacal calendar first of all, we should ask the question of why should the Picts choose to give the reader of the panel this particular range of dates. The answer to this could lie in the overall context of the panel. Taken as a whole, the Shandwick stone is undeniably proclaiming itself as a Christian monument and it is within the Christian context that we must view the panel. This at first may seem strange, given that the panel contains figures that appear more pagan than Christian but it is very much part of the history of Christianity to evangelise new peoples and cultures, without totally subsuming aspects or even the symbols of older belief systems. If we examine modern Christianity there are many traces of Roman deities to be found, thinly disguised as patron saints. In Scotland and Ireland, Celtic deities and religious rituals abound. Brigid, for example, is commemorated in Scottish and Irish place names such as Kilbride and is associated with holy wells. If we consider the dates corresponding to the heliacal rising of the stars discussed above, these appear to encompass a nine-month period, culminating around midwinter. A possibility therefore exists that these stars are arranged in the form of a procession, starting with the spring and inevitably leading to Christmas Day. Perhaps, the panel represents therefore the period of time from the 'Annunciation' on 25 March, when the Angel Gabriel told Mary of her forthcoming pregnancy, to the birth of Jesus on Christmas Day.

What of the other possibility that the panel represents the procession of stars on a particular night, therefore clearly identifying a specific date? If the panel is read from left to right, then we would expect to see Gemini rising at sunset and Sagittarius and Scorpio rising just before sunrise. This actually occurs at midwinter and once again 25 December fits well with this.

It would seem therefore that both a heliacal model and a model invoking stellar progression over a particular night support the possibility that the panel is pointing to the date of the Nativity around or just after midwinter. As a potential marker for this event, and applicable for both the above models, the star Dabih rises heliacally with the Sun on 23 December, and in fact would be observed a couple of days later at dawn. Perhaps this star to the Picts heralded Christmas Day, which would also seem fitting when we remember the significance of the star of Bethlehem. It is therefore possible that the panel is actually a calendar, counting down from the Annunciation to Christmas and therefore in perfect harmony with the Christian cross on which it sits.

The Shandwick Symbol Pair

Astrology, with its deeply embedded pagan beliefs, surprisingly survived the onslaught of Christianity and has been almost inexplicably tolerated by the Church down the centuries. This may have some bearing on our exploration of the Shandwick stone and may help us in our understanding of why pagan elements come to sit side by side with Christian symbolism.

Immediately above the hunting scene there is another panel, a symbol panel, on which is carved perhaps the best known of the symbols, the so-called Pictish beast or elephant. Is it possible that there is a relationship between the two panels? The combination of this panel with the hunting scene could provide clues in understanding both the Shandwick stone and the Pictish symbols themselves.

The Shandwick elephant symbol is typical of other such symbols found on other stones; there are about two dozen examples so far found. It depicts a strange and unearthly beast. It has a wispy, ethereal quality to it. It lacks substantial feet and instead its legs end in whirling patterns. A curved horn or perhaps a mane emerges from the head of the beast and sweeps backwards. The head is lowered and it possesses almost beak-like jaws. Apart from its vague elephantine identity, other alternative origins have been suggested for this symbol. Other authors, for example, have suggested that it represents a dolphin. In addition, Elizabeth Sutherland believes that the 'beast' might be a pictorial representation of the legendary Scottish 'kelpie' or water beast. For the moment, though, we will refer to the elephant by the simple title of the beast.

While the creature dominates this particular panel, it is not the only figure cut into this portion of the stone. There are three much smaller figures below the beast. These provide the clues that enable this symbol to be identified and, although it is at first a surprising identification, it fits well within the context of the hunting panel.

Just below the head of the beast there is a small but unfortunately damaged four-legged animal, which could be a centaur. In addition, sandwiched between the beast's legs are two sheep or rams. Following on from the logic of the panel beneath these creatures, a simple proposition can be put forward. These two rams could represent the classical constellation of Aries. This zodiacal constellation is made up of just a few

14. Shandwick stone (Pictish beast symbol), Shandwick, Easter Ross. (© Iain Forbes)

mainly faint stars, but is dominated by two bright stars – Hamal and Sheratan. These two stars are regarded as 'twin' stars due to their similar appearance and proximity to one another. If we hypothesise that the rams might represent Aries, then we have the possibility that the beast also represents a constellation, asterism or star. If we could provide evidence for this, we would therefore be at the threshold of understanding at least some of the meaning of one of the Pictish symbols, perhaps for the first time in over a thousand years.

If we build a timeline for the beast's panel, in the same way as we constructed one for the hunting panel below, then we might be able to identify candidate stars. Hamal rose with the Sun on 30 January AD 700 and Sheratan would have risen on 4 February. If we consider the positioning of the two rams, then this would imply that the first portion (the left-hand side) of the beast would correspond to an earlier heliacal rising of a prominent star – assuming, of course, that this panel follows the same rules as the hunting panel. The first problem is in establishing this start date for the left-hand side. This problem may not be as hard as it first seems. We have built a reasonable hypothesis that the panel below covers a time period between approximately the end of March and around 25 December. It might be reasonable to assume that any stars that may be represented by the beast occur in this time frame, or perhaps just after. We have already seen that Hamal and Sheratan fit beyond this time frame, and therefore we should examine the behaviour of prominent stars between 25 December and the beginning of February if we want to reveal the possible identity of the beast.

The figure furthest to the right on the Shandwick hunting panel is the goat man, whose identity we are unable to pinpoint with any certainty. As we have seen, on 17 December, Algedi in Capricorn rose followed by Nunki in Sagittarius on 22 December. Dabih in Capricorn, which is significantly brighter than Algedi, also rose on 22 December. Then on 27 December, the next zodiacal sign would have started to rise, led by its two brightest stars. This sign is Aquarius and the two stars are Sadalsuud and Sadalmelik. Following these two stars, the next prominent star to rise was Atik in Perseus, on 24 January, followed by Hamal and Sheratan. A further star in Capricorn (Deneb Algedi) rose on 5 February. No major stars would have risen until the Pleiades on 25 March – around the hypothetical start of our sequence in the hunting panel. It is also worth noting that the Sun was between Sagittarius and Capricorn on 25 December.

These dates leave us with very few possibilities. If we are confident that the two rams signify Aries, we are left with the constellations of Capricorn, Aquarius and Perseus. In the light of this sequence of heliacal risings between 17 December and 25 March, it is a real possibility that the beast represents one of the two zodiacal constellations from the three possibilities, either Capricorn or Aquarius. If we reject the identification of the goat man as Capricorn, instead choosing to identify him as Centaurus, then the most likely candidate for the beast would be Capricorn. If Aquarius was viewed by the Picts as the beast, then there would seem to be no commonality between the classical figure of the water bearer and the Pictish version. In Babylonia, this constellation was simply visualised as a water jug or pot, from which flowed water. Perhaps it is also significant that next zodiac symbol to follow Sagittarius, and traditionally associated with the winter solstice, is Capricorn.

CHAPTER 8

GIANTS, STARS AND SYMBOLS

Another Astronomical Calendar?

During the course of the last few chapters, we have explored in detail the Shandwick stone, and specifically the meaning of the hunting panel. On artistic merit alone there is no doubt that the Shandwick stone is an extraordinary monument. Despite its creation during the supposed Dark Ages, we have found that there are previously unimagined levels of complexity within the imagery. The cross slab seems to exhibit a curious mix of Christian symbolism, but also seemingly impenetrable pagan symbolism. As a result of an analysis of the imagery, we have developed a working hypothesis that the hunting panel actually represents a calendar that is integral to the meaning of the stone as a whole, a calendar based on the movement of the night sky. It has been argued that there is a strong possibility that it may even be counting down to a specific date, rather like an advent calendar. This date appears to be around the winter solstice and, in the context of the rest of the Christian message of the stone, this is most likely to be the Nativity. The starting date, around the vernal equinox, may also be significant. In the Christian context, this represents the day of the Annunciation by the Angel Gabriel to the Virgin Mary that she would be carrying the son of God. Significantly, the prominent Pictish symbol above the hunting panel may well be linked to the imagery below, perhaps representing a constellation associated with the winter solstice (with Capricorn as the most promising candidate). This figure, the Pictish beast, may have been a very potent symbol of Christmas to the Picts, in the same way as pagan symbols, such as the Christmas tree and Santa Claus, are instantly recognised as an integral part of the Christian holiday of Christmas.

The implications of these rediscovered levels of complexity are enormous. The Picts, previously dismissed by many as barbarians, would now seem to have been deeply interested in astronomy and appear to have had a sophisticated understanding of the heavens. Furthermore we have uncovered evidence that while some of the constellations they recognised differed significantly from those of Mediterranean cultures, others shared considerable commonality with other European traditions. This suggests the possibility that astronomy may not have been the sole preserve of the classical cultures. There may have been a significantly different form of astronomy associated with northern Europe, with its own ancient pedigree. There is still a great deal of mystery about the nature and function of the imagery used on the stone, with the tantalising possibility that the Pictish symbols displayed on the Shandwick stone are not only integral to the stone's message but may relate to a specific calendar date or to the night sky in some way.

Other Pictish monuments also display complex scenes and it would be desirable to turn our attention to other examples in order to identify other instances where there may also be an astronomical or calendrical influence. We should also attempt to apply the same techniques to these, in order to ascertain whether other stones carry astronomical information. We could also aim to ascertain whether such information can be used to further our understanding of Pictish astronomical ideas, to relate these ideas to those of other cultures, and explore further the hypothesis that the symbols might also relate in some way to astronomy.

A Celestial Giant

The Golspie stone is an 8-foot Pictish cross slab, housed in Dunrobin Castle museum in Sutherland in the north of Scotland (see picture 9). It originally stood in nearby Golspie kirkyard. Unlike the Shandwick stone, it does not appear to carry any obvious Christian symbolism or message and therefore it is possible that it pre-dates the establishment of Christianity in the area. What is interesting about this stone is that it depicts a scene where classic Pictish symbols are mixed together with figures. It is this mixture of symbols and figures that could provide further insight into the purpose and meaning of the Pictish symbols.

Some regard most of the carvings, including the animals and the peculiar human figure, as symbols and have attempted to pair these. There would, however, seem to be very little justification in such an approach. The top two well-recognised symbols, seem to form a natural pair. Immediately below them is a human figure. There is no record of a human figure forming part of any symbol pair. The dog- or lion-like figure could be interpreted as the known wolf symbol, but is not particularly wolf-like. There are no known examples of symbols pairs incorporating intertwined sea serpents. There are, however, recognised pictographs carved on the stone that are known to occur in symbol pairings. These pictographs are much smaller than the pair at the top of the stone as are the crescent, the flower and the double disc. It is difficult to tell whether or not these symbols are part of any pair, given the confusion of figures. It is more likely that the top two symbols therefore probably represent a true symbol pair, relating closely to the scene set out below. The second of these two symbols is the same beast symbol that we came across in relation to the Shandwick stone.

The most striking figure on the stone is that of a strange-looking man holding a knife and axe in front of him. The axe is extremely unusual in two respects. Firstly the blade of the axe is very narrow and seems completely impractical. Secondly, the axe shaft has a distinct and unusual curvature to it. The giant has long hair and a long beard. His nose and eye are disproportionately large, as is his eyebrow. He wears a short kilt, well above the knee, and he has a belt at his waist. He wears no shoes or leggings. This is no ordinary man and is really quite frightening. He is the sort of figure you might imagine the bogeyman resembles.

The Golspie stone may not be the only place where this figure is represented, as on the so-called Rhynie stone there is another, even more malevolent, human-like figure.

This figure demonstrates a number of strikingly similar characteristics to the Golspie man. The Rhynie man also has long hair and a long beard; likewise he carries an axe and possesses a disproportionately large nose, eye and eyebrow. He also sports a short kilt and belt, and appears to be barefoot. He does, however, differ from the Golspie man in two respects. Firstly, he is clearly balding. Secondly, his mouth is open, revealing sharp, pointed teeth.

To the right of the Golspie man is an animal that has been interpreted previously as a dog, or a lion, and just below this figure is a fish. The possible lion and the fish figures have been viewed by some as Christian symbols deliberately placed in opposition to a pagan male figure. In regard to the dog- or lion-like figure, it is difficult to ascertain what it actually represents. The overall shape of the figure suggests the form and bearing of a canine, rather than that of a feline, particularly the presence of a long muzzle. It has, however, some similarity to other examples of carvings that have been interpreted as lions, such as the one that appears on the Papil stone from Shetland. The presence of claws does little for either case as all big cats, with the exception of cheetahs, have retractable claws. Dogs of course cannot retract their claws, but they are not as pronounced as those shown on the Golspie stone. It is therefore possible that this figure's features have been deliberately exaggerated, perhaps to emphasise an unworldly aspect to the creature. Below the fish are three seemingly abstract Pictish symbols: the double disc, a crescent and the so-called flower symbol. At the very bottom of the stone are two intertwined serpents. These have been described by Elizabeth Sutherland as adders, but this interpretation is doubtful, as both serpents have fish tails. The serpent with its head to the left has two eyes, while the right-hand serpent is showing just one. As well as the figures and symbols carved on the stone, along the top and side of the stone is carved an example of Ogham (a form of writing originating in Ireland). This consists of simple up and down strokes, presumably written in Pictish rather than Irish, and is unfortunately indecipherable.

We can divide the carvings, below the rectangle and beast symbols, into two categories. Firstly, there are the animal or human-like figures – the man, the lion or dog, the snakes, and the fish. Secondly, there are the three abstract or semi-abstract designs. The fish could be interpreted as either an animal figure or as a symbol.

If the figures on this stone represent constellations or stars, can we find any evidence for this? If they are indeed astronomical in nature, can we ascertain which constellations or stars are depicted? Finally, if we assume that this stone also exhibits a timeline, running from the left-hand side to the right-hand side, can we establish the approximate start and finish dates? Perhaps the first step is to examine figures that resemble known classical constellations.

The Golspie Man

If we start with an examination of the rather grotesque male figure, with its short tunic, belt and prominent eye, the constellation that springs to mind almost immediately as a possibility is that of Orion – the celestial giant with his belt of stars. The general proportions of the Golspie figure and that of the constellation seem similar, and both seem to give the general sense that they are both giants.

15. Rhynie stone, Rhynie, Aberdeenshire. (© Crown Copyright: RCAHMS. Licensor www.rcahms.gov.uk)

Orion, the hunter, is one of the best-known constellations in the sky. Its huge outline dominates cloudless crisp winter nights, rising after dusk. It is formed by an impressive collection of stars, with no fewer than five of the thirty-three brightest stars in the entire night sky forming the bulk of its shape. The most obvious feature of the constellation is the belt, which is made up of three stars in a row, close together, and roughly equally spaced. This triplet consists of the stars Alnitak, Alnilam and Mintaka. This belt defines the giant hunter's waistline. His left-hand shoulder is defined by the star Betelgeuse, the luminous red giant and the tenth brightest star in the sky. His right shoulder is defined by Bellatrix. Two further stars, Saiph and (the spectacularly luminous blue giant) Rigel, define the hem of Orion's short tunic. To the right of the main bulk of the constellation, Orion extends an arm, holding what is usually regarded as a lion skin or more occasionally a fishing net. Orion in Greek mythology is a giant with strong associations with the sea, not surprising given that he is the son of the sea-god Poseidon. As befits his parentage, he has the power to walk on water. This giant hunter tries to rape Merope, and is punished by having his eyes put out. His sight is eventually restored by the rising Sun.

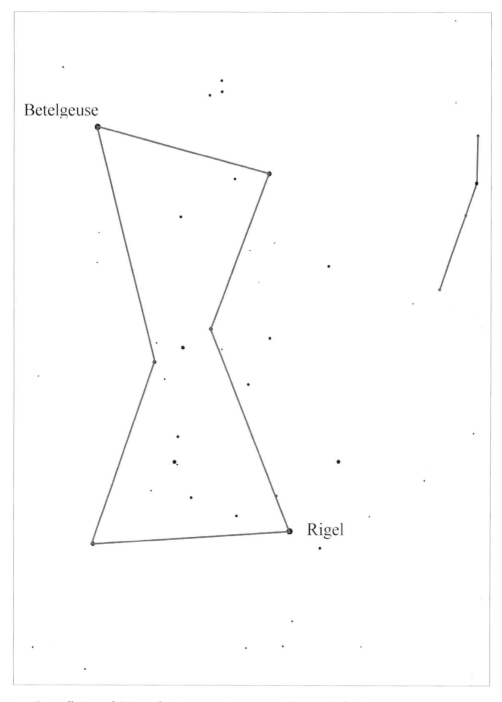

16. Constellation of Orion, showing prominent stars. (© Iain Forbes)

A raw comparison of the Golspie image to the Orion constellation reveals some clear similarities between the two, although not perfect. The most obvious features in common are the belt and short tunic. The position of Betelgeuse could approximate to the Golspie man's shoulder, while Rigel and Saiph define the tunic's hem. Bellatrix would correspond roughly to the end of the figure's beard. There is, to the right of the main body of Orion, a line of stars that include Tabit and Thabit. These seem to approximate to the axe held in the Golspie figure's hand. Perhaps significantly, this line of stars has a slight curvature to it. This is mimicked almost perfectly by the otherwise inexplicable curvature to the Golspie man's axe. There is no logical explanation for this peculiar feature other than the possibility that the artist is deliberately making a link between the axe and the corresponding arrangement of the bright stars, to the right of the main body of Orion.

The stars Pi5 and Pi6 also correspond well with the knife in the figure's hand. Above the main body of Orion, a cluster of stars could well correspond to the man's face. These are traditionally identified as Orion's head. The cluster is dominated by the star Meissa. This star corresponds well to the rather prominent eye of the Golspie figure – an eye that would seem to be overexaggerated and we should be cognisant of the prominence given to Orion's eye in legend.

There would therefore seem to be a number of features that might suggest that the male figure on the Golspie stone could be identified with the constellation Orion. Clearly, evidence for further links to constellations on the stone would help to establish whether or not the figure actually does represent Orion.

The Golspie Animal Figures

Looking at the other figures on the panel and reading from left to right, we would expect that the two serpents at the bottom of this stone panel should equate to a star or stars rising at approximately the same time as Orion. By far the best candidate for the two serpents becomes immediately obvious when this portion of the night sky is examined. Close to and below the ecliptic, lies the constellation Hydra – its stars rising around the same time as Orion. This exceptionally long constellation starts close to the constellation Cancer, and meanders roughly parallel to the ecliptic, past Leo, finally terminating level to the boundary between Virgo and Libra. Our fish-tailed Golspie serpents would seem to fit well with the notion of the water serpent or hydra, but this fit does not need to rely solely on the presence of the fish tails. The constellation Hydra is basically a line of stars that noticeably zigzag through the night sky. The intertwined serpents would seem also to convey this effect. Let us consider for a moment why the left-hand serpent has two eyes, while the right hand has only one. The answer to this problem is actually very obvious. The first portion of the constellation to rise above the horizon comprises two bright stars close together; it is easy to see these as the eyes of two serpents and indeed these are the stars recognised as the eyes in the classical constellation. Along the length of Hydra, there are no other pairs of bright stars that would allow the second putative serpent to have more than one eye.

The two eyes of Hydra, comprising Epsilon Hydrae and Zeta Hydrae, would have risen in Golspie on 28 July and 30 July respectively. Its brightest star, Alphard, would have risen on the 20 August. Modern astronomical charts place the terminal star as Pi

Hydrae, midway between Virgo, Libra and Centaurus. This star rose in the north of Scotland in AD 700 on 23 October.

If the star Meissa, in Orion, and the Hydra's tail mark the approximate beginning and end of the scene's time frame, then we could therefore postulate that it runs from around the end of June to roughly the end of October.

Clearly there are far too many rising stars to be included as candidates for the small number of figures and symbols on the Golspie stone. We could, however, concentrate on constellations containing only the very brightest and attempt to whittle down the list to seven. If we do this we are left with; Orion, Canis Minor, Leo, Canis Major, Hydra, Bootes and Virgo. The brightest stars in these constellations rise in the following order: Bellatrix, Betegeuse, Alnilam, Alnitak, Rigel (all Orion), Procyon (Canis Minor), Regulus (Leo), Murzim and Sirius (Canis Major), Alphard (Hydra), Wezen (Canis Major), Arcturus (Bootes), Adara (Canis Major) and finally Spica (Virgo).

If we are reasonably confident that the human-like figure corresponds to Orion, then it is very possible that the animal to his right corresponds to one of Orion's hunting dogs. The most likely candidate constellation therefore would be Canis Major, with Sirius as its principal star. This star, known as the 'dog star', was regarded by many cultures as one of the most important stars in the sky. The Egyptians revered it and saw it as the herald of the Nile floods, which brought renewal to the soil of ancient Egypt. It would appear that most Western people saw this star and its constellation as a dog, usually closely associated with its master Orion. Sirius would have risen on 8 August.

There is no obvious classical zodiac constellation that could provide a match for the fish figure on the Golspie stone within the timeline suggested above. This might imply that this represents a completely different interpretation of a classical constellation. It is also possible that the figure, like the crescent, double disc and flower, represents a classic Pictish symbol. The order of the figures on the stone, from left to right is as follows: the serpents and man, double disc, the fish, the lion or dog, the flower-like symbol and finally the crescent symbol. If we compare this to our list of constellations containing the brightest stars, there would seem to be no obvious match. If we were to accept that Orion, Hydra, and Canis Major are already matched with figures on the stone, we would be left the choice for the fish of Canis Minor, Leo, Bootes and Virgo. If we are only considering the constellations that are found in the 'waters' below the ecliptic, then we would be left with just Canis Minor.

We have previously noted that Meissa, Bellatrix and Betelgeuse, all in Orion, would have risen in late June and would be followed by the belt stars in mid-July. The first stars of Leo actually would have risen prior to the belt stars, in early July. The next bright stars to rise are those of Canis Minor, seen by the Greeks as the smaller of the two hunting dogs of Orion. This constellation is basically made up of just two stars. Gomeisa, the dimmer of the two, would have risen first in the north of Scotland on 15 July. The second star, Procyon, which is by far the brighter – its magnitude of 0.4 makes it in fact the eighth brightest star in the sky – would have risen on 21 July. Procyon, a Greek name, means 'before the dog' and indicates that its acts as a herald for the 'dog star', Sirius. For this reason classical authors viewed this constellation as the little dog or Canis Minor. Its proximity to Eridanus (the river), according to Richard Hinckley Allen, may have led the civilisations on the Euphrates to see this as the 'water-dog'. After the stars of Canis Minor, the stars of Hydra's head rose at the end of July. Leo rose at the very beginning of August. Eight days later the principal star of Canis Major, Sirius, would have risen.

Is it possible, given the brilliance of the star Procyon, that the fish might actually be a Pictish representation of the small constellation of Canis Minor? It is not beyond the realms of possibility to see Procyon as the head or eye of a fish, with the other star being seen as a tail.

The Symbols

Perhaps an obvious difference between the scene on this stone and that on the cross slab from Shandwick is that there are far fewer figures. This might imply that the artist was being highly selective about the constellations he wished to include. Indeed there is only one human-like figure and only three animal figures. It is therefore imperative that we try to establish the logic behind the selection of these particular figures and also explain why the three abstract designs, which are also known Pictish symbols, are not only included but found alongside the figures. There are of course a number of parameters that the sculptor may have been using in the choice of which figures to include. These could have been sacred or mythological parameters. For example, some particular constellations or stars may have had particular religious significance or appear as characters in Pictish mythology. Another possibility is that they were simply interested in stars or constellations found in the same area of the sky, or within a certain distance of the ecliptic. Finally, they may have been specifically interested in particularly bright stars, visible even on hazy nights.

The relative lack of success in pinning down zodiacal matches to our Golspie figures might lead us to conclude that not only does the Golspie tableau exclude northern constellations, but also zodiacal constellations. This would contrast therefore with the Shandwick stone's depiction of apparent northern and zodiacal figures. A possible explanation is that northern and zodiacal constellations are represented on the Golspie stone but, instead of being depicted as figures within a tableau, are represented by the seemingly abstract classic Pictish symbols – the flower, the crescent and the double disc. We already know that classical Western astrology utilises animal, human, abstract and semi-abstract symbolism. So, for example, the planet Venus can be depicted as a woman, or as a symbol (the female gender symbol). This also applies to all the other planets. Similarly, the signs and constellations of the zodiac can likewise be displayed in two distinct forms. Aquarius, for example, can be a male figure pouring water from a vessel or two parallel wave-like lines. It is the choice of the astrologer or artist to use whichever form, picture or symbol, is most appropriate for the setting. Therefore Aquarius will be displayed as the human-like 'water bearer', or even a pouring jug in a magazine horoscope intended for the general public, but in astrological charts, which the average person in the street would not be able to understand, would include the simpler double-wave symbol. If we think about the possibility of dual pictorial systems in the context of the two stones that we have examined, zodiacal animals and human figures may well have fitted well with the Shandwick hunt in the mind's eye of the sculptor. However, for some reason these did not fit well within the context of a scene containing the Golspie man, the fish and the lion or dog figure. It may have been that the constellations or stars represented by the apparently abstract symbols were still important enough to be carved within the scene, even if they clashed in some way with the other figures.

With the possibility that the southern constellations, of Orion, Hydra, Canis Major and Canis Minor, may be depicted on the stone as figures, can we identify the three remaining symbols? Gemini would have risen already, ahead of Orion's first stars prior to late July in AD 700, and therefore we would expect it to be absent. The next constellation of the zodiac to have risen was Cancer, the crab, and the most indistinct zodiacal figure. This constellation contains no bright stars and would seem to be an unlikely candidate given our hypothesised emphasis on spectacular stars. The next zodiac sign to have risen would have been Leo. As mentioned before, its alpha star, Regulus, rose in northern Scotland on 1 August around AD 700. We have already noted that this star is one of the brightest in the sky. Following Leo were the stars of Virgo. Spica, Virgo's brightest star, is also exceptionally bright. From these four zodiac constellations, if we rule out Gemini on the basis of timing and Cancer on the basis that it lacks any significant stars, we are left with Leo and Virgo as possibilities. This would leave one symbol, the flower, unmatched. However, from our list of constellations that possess exceptionally bright stars and that would have risen in our time frame, there is one unmatched constellation, Bootes with its star, the third brightest in the night sky, Arcturus.

Given the position of the symbols, relative to each other and the other figures, a reasonable hypothesis might be that the double disc indicates Leo, or its star Regulus. The crescent might correspond to Virgo, or its star Spica. Finally, the flower might correspond to Bootes, or its star Arcturus. All of these three are from on or above the ecliptic and are particularly bright stars.

Winter Symbol

The Golspie stone therefore seems to be less straightforward than the Shandwick stone. It is most likely that the figures on the stone represent constellations or bright stars from below the ecliptic. The abstract symbols might also represent exceptional stars or constellations from on and above the ecliptic. Given the differences between the Golspie and Shandwick stones, could they represent two distinct 'worlds' populated by different characters? The concept of the heavens populated by heroes and gods is one that is familiar to us, through Graeco-Roman culture, and likewise the concept of an underworld as the resting place of the dead, reached by river. Did the Picts have a similar concept, and did they see the ecliptic as the boundary between these two worlds? It would certainly seem possible from the evidence from these two stones that they did. The northern portion of the sky, as perhaps depicted on the Shandwick stone, would be associated with the summer months, a time of life and abundance, a time for pleasures and sport. In contrast, the southern portion of the sky, comprising the sub-ecliptic stars, may well have represented the other world – a view that would not be foreign to the Greeks, the Irish or Brythonic Celts. This would seem to be a world ruled over by the constellation Orion. He perhaps represents a god of death, with his axe and dagger. His companion, the hound, is suitably menacing. It is a world of death and foreboding. Orion is often referred to as the great winter constellation, dominating the sky when the ground is frozen and life is on hold. Orion holds court in the night sky when days are at their shortest and the Sun is at its weakest, a point particularly relevant to northern Scotland. This is the time of year when life itself seems to be on the wane. It seems likely that the constellation of Orion, as represented on the Golspie stone, therefore has a strong association with winter. From the perspective of northern Scotland, with its very short and cold days and in contrast to the near constant brightness of the summer sky, such a wintry character may have featured heavily in the psyche.

We can look at Orion's potential role as a winter symbol if we model the night sky as seen by the Picts. In our original attempt to make sense of the stone, the first star we looked at was Meissa (Orion's eye). This would have risen, heliacally, on 26 June in AD 700. This was a few days after the summer solstice, almost exactly six months prior to midwinter and the rising of the stars of Capricorn and Aquarius. Returning to simulations of the night sky, if we model sunrise a few days after the winter solstice in the Pictish period, we find that as the Sun set, Meissa, Orion's eye, rose in the east. A few days before that at the winter solstice on 17 December, the first bright stars of Orion rose as the Sun set (Tabit and Thabit). Orion would have started to appear in the dawn sky at the summer solstice, and as the months progressed towards midwinter, it would have been visible for an increasing portion of the night. By the winter solstice, it would have risen at sunset and dominated the winter night until finally setting at sunrise. In effect, as a symbol of winter, Orion was at the height of power. The emphasis of Orion, as a starting point for the timeline on the stone, may therefore be indicating the importance with which the Picts viewed this winter symbol. The stone may therefore be counting down to an important event that involves their interpretation of the Orion constellation.

It would seem that for both scenes found on the Shandwick stone and the Golspie stone a number of basic rules apply. Both stones may indicate a timeline from left to right. The carvings on both do not represent a star atlas or a snapshot of the night sky as such, but rather place the constellations in the approximate order in which their brightest stars rise with the sun. Extrapolating from the subject matter of the two different monuments and the lack of any overlap between their scenes in terms of figures, it would also seem that mixing constellations from above the ecliptic with those below the ecliptic may not, for whatever reason, have been acceptable to the Picts. Finally perhaps the most important possible rule is that the associated Pictish symbols also seem to relate to the timeline of the tableau, therefore providing evidence, for the first time, that Pictish symbols relate to a celestial calendar and may represent constellations or prominent stars.

Identifying a Pictish 'Orion'

From our interpretation of both the Shandwick stone and the Golspie stone it would seem that, whether for Christian or for pagan reasons, the Picts thought it was important to record key celestial events in relation to the calendar. It would be useful to explore further the motion of Orion in the night sky in the early Middle Ages in Scotland, to ascertain what role this constellation may have had within the Pictish calendar.

During the Pictish period, we know already that Orion would have started to heliacally rise at midsummer and that, around midwinter, Orion would have risen as the Sun set. This would, however, leave us with two other events involving Orion and the Sun. These would relate to Orion setting with the Sun (heliacal setting) and Orion setting as the Sun rises. If we follow Orion's path through the sky from midsummer, Orion rises further and further ahead of the Sun; by mid-October it was rising in the early evening. However, of more interest is when it sets. On 19 October in AD 700, Rigel was setting in northern Scotland as the Sun rose, the 'belt' stars set on 30 October, Meissa on 9 November and Betelgeuse on 10 November. The end of October was of great significance to the Celts, marking the festival of *Samhain*, the end of the summer. This festival has come down to us as the Scottish festival of Halloween, now celebrated across the world. It is of course associated with spirits, ghouls and ghosts, at the point in the year when our world and the spirit world supposedly come into contact. Is the heliacal setting of Orion's belt within twenty-four hours of the Celtic festival of *Samhain* a coincidence? If the Golspie man represented some sort of god of the other world, emerging to dominate the winter sky, then this constellation's opposition to the sunrise around *Samhain* might well signify the start of winter. If Orion played a major role in defining the year, then we also have to look at the Celtic festival that defined the start of summer – *Beltane* or May Day. Moving the simulation of the sky of northern Scotland forward to around *Beltane* in AD 700, we find the 'belt' stars of Orion set with the Sun just prior to *Beltane*.

How should we interpret all this? Just before *Samhain*, the rising Sun would in effect overpower Orion, while the constellation was high in the sky, while at *Samhain* the Sun would lose its ability to dominate Orion and it would only be a matter of time before Orion would triumphantly rise as the weak midwinter Sun set. The tables would be turned, however, as *Beltane* approached. Orion would become progressively harder to see in the sky. By midsummer, the Sun would have been its strongest, with Orion completely invisible. Perhaps the behaviour of Orion was used, possibly along with other constellations, to mark both *Beltane* and *Samhain*, as well as to mark the solstices. In effect it would have marked the turning of the seasons and crucially would therefore have served to link the solstices with a sidereal Celtic calendar. Orion therefore may have been of prime importance to the Celts and their belief system. This would provide an explanation as to why the Celts celebrated the so-called quarter days, which at first glance have little bearing on the solstices and equinoxes, but would seem to be in fact intrinsically linked via Orion. The appearance of a possible Orion figure on Pictish stones might further support the idea that the Picts were also interested in the Celtic quarter days.

While we can now match a putative Pictish Orion figure to astronomical events at key points in the calendar, and even suggest that this figure might represent a god of the other world, we still, however, have only a little evidence to suggest that the Picts saw any significance in Orion's celestial behaviour surrounding the very Celtic festivals of *Samhain* and *Beltane*. Likewise, there is no evidence at present to suggest that their neighbours, the Irish and Brythonic Celts, observed Orion and linked its rising and setting to their festivals.

If we could link a Pictish Orion to a Celtic mythological figure, which clearly relates to *Samhain* or *Beltane*, we might then uncover a previously unknown and strong cultural link between the Picts and the other Celtic peoples of Britain, Ireland and the continent. We may therefore be able to provide evidence that the Picts were culturally 'Celtic', if we are able to show that an Orion-like figure was not only important to the Picts and their calendar, but also to that of other Celts. There are two ways to approach such a search. Firstly, we should look for figures in Celtic literature whose descriptions are close to the pictorial representation of the Golspie man. Secondly, we should search for any such figures associated with the Celtic festivals. We can proceed by recapping the principal features of the two Pictish figures from Golspie and Rhynie. The grotesque and exaggerated features of the two figures might suggest that both represent giants. In the same way that Orion is referred to as a celestial giant, dominating the night sky and dwarfing many of the other constellations, the Pictish figures might have been intended to convey the notion that they too are celestial giants. The grotesque features add to this impression and are in keeping even with our modern idea of fairytale giants. The specific features we must focus on are the prominent eyebrow, the large eye, the excessively large nose, the beard and long hair. Both figures also menacingly carry an axe although the Golspie man does not possess the Rhynie man's sharp teeth; or rather these are not displayed. The clothing is distinctive and, as we have seen above, probably relates to the identification of the figures with the constellation.

Who then are the giants of Celtic mythology and do they in any way resemble these two Pictish figures? The most obvious place to look in the Irish tradition is among the mythical race of giants, the Fomorians. They are depicted in Irish mythology as evil and misshapen, often with missing limbs or eyes. According to Miranda Green's *Dictionary of Celtic Myth and Legend*, their name means 'under-demons' and they fascinatingly represent the chthonic powers of darkness and winter. Other sources, such as *The Ultimate Encyclopaedia of Mythology*, describe them as sea-gods, who emerged from the sea 'violent and misshapen'. They are described in Irish origin stories as battling with another supernatural race, the *Tuatha Dé Danann*, for control of Ireland. The leader of the Fomorians is Balor, whose single eye could bring death to his enemies. This monstrous weapon was covered by an eyelid that took four servants to lift. Peter Beresford Ellis, in his *Dictionary of Celtic Mythology*, describes him as a 'god of death'. He was eventually killed by his own grandson, Lugh, god of light, at the second battle of *Mag Tuired*. Is it a coincidence that in Greek mythology there is also an emphasis on Orion's eye? Balor's apparent dominion over the sea and the underworld could indicate a possible connection to an Orion-type figure and we must remind ourselves not only of the links the Greek Orion has to the sea but of the constellation's location below the ecliptic close to the 'aquatic' constellations. The battle between Lugh and Balor could therefore be interpreted as a narrative on a forgotten eternal 'battle' between the Sun and the great winter constellation for dominance of the sky. Furthermore, and perhaps significantly, the Fomorians are also credited with introducing the Celtic festival of *Samhain*, or Halloween, to Ireland. Perhaps most significantly, we even have date for the battle between Lugh and Balor – *Samhain*, when the Sun and Orion were in opposition at sunrise. We therefore have some strong evidence of a relationship, in the Irish tradition, between a monstrous giant, in this case the Fomorian giant Balor, and the Celtic festival.

Balor, the chief of the giant Fomorians, has a Welsh counterpart in Yspaddaden Penkawr, the father of Olwen. He too is described as monstrous, and the story focuses on his peculiar eyes, which like Balor, required help in order to be opened. He is described as having one or sometimes two eyes. These, however, lack the special powers of Balor's eye. While it is Balor's eyelid that droops over his eye, in Yspaddaden's case it is his prominent eyebrows that limit his vision. It is in this connection that we should note the 'larger than life' eyebrows of the Rhynie man. If elements of the story of 'Culhwch and Olwen' carry astronomical significance, then it is feasible that the character Yspaddaden could also represent a celestial figure. Could the Golspie man and the Rhynie man be the Pictish equivalent of the Welsh Ysbaddaden and perhaps also the Irish Balor?

Another figure that has some echoes with the notion of a Pictish other-worldly figure is the god Bel. In Welsh mythology, Bel is one of the chief figures in the Celtic 'pantheon' of gods. However, interpretations of Bel and his Irish incarnations of Bile or Beli, or the Gaulish version, Belenus, are confused. In Welsh mythology he is the husband of Don, the mother goddess, known as Danu in Ireland. This god has echoes in the Graeco-Roman tradition, as he gives rise to the first men in much the same way as Dispater or Jupiter. Bel also rules over the other world. He was apparently viewed as a god of death, but the interest here is in his connection to *Beltane*. The similarity between the name of the Irish king of the Fomorians, Balor, and Bel may also hint that they may be one and the same. There have been two suggestions as to the origin of the name Bel. The first suggestion is that the name relates to death, the second that it relates to light. *Beltane* has therefore been interpreted as the festival of the 'bright fire' or the festival of 'Bel's fire'. If there is a real connection between Orion being seen as the god of the other world and May Day, then this might revive the possibility that *Beltane* is linked to the god of the other world.

In a previous chapter, we also explored a Welsh tale that seemed to have some parallels with both the story of Castor and Pollux and the giant Geryon's cattle, as well as the Irish tale *Táin Bó Cúailnge*. This tale of Nynniaw and Peibaw, may also provide a clue as to the identification of both the Rhynie man and the Golspie man. As we have seen previously, in one version of the tale, God transforms the two brothers into two oxen or cattle, but in another version of the tale, a giant, Rhitta, defeats the brothers and also lays claim to the night sky and all its stars. This strange portion of the story puts great emphasis on the removal, as punishment, of the beards of Nynniaw and Peibaw by the giant with his knife. He also removes the beards of twenty-six other kings. As suggested previously, these kings and the two brothers may represent stars stationed along the Moon's path. Ultimately, Rhitta's own beard is removed by Arthur and his allies. In Welsh, Rhitta's name is usually given as 'Rhudda Gawr' and means 'the red giant'. Could this be reference to the bright red star in Orion, Betelgeuse? In this tale, wintry metaphors are used to describe Rhitta's devastating attacks on his enemies – descriptions that would fit very well with the idea of Orion dominating the winter sky and being the very Celtic symbol of winter. Could the bearded Golspie man, with its possible link to Orion, be a Pictish Rhitta?

Astronomical Imagery on the Golspie and Shandwick Stones

It would seem therefore that there is a high probability that the Golspie stone, like the Shandwick stone, carries a pictorial calendar relating to the movements of the stars. Both show scenes that at first glance are a jumble of figures, with no logical structure, but on closer inspection, and with astronomy in mind, are likely to show significant structure. The principal difference between these two Pictish monuments is that while the Shandwick hunting panel appears to display constellations from the northern portion of the sky, the Golspie stone seems to be focussed on southern constellations. It also, however, incorporates the enigmatic Pictish symbols into the scene, suggesting that these too relate to stars or constellations. It is also worth emphasising that both the Golspie stone and the Shandwick stone display figures that have resonances with characters from other cultures. The Shandwick stone in particular has figures that relate to classical zodiacal constellations, as well as other constellations that were recognised by other European cultures and figures that seem to relate to the mythology of other cultures. In the case of Golspie, the human-like figure may relate to Orion from Greek mythology, but also to mythical figures from Celtic stories. Similarly, it is fascinating that the Picts, like the Greeks, may also have viewed the constellation Hydra as water serpents.

In terms of Pictish studies, what we have uncovered so far from the examination of these two stones would seem to indicate a very strong astronomical aspect to their content. Furthermore, there is more than a hint that the accompanying symbols also relate to astronomy in some way, a theme that we will consider further in the coming chapters.

CHAPTER 9

THE PURPOSE OF THE SYMBOLS

Pictish Astronomical Calendars

Our analysis of both the Shandwick and Golspie stones has already led to a greater understanding of the Picts. The inference from this analysis is that they possessed at least a reasonably sophisticated knowledge of the night sky. Crucially, the apparent structure of the Shandwick panel suggests that the figure's position within the scene (from left to right) reflects the order in which prominent stars rise, rather than a straightforward map of the night sky. This would further suggest that the sculptor may have devised the scene as a pictorial calendar. If the stars have been correctly identified, then it is likely that the sequence is indicating a particular event in the Pictish calendar, most likely around midwinter, with the Nativity being a strong possibility. The Shandwick tableaux would therefore fit perfectly with the rest of this overtly Christian monument.

The tableau from the Golspie stone has in addition provided an unparalleled opportunity to gain a basic understanding of the meaning and purpose of the symbols. The figures carved on the stone would also appear to represent prominent stars within constellations, again arranged in a sequence from left to right, again according to the order of rising. However, it is the integration of Pictish symbols into this celestial scene that offers the most dramatic opportunity to achieve a breakthrough in understanding their meaning. The most obvious conclusion to draw is that these particular Pictish symbols also relate in some way to the night sky and could correspond to stars, constellations, or planets and therefore may also be associated with a calendar. This possibility provides for the first time an indication as to what the basic function of the symbols might be.

The analysis of the stone has allowed us to postulate that the hideous Golspie man appearing in the scene actually corresponded to the southern constellation of Orion and indeed we found similarities between the Golspie man and the constellation of Orion morphologically. Similarly, other figures on the stone were then matched with the rising of prominent stars that follow on from those of Orion. Perhaps most excitingly, not only were we able to match the figures to specific stars, but we were also able to attempt to match the symbols that appeared among the figures. Therefore the position of one of the symbols, the double disc, on the stone might correspond to the rising of Regulus, in the constellation Leo. The flower symbol's position may have corresponded to date of the rising of the third brightest star in the night sky, Arcturus, in the constellation of Bootes. The crescent symbol might represent another prominent star, Spica, in the constellation of Virgo. It is of major significance that these three Pictish symbols, which normally appear in symbol pairs, may actually represent stars. Their basic function may be astronomical but one that was intimately associated with a Pictish calendar. Our own modern calendar is of course based on a solar year divided into months, and while not entirely satisfactory (we have to incorporate an extra day every four years to keep our calendar accurate) it functions reasonably well. Although our modern calendar is solar, we still choose to subdivide the year into months. This is a legacy of older calendars that were based on the cycles of the Moon, hence the word months. Other calendars are wholly based on lunar cycles, for example the Islamic holy calendar. While others have sought to integrate fully the annual progression of the Sun with the lunar cycles and as such were incredibly complex, with entire extra months having to be added every few years. An example of a lunisolar calendar is the (primarily religious) Hebrew calendar.

If the individual symbols represent stars or constellations, and appear on the Golspie stone in the context of some form of astronomical information relating to a calendar, could the symbol pairs scattered across the Scottish landscape have a similar function? Are they indicating a particular year and month or is some other calendrical information encoded? It is worth remembering that calendars functioned in the past not just to keep track of the days in the year, but were intimately bound to the rhythms of everyday life. In addition, as they were governed by the movement of the Sun, Moon, stars and planets, they also had a divine or supernatural aspect, and were intrinsically linked to the gods. One major function was that they were used to govern the timing of holy festivals. The ability to accurately keep track of the days of the year and the position of the planets in the night sky also enabled the development of the art of astrology. The course of a person's life was thought to be determined by the positions of the celestial bodies on the day of their birth and people sought guidance on how to conduct their lives according to their birth charts. Some days in the year were considered luckier than others for particular activities, and again this depended on the planets. We therefore have the further possibility that the information encoded by the Pictish symbols was not only astronomical, calendrical and perhaps of religious significance, but may also have been used in an astrological setting.

Perhaps the first step to take in trying to determine if there could be an astrological aspect to the Pictish symbols, is simply to consider their total number. In the case of the Western zodiac, the year was divided between just twelve 'signs'. If the Pictish symbols form part of an astrological system, each symbol representing a key constellation, then we might only expect twelve symbols if they recognised twelve zodiac signs. In this case, if the double disc corresponded to the whole constellation of Leo, then the appearance of this symbol in a pairing might be telling us that the symbol pair related in some way to the month of August, when the Sun was in Leo. In reality, as we have seen, the actual number of Pictish symbols is in the high twenties for either position within a pair and this would seem to rule out the symbols approximating to a month. However, when considering ancient calendars we quickly can find extra levels of unexpected complexity. The ancient Babylonians, when devising their calendar, divided the circular ecliptic into 360 portions or 'degrees'. Each degree represented one day in their year (hence our use of 360 degrees in mathematics). Each degree corresponded to their estimation of the relative distance travelled by the Sun per day against the 'fixed' star background. They then subdivided this celestial circle into thirty-six portions of 10 degrees each. These 10-degree segments are sometimes referred to as decans, and were each represented by a prominent star. Three decans correspond to one month, or one zodiac sign of 30 degrees. If the Picts recognised a similar division within the month, then clearly they would require thirty-six symbols to account for all decans. Clearly the number of symbols that appear in pairs is significantly short of this.

Another possibility is that the Pictish symbols relate to a lunar or lunisolar calendar and represent not the solar houses, or indeed subdivisions of these, but rather represent 'lunar mansions'. In such a system there would be typically twenty-seven or twenty-eight subdivisions of the ecliptic, one for each day of the so-called sidereal lunar month. This sidereal lunar month is approximately 27.3 days long and represents the number of days the Moon takes to make one full circuit of the ecliptic. It should be pointed out that the cycle of lunar phases is slightly longer than this with, for example, the time taken from one full Moon to the next full Moon corresponding to 29.5 days; this time interval is referred to as the synodic lunar month. The difference between the synodic and the sidereal month is accounted for by the change in the Earth's own position in its orbit during that time period. Because the lunar sidereal month is not exactly twenty-seven days, a lunar month could be deemed to be twenty-seven days or twenty-eight days, and therefore a system utilising lunar mansions would tend to normally use twenty-seven symbols, but on occasion add one extra symbol.

Each lunar mansion would define the position of the Moon each night, and would in all probability be represented by a particular bright star or specific portion of a constellation. This type of system forms an important part of the ancient Hindu (or Vedic) astrology system, where each lunar house or mansion is referred to as a *nakshatra*. In a similar way to Western solar astrology, each mansion has its own ruling planet. The word *nakshatra* is derived from the Sanskrit meaning 'star cluster' and these are thought of as the 'star wives' of the god of the Moon, Chandra. The number of *nakshatras* (twenty-seven or twenty-eight) would also seem to correspond well to the known number of Pictish symbols. These twenty-seven or twenty-eight stars are not, however, necessarily close to the ecliptic. The Moon's path is somewhat erratic compared to that of the Sun. This results in the Moon entering or passing close by to stars or constellations further from the ecliptic than the traditional Western zodiacal constellations. Therefore we see in the Vedic system individual *nakshatras* being represented by prominent stars of constellations at some distance from the ecliptic and the Western signs of the zodiac. For example, the Vedic system recognises the non-zodiacal constellation of Bootes and its alpha star, Arcturus, as the *nakshatra Sveti*. Previously we discussed the possibility that the Pictish flower symbol, based on its relative position to other figures and symbols on the Golspie stone, might represent the constellation Bootes. The use of the star Arcturus, in the constellation Bootes, as a lunar mansion in the Vedic system might encourage us further to view the Pictish flower symbol as representative of the star Arcturus.

The Mirror and the Comb as Astrological Symbols

The relatively large numbers of symbols used within the pairs seem to indicate that we are dealing with a reasonably complex system. This complexity would seem to be added to by the addition of two other apparently optional symbols, which would seem to act as adjuncts to the main pairing – the mirror and comb symbols. While we now have a working hypothesis that the principal symbols represent particular stars or parts of constellations, and were used in some calendrical context, how could these two additional symbols possibly fit with such a hypothesis? What role could these possibly have in an astrological setting, and why were they used on some occasions, but not at others? Clearly, any hypotheses or theories regarding the function and specific meaning of the Pictish symbols has to account for the use of these two symbols, and also has to be able to explain adequately why these additional symbols take the specific form of a mirror and comb. Before going on to an investigation of the possible meaning of the main Pictish symbols, we will therefore address the role the mirror and comb symbols may have fulfilled and consequently show how they help elucidate the broader meaning of the mainstream symbols.

The mirror and comb symbols do not seem to be mainstream symbols but appear to be supplementary to the other symbols. They are usually smaller than the principal symbols, and appear typically below the main pairing. The mirror can appear on its own or with the comb, but there is no clear example of the comb appearing by itself, suggesting some form of logical coding or stratification. It may be that these two symbols were intended to convey additional information to the viewer about the combination of the mainstream symbol pairs – they may act as qualifiers, providing further clarity to the message. An example of a stone bearing a mirror and comb alongside a symbol pair can be found in the picture of the Aberlemno 1 stone (picture 1).

The most obvious place to start is the widely held notion that the mirror and comb somehow convey a feminine aspect to the interpretation of the symbols. According to previous theories on their function, if the two symbols represented someone's name, then the mirror could indicate that the name was that of a female. Such an interpretation does not, however, explain the extra potential coding suggested by the addition of the comb symbol in a large number of cases. The 'female hypothesis' would of course be dependent on the Picts associating both these objects with femininity, an association for which we have no clear evidence. Why wouldn't these objects also be an important item in male grooming? Mirrors would also have been relatively rare and therefore a status symbol and it is just as likely that a mirror symbol conveys the notion of this status. The comb, however, would seem to be a much more common item, and it is telling that it occurs only in the presence of the mirror.

The mirrors depicted appear to be typical of early medieval mirrors, and similar examples of these can be seen in various museums in Scotland and further afield, although some of the specific mirror designs carved on Pictish stones have not been found by archaeologists. The mirrors found are clearly opulent objects, often richly decorated and would have been considered a very desirable accessory. The combs, which can consist of a single or double row of teeth, are much more common and can be made out of materials such as wood, bone or rare and more valuable materials such as ivory.

Perhaps the first relevant question to ask is, given the astronomical symbolism we have been exploring, how could these two symbols possibly fit with a calendrical, astronomical or astrological interpretation of the Pictish stones? We could start with a relatively simple hypothesis; if the mirror is a symbol of value then its presence may tell the person viewing a particular stone that the astrological significance of the symbol pair it accompanies is higher than usual. Likewise, the addition of a comb could mean that the combination of symbols is of particular significance. This possibility might explain why mirrors are often associated with a rodded double disc, but there is no clear example of a mirror accompanying the simpler double disc without a rod. If we assume for the moment that a rodded version of a symbol had a higher status than its non-rodded counterpart, and if the mirror's function was to convey the importance of the two symbols it accompanied, then a mirror and simple double disc occurring together would indeed be less likely.

The use of the mirror might be analogous to the underlining of a particularly important passage in a book, and the addition of the comb could be viewed as the process of highlighting to the underlined text. Such an interpretation would fit with the astrological hypothesis, but could also be adapted to other theories. For example, if the symbols represent lineages, as proposed by Anthony Jackson, the presence of the mirror and comb could signify that the union of the two lineages depicted is of particular importance.

There is, however, a significant feature of mirrors that adds weight to the notion that the Pictish symbols are astrological in nature: the fact that mirrors have attached to them a considerable folklore connecting them to future events. This folklore is still very much extant and it is still a commonly held belief that breaking a mirror will bring seven years of bad luck. If we ask ourselves why the breakage of a mirror would have such dire consequences for the future, the mundane answer would be that, going back in time, the mirror, at least one made of glass, was originally a very valuable and fragile object and of course in this sense it would be 'unlucky' to smash one. This doesn't explain why you would then experience further bad luck for many years to come. If breaking a mirror is unlucky, is there an implication that the intact mirror is somehow lucky or even associated with the supernatural in some way? And if this was true why would this be the case? The very concept of luck is interesting in itself. In *Chambers Dictionary*, luck is defined as 'fortune: good fortune'. Furthermore fortune is defined as, 'What ever comes by lot or chance: luck: the arbitrary ordering of events: a prediction of one's future.' Did the mirror originally have some sort of supernatural role, perhaps in fortune telling or in predicting the future? If it did, then the mirror's presence among astrological signs would make perfect sense.

Delving into this aspect of the mirror as an object with potential supernatural uses, it soon becomes obvious that there is more to the mirror than meets the eye. We could start with some word games, and look at the English verb 'speculate' and trace its meaning and origins. *Chambers Dictionary* tells us that 'speculate' means, 'To reflect: to theorise: to make conjectures or guesses.' Its origin is from a Latin root listed as *specere*, 'to look at'. Right underneath the entry for 'speculate' is another related word, 'speculum', formed from exactly the same Latin root. Nowadays the use of this word is confined to medical terminology, and interestingly enough is a rather fancy word for a mirror, and indeed was borrowed straight from the Latin common word for a mirror, *speculum*. Both words are from the same root, but it does not necessarily follow that the word 'speculate' might be derived from *speculum*, but it is an intriguing possibility. In the *Penguin Dictionary of Symbols* the reader, however, is left in no doubt as to the connection between mirrors and speculation. Here is the opening paragraph:

Mirror

The Latin word for mirror (speculum) has given us the verb 'to speculate'; and originally speculation was scanning the sky and the related movement of the stars by means of a mirror. The Latin for star (sidus) has also given us the word 'consideration' which, etymologically, means to scan the stars as a whole. Both abstract nouns which now describe highly intellectual activities are rooted in the study of the stars reflected in mirrors. It follows, then, that mirrors, as reflecting surfaces, should be the basis of a wealth of symbolism relating to knowledge.

The link between divination, the mirror and, importantly for us, the stars and planets, is therefore clearly stated. Similarly, in Jack Tresidder's *Dictionary of Symbols*, the entry for 'Mirror' states the following:

Almost everywhere, mirrors have been linked with magic and especially with divination because they can reflect past or future events as well as present ones. Shamans in central Asia aimed mirrors at the Sun or Moon in order to read the future.

Indeed the use of mirrors for divination appears to have been widespread; according to the *Penguin Dictionary of Symbols*, 'The use of the mirror is one of the oldest forms of divination and Varro says that it originated in Persia.' It also quotes a story about Pythagoras using a mirror to read the future by pointing it at the night sky: 'According to legend, Pythagoras had a magic mirror which he, like the Thessalian witches, would turn towards the Moon before reading the future in it.' Furthermore, the entry on mirrors in this dictionary goes on not only to reiterate the mirror's use by Shamans in central Asia, but also to note that 'shamanistic robes were often decorated with mirrors'. This practice should also remind us of the stereotypical image of the gypsy fortune teller, whose attire was decorated with small reflective discs.

According to the *Penguin Dictionary of Symbols*, the Muslim world also seems to have viewed the mirror as more than just an object to reflect a person's image: 'The magic mirror which enables its user to see past, present and future is, in any case, a classic theme of Muslim literature.' This same basic theme of mirrors, divination and magic seems to pervade many cultures, including European culture where the magic mirror appears centrally in the folk tale 'Snow White': 'Mirror, mirror, on the wall, who is the fairest of them all?'

Even in Scotland, it would appear that mirror divination may well have survived the centuries and was strongly associated with Halloween. In *The Book of Hallowe'en*, published in 1919, Ruth Edna Kelley describes the custom of young women who would look into moonlit mirrors on 31 October in order to see their future lovers or husbands. There is also strong evidence of similar customs having been common in the USA, and indeed Halloween cards from the first half of the twentieth century in America show this very practice.

So it would seem that in different times and different places the mirror has been fundamentally associated with divination, and particularly sky divination. There is also unambiguous evidence of the mirror symbolising supernatural knowledge. It no longer seems far fetched to view the Pictish mirror symbol as an astrological symbol, fitting perfectly well with other astrological symbols. This would explain elegantly why this seemingly mundane object should be found carved beside the almost other-worldly Pictish symbols. The possibility that the mirrors depicted on Pictish stones have an astrological context would also seem to be reasonable in the context of other Eurasian cultures. We should therefore consider the idea of the reflection in the mirror being not simply photons bouncing off the silver layer behind the glass back to our modern eyes, but perhaps as our ancestors saw it, as a glimpse into another place. Water also has reflective properties, and it is interesting that the Celts cast offerings into lakes and springs, perhaps passing these precious objects through the reflective surface into the other world. The mirror may therefore have been almost a kind of portable reflective substitute for water, allowing a druid or priest to peer in to this alternative spiritual world at any time, now replaced by the fortune teller's almost stereotypical crystal ball.

Combs have been around for an exceedingly long time, and have a dual function as both a tool to untangle hair and also to remove parasites. In European folk traditions they also appear as magical objects, for example as an essential accessory for mermaids; the creature is often depicted combing her hair in a hand mirror. The mermaid's comb is frequently described as golden and provides any human who manages to acquire the object with the ability to control the creature – a recurring theme in Scottish tales of mermaids. In Hans Christian Andersen's *The Snow Queen*, a golden comb when pulled through the victims' hair makes them forget. In a tale collected by the Grimm brothers, 'The Nix of the Mill Pond', a golden comb is used by a wife to summon her husband from the mill pond, where he had been taken by a beautiful woman who lived in the water. Perhaps this is really about summoning her husband back from the spirit world, through the reflective surface of the mill pond, the comb being used to control the will of spirits to do a mortal woman's bidding. In Ireland, banshees – female spirits whose appearance signals a forthcoming death – also possess combs, although these are silver rather than gold. Combs and the act of combing therefore seem to be associated with females from the other world and possess magical qualities relating to control of their supernatural owners or victims, or perhaps to signal a supernatural prophesy. If we regard the mirror as providing a portal into the other world, with the reflection literally symbolising a window into that world and the comb or the act of combing as part of the process of divination, then the purpose of these two symbols becomes clearer: the mermaid or banshee is divining the future, perhaps foretelling a specific event using the tools of her trade, passing that message from the other world to our own.

In the context of the Pictish symbols, the comb might therefore represent some or all of these elements: contact with the other world, a feminine aspect, a symbol of control over the spirits or perhaps a symbol of prophecy. Previous authors have suggested that the mirror and comb, in the context of the Pictish stones, might be marriage symbols and, given the above, it is possible that the comb may well represent a symbol of matrimony. Alternatively, and more likely, it might represent control over the other world and relate to death, and the passage of the spirit, or suggest that the message conveyed by the symbols originates in the other world. The significance of the mermaid's comb being made of gold and that of the banshee being made of silver might also evoke solar and lunar symbolism respectively. Unfortunately, in the context of Pictish carvings of combs, there is no way of knowing what material they were supposed to be made of.

In Welsh mythology we have already encountered a golden comb in the story of 'Culhwch and Olwen'; it is one of the objects demanded by Ysbaddaden the giant and is eventually retrieved from behind the ears of the Boar King, the Twrch Trwyth. If this particular character has celestial origins, as suggested, then it is possible that the comb, as well as the razor and shears for that matter, are also connected to objects in the night sky, or at the very least seen as items linked to the other world.

However, one idea, which seems to have been overlooked more recently, may well help shed further light on the presence of combs on Pictish stones and was published in the *New York Times* in September 1888:

> THE MYSTERY OF THE COMB – It would be curious to know what mystic meaning our forefathers attached to so simple an act as combing the hair. Yet we learn from old church history that the hair of the priest or Bishop was thus combed several times during divine service by one of the inferior clergy. The comb is mentioned as one of the essentials for use during a high mass when sung by a Bishop, and both in English and foreign cathedrals they were reckoned among the costly possessions of the church. Some were made of ivory. Some were carved, others gemmed with precious stones. Among the combs specially known to history are those of St. Neot, St. Dunstan, and Malachias. That of St. Thomas the Martyr of Canterbury is still to be seen in the Church of the Sepulchre at Thetford, and that of St. Cuthbert at Durham Cathedral. From sundry references in old legends to the use of the comb in divination, and from its appearance in combination with pagan emblems on rudely sculptured stones in various parts of Scotland, it seems probable that this was one of the objects of pagan veneration which early Christian teachers deemed to be prudent to adopt, investing it with some new significance.

Apart from the reference to the comb's use in divination in old legends, and therefore possible further evidence for an astrological role, the principal insight into the importance of the use of combs in early Christian religious ceremonies is fascinating. Indeed many ornate ceremonial or liturgical combs have been identified as associated with bishops or saints, including that of the founder and patron saint of the city of Glasgow St Kentigern, and it would appear that the comb was one of the few possessions owned by senior members of the clergy. In some cases, the combs have a small hole, suggesting that they may have been worn around the neck or attached to vestments. Combs are apparently still an important feature of the consecration of bishops, as laid out by the Catholic Church. So why are combs used at all in a religious context, and how did they come to be adopted not just in any ceremony but in 'high' masses? The combing of the bishop's hair at key points may indicate some sort of purification. Purifying the bishop's hair by combing it may have been thought to bring the bishop closer to god and, if the author of the extract from 1888 was correct, pagan priests or druids may have also used the comb for a similar purpose, presumably purifying themselves for communication perhaps not with 'god' but rather with the spirit world. This scenario would also neatly explain the purpose of the comb in the hand of the mermaid. In this case the mermaid is not only able to see into the spirit world via a reflection in her mirror but also, by using the comb, is facilitating communication between our world and that of the spirits. If the comb really does have a role in helping an individual to get closer to the divine or to the spirits, then the use of the mirror and comb could well be communicating this function to us. The presence of the mirror alone would lend some spiritual weight to the importance of the event commemorated on a stone, but the presence of both symbols clearly is something special.

If the comb came to be closely associated with the early Christian clergy in Britain, then it is possible that it was already associated with pagan priestly orders, including perhaps the druids. As it seems to be particularly associated with bishops then likewise the comb may have been associated with a druidic elite; the arch druids. The symbols of the mirror and comb may therefore, in the pre-Christian era, be the mark of a high-ranking druid later adopted, in the early Christian era, as the mark of a bishop or saint who would also presumably want to emphasise their superiority. As the design of the mirror and comb varies from stone to stone, they may even represent depictions of real liturgical combs and mirrors possessed by particular individuals. If this was the case then it may be possible in the future, although the chances are slim, to match combs found buried with senior clergymen in Pictland to stone representations of specific combs or to date stones with the same designs to the same time period.

Finally, there may also be evidence of further sets of qualifiers, other than the mirror and comb on stones in Pictland. On the Abernethy stone (picture 6) what seems to be a hammer and possibly an anvil appear on the stone. Blacksmith's tools and the ability of the blacksmith to work with iron have long been linked to the supernatural and luck, and is best manifested in the folklore surrounding horseshoes. At Gretna Green in southern Scotland, blacksmith's tools are still used to symbolically marry couples.

CHAPTER 10

HIGH-STATUS SYMBOLS:
V-RODS AND Z-RODS

Associated Symbols

In this chapter we will start to examine individual Pictish symbols in depth and in reference to their potential astrological significance. It is clear from even a casual examination of the symbols that they can be grouped in a number of different ways. For example, they can be divided into categories such as animalistic, abstract and symbols that portray familiar objects. Another common classification is to divide the symbols into so-called rodded or non-rodded forms. The rodded symbols seem only to add further complexity and mystery to the symbols and transcend the more obvious categorisation. This group comprises designs that are often embellished with a an arrow or spear-like rod, taking the form of either a 'z' shape or 'v' shape, which cross or divide the symbol symmetrically. These symbols can be animalistic or seemingly abstract. The addition of rods to some of the designs has long fascinated anyone who has taken an interest in Pictish symbols. Their function, as in the case of the supplementary mirror and comb pictographs, has to be explained in the context of any hypothesis or theory regarding the symbol system. As there are only five known symbols that are found in a rodded form, then this might suggest that these particular symbols are of some significance. In a possible calendrical or astrological context it might be hypothesised that these seemingly special symbols take on greater significance at certain times, and this is signalled by the addition of a rod.

The Double Disc
The solar symbolism of this design was noted as long ago as 1893 when the Earl of Southesk interpreted the two conjoined discs as representing the Sun and the Moon. Representations of the Sun as a disc are of course commonplace in Europe and elsewhere, and appear as far back as the Bronze Age, while the Moon is almost universally represented by a crescent shape. If we are looking for an astrological connection for this symbol, it is obvious that it is the Western astrological symbol for the Sun that seems to resonate most with the Pictish double disc. This classic astrological symbol is generally regarded as dating back to the infancy of astrology in the Middle East and has persisted up to the modern day. It consists of a simple disc or circle with a dot in the middle. The possibility that the Pictish double disc contains similar solar symbolism is considerably enhanced when we examine, among others, the so-called 'Dunnichen stone'. The double disc on this stone (see picture 3) has many of the features of the typical symbol, including a z-rod, but as well as concentric circles

with dots in the middle, each of the two discs appears to have what may be depictions of the Sun within them. The z-rod appears to be spear-like in its proportions.

If we postulate that the double disc is solar in nature then how could this relate to the possibility that, as arose in our discussion of the Golspie stone, the double disc might correlate with the stars of the constellation Leo? The answer to this question is surprisingly simple and can be found in Western astrology. Returning to the zodiac, we find twelve constellations that occur along the Sun's path or ecliptic. These serve to divide the year into twelve portions, one for each solar month. The Sun during the course of the year appears to move through each constellation in turn. On a particular date, for example a birthday, the Sun's position could be adjudged to be within a particular zodiacal sign. So for example, if a person was born on 1 May in the first millennium AD, the Sun would have been in the constellation Taurus, and therefore their star sign, or more accurately 'Sun sign', would have been Taurus the bull. Unfortunately, over time astrology has become completely 'unhitched' from astronomy, due to the phenomenon of precession (the Earth's slow wobble on its axis). Today the Sun's position on the ecliptic would no longer coincide with the date range given by the astrologers for each zodiacal sign. This strange situation now means that when somebody is born on 1 May, they believe that their 'star sign' is Taurus, but in fact they would have been born with the Sun in the middle of Aries.

The Sun's position within each constellation is of course only a starting point for an astrological reading. Astrologers also look at the relative positions of the planets in relation to each sign and in particular to your star sign. The presence of each planet within a zodiacal sign can have a positive or negative effect depending on a set of rules. For example, Taurus is said to be ruled by the planet Venus and the influence of the 'planet of love' would be thought to bestow all sorts of interesting benefits. This influence would be at its strongest when Venus's position on the ecliptic coincided with the constellation Taurus at a person's birth. Astrologers refer to Venus as the ruler of Taurus, and Taurus as Venus's house. Similarly, each of the other zodiacal constellations is said to be ruled by a particular planet, and each zodiac sign represents the house of its ruling planet. Up until 1930, when the three recently discovered planets of Uranus, Neptune and Pluto were added to the astrological system, the astrological planets taken into consideration were Mercury (ruling over Virgo and Gemini), Venus (ruling over Libra and Taurus), Mars (ruling over Aries and Scorpio), Jupiter (ruling over Pisces and Sagittarius) and Saturn (ruling over the neighbouring signs of Aquarius and Capricorn). In addition the Sun and the Moon were each thought to rule over one sign each and were also confusingly counted as 'planets'. The Moon ruled over Cancer, while the Sun, interestingly enough from the point of view of our double disc, ruled over Leo.

The organisation of the zodiacal signs in relation to the year and the planets is very interesting, and helps us not only to get into the mind of ancient astrologers but gives us clues as to the ancient origins of the zodiac. The Sun's house, Leo, corresponds in modern astrology with the period from 23 July to the 23 August but peculiarly these dates do not correspond with the Sun's maximal strength at midsummer, as one might expect, but towards the end of summer when the power of the Sun is already fading. The reason for this lack of correspondence can be explained once again by precession.

If we turn the clock back to roughly 2500 BC, we can then explain the relationship between the ruling planets and the zodiac signs. If we were to look at the sky at that time we would find that, firstly, the summer solstice occurred on 15 July (and not in June when it occurs today) but crucially that this date also corresponded to the Sun's presence in Leo. It is therefore likely that the system of planets and their houses had its origin several millennia ago. The Moon's house, Cancer, sits beside Leo, and the other planets are then distributed symmetrically on either side of these two in the same order as their distance from the Sun. Mercury therefore rules the houses on either side of Leo and Cancer, while Saturn rules the two houses furthest away. It is no coincidence that the Sun is associated with life while Saturn, whose house corresponded to the midwinter solstice in 2500 BC, is associated with death and senility. In other words the solar imagery associated with Leo probably derives from around a period some 4,500 years ago when the summer solstice occurred in that constellation. Similarly the winter solstice was, and still is in Hindu culture, associated with Capricorn and its ruling planet, Saturn.

Returning to the Pictish double disc, the most obvious question to ask, and probably the most awkward, is why there are two discs. As was mentioned above, the Earl of Southesk tried to explain this in terms of one disc representing the Sun and the other the Moon, and this certainly is a reasonable hypothesis. Other authors have not really tried to consider this problem, sticking with the vague notion that there is possibly a solar element to the pictograph. In the light of a possible connection with the constellation Leo, a reasonable explanation might be that this double disc is expressing a duality connected with the Sun residing within the 'Sun sign'. The Sun in this scenario takes on a special aspect; it is in its own domain and while the solstice no longer coincided with the Sun in Leo by Pictish times, and therefore the Sun would have not been as physically strong, the association between planets and their houses may have already been fixed.

Another explanation is that one disc may represent the start of a cycle of months or even years, the second the end of the cycle, the interconnection of the two discs demonstrates the never-ending cycle of time. At another level, the solstice is the midpoint of the Sun's cycle where it can exert its maximum power – the midpoint between the equinoxes. Each disc might therefore also represent the Sun at the spring and autumn equinox. However, this hypothesis on the origin of the double disc symbolism relies on the notion of the establishment of double disc imagery thousands of years prior to this symbol being committed to stone in Pictland and unfortunately there are no other examples of this anywhere else from an earlier time. If this explanation is correct, then it is very possible that the origins of the double disc symbolism would have been forgotten by the Picts, or modified to relate to the four great Celtic festivals of *Imbolc*, *Beltane* and *Samhain*, and perhaps specifically *Lughnasa* when the Sun travelled through Leo. We have also seen from the Shandwick stone that the heliacal rising of particular stars may have had some importance to the Picts. In the case of Leo, this would most likely apply to its alpha star, Regulus. The interesting fact about Regulus is that it is almost unique in that it is a bright star lying very close to the ecliptic. The relationship between Sun and Regulus, with the Sun almost eclipsing Regulus, could also provide an explanation for the double disc symbolism.

Lastly, the so-called 'Newton House Stone' displays a very unusual form of the double disc; a crescent-shaped notch is carved into each of two discs (see picture 7). If the discs of this symbol do actually represent the Sun, could it be that these notches represent solar eclipses, with the Moon partially eclipsing the Sun? If this was the case and the notches are accurate representations of an actual astronomical event or events, then it might be possible to produce a list of candidate eclipses that correspond to the Newton Stone's double disc and therefore specific dates for the creation of the stone.

The Crescent
The most obvious difference between the crescent and the other common symbols that appear in rodded forms is that the rod is v-shaped rather than z-shaped. The typical v-rod is of quite different proportions to the z-rod, with its large tip and tail and short shaft suggesting that it might represent an arrow rather than a spear.

The crescent symbol would seem at first glance to be the most obvious representation of a celestial symbol. If other authors have noted the solar symbolism of the double disc, why has more emphasis not been given to the potential lunar symbolism of the crescent? If the two most common symbols potentially exhibit astronomical or astrological symbolism, then one might expect that this would be viewed as highly significant and at the very least as a starting point to explore possible astronomical connections.

Other suggestions for the identity of the crescent include a drawn bow (presumably to match the arrow-like v-rod), a shield viewed from the side (this seems highly unlikely), and a depiction of Pictish jewellery on the basis that crescent-shaped plaques, which may have been worn, have been found.

Perhaps the reason for the failure to address potential astronomical symbolism lies in the way the crescent is presented. In the majority of situations the crescent is depicted with its 'horns' facing downwards. This may seem to the many that have casually observed the Moon in the night sky as a very unnatural position for the Moon. There are, however, rare occasions when the Moon does lie with the 'horns' pointing downwards, although this is not visible in the glare of the Sun. This phenomenon occurs at the new Moon at around sunrise, particularly when the Moon is close to the ecliptic. Two variables determine the angle between the crescent new Moon and the horizon. The first is latitude and the other is the Moon's position in relation to the ecliptic. As mentioned previously, the Moon's path through the sky is sinusoidal in relation to the Sun's path. The Moon at times can be several degrees above or below the path that the Sun takes. An eclipse of the Sun takes place when the Moon position coincides exactly with the ecliptic at the transition between the old and new Moon. If the new Moon is at its maximum distance below the ecliptic a few days after it passes the Sun's position, then the angle between the crescent and the horizon is decreased. As you travel further north, the angle between the ecliptic and the horizon at Sunrise varies depending on the time of year. The angle is at its maximum at the time of the autumn equinox, midway between the summer and winter solstices. In AD 700 this would have occurred at sunrise in September. However, it is unlikely that this phenomenon was observable.

If the Pictish crescent resembles the orientation of a rising new Moon at the autumn equinox, it is perhaps also pertinent to examine the nature of the crescent itself as portrayed on the Pictish monuments. While there is some variation in the crescent phase, they all appear to depict a waxing crescent Moon, approximating to four or five days after the new Moon. So it is possible that the new Moon had some significance to the Picts; perhaps the first glimpse of the new crescent Moon in the sky marked the beginning of a new lunar month, in a similar way to Islamic astronomers who look for the first glimpse of the crescent moon to mark the end of the holy month of Ramadan and the beginning of the festival of Eid.

As with the double disc, it is possible that the crescent Moon was associated with a particular zodiacal constellation or star, and the most obvious place to start looking is the familiar Western zodiac. If the double disc, with its solar symbolism, could be associated with the constellation and zodiacal sign of Leo, should we not be considering the possibility that the crescent represents the Moon's zodiacal house? In Western astrology the Moon's house is the sign Cancer. This constellation sits beside Leo on the ecliptic and the Sun would have crossed it during July in AD 700. The constellation Cancer is envisaged in the sky as a crab, a creature that inhabits the littoral zone between the sea and the land – the part of the world that seems to be most influenced by the Moon.

While Western astrology may well recognise Cancer as the Moon's house, we must remember that the form of astrology people used in Europe is not the only form still practised in the world. Vedic astrology, with its roots in ancient India, provides us with an alternative system. As we have discussed previously, this form of astrology places emphasis on a lunar aspect to astrology and consequently divides the sky into twenty-seven or twenty-eight *nakshatras*. If we examine these, we find that Leo's primary star, Regulus, is recognised as the Sun's house (as in Western astrology), but the stars of Cancer in the Vedic system do not relate to the Moon. In fact the stars of a portion of the next constellation, Virgo, are seen as a lunar mansion ruled by the Moon (there are two other mansions). While Cancer's link to the Moon may revolve around the idea of tidal motion, Virgo's link to the Moon may stem from the phenomenon of an equinoctial new Moon, in particular the so-called 'harvest Moon'. Many people will have heard of the harvest Moon but know little about what this actually means. In the first millennium AD, the autumnal equinox would have coincided with the Sun's position close to the principal star of Virgo, Spica. If we examine for a moment the relationship between the Sun and the new and full Moon, this will help us to understand the harvest Moon phenomenon. The new Moon around the autumnal equinox will rise, like the Sun, steeply due to its apparent proximity to the Sun on the ecliptic. At this point, the Moon in its orbit is between the Sun and the Earth – the position necessary for a solar eclipse. The full Moon occurs when it on the opposite side of the ecliptic from the Sun, when the Earth is between it and the Sun – the position necessary for a lunar eclipse. At the autumnal equinox in the northern hemisphere this major difference in the full Moon and Sun's relative positions on the ecliptic means that while the Sun rises more steeply than at any other time of the year, the full Moon in contrast rises on a very shallow trajectory. This results in three familiar attributes of the harvest Moon. Firstly the Moon's path skims the horizon, never rising significantly. Secondly, the Moon will appear to rise at roughly the same time every evening (normally there can be up to fifty minutes or so difference in moonrise every night). Thirdly, because the Moon never rises very high in the sky it retains a reddish glow (due to us viewing the Moon through many miles of atmosphere, akin to the reddish colour of the Sun at sunrise or sunset). These three peculiarities of the Moon's behaviour around the autumnal equinox would have provided a marker for harvest time and, as far as the crescent symbol goes, provides another possible link between the Moon and Virgo – the constellation inextricably linked to the harvest.

The Notched Rectangle

Various ideas have been put forward as to what the notched rectangle might represent (see picture 3). The two principal notions are that it might be a chariot (to try to partly explain the circles or semi-circles found within some of the examples) or that the symbol could be representing a house or broch. Brochs were a type of stone tower, unique to Iron Age Scotland, and are often associated with the Picts or at least their ancestors.

The obvious starting point for trying to identify what this symbol might represent is to try to match the symbol to astronomical constellations or stars. If we start with the observation that this symbol, like the double disc and crescent, is often rodded, a reasonable guess might be that this symbol may represent a prominent star or constellation lying close to the ecliptic. William Forbes, has pointed out that the general shape of the symbol was reminiscent of the constellation Gemini. Apart from the shape and the proximity of Gemini to the ecliptic, are there any more clues that might help identify the notched rectangle as a putative Gemini symbol? One feature of the symbol is the presence in many of the examples of a pair of circles or circular notches. If the hypothesis that the notched rectangle represents the constellation Gemini is correct, could the circles or circular notches actually represent specific stars? An examination of Gemini reveals that the ecliptic cuts diagonally across Gemini, separating two prominent stars within the constellation, in a way that is very reminiscent of the diagonal rod and the circles of this symbol (with the two stars on either side of the ecliptic). The diagonal is mirrored in relation to the majority of the examples of the notched rectangle, with it cutting the constellation from top left to bottom right. However, there are cases where the diagonal of the symbol and the ecliptic match each other in orientation and direction. So it is possible that the notches/circles, in the context of the rod, may correspond to stars close to the ecliptic. The phenomenon of mirroring, which occurs in this and in other symbols, would seem to add another layer of complexity to Pictish symbolism.

There is another piece of information that may significantly contribute towards this debate on the origins of the symbolism of the notched rectangle. So far, it has been suggested that this symbol relates to the constellation Gemini, and in particular to the stars Castor and Pollux, and we have noted that some authors have seen this symbol as representing a house or fortress, or more specifically a broch. In this interpretation, the notch is seen as a doorway, and this certainly seems to make some sense. In the case of the notched rectangle found on a stone from Arndilly in Moray, the presence of

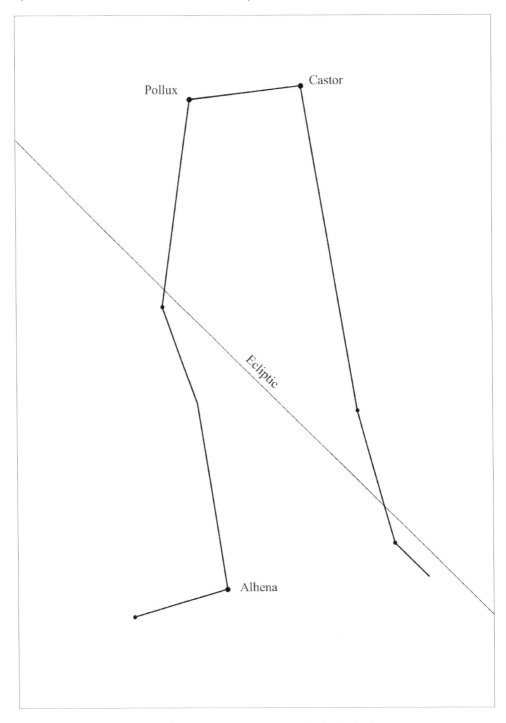

17. Constellation of Gemini, showing prominent stars. (© Iain Forbes)

a striped band across the top of the rectangle might also remind us of a roof. However, perhaps the most startling piece of evidence that this symbol might represent a house or broch comes once again from Vedic culture. The Vedic lunar mansion *Punarvasu* corresponds to the two principal stars of Gemini, Castor and Pollux. It is symbolised by either a quiver or, more interestingly from our point of view, a house. To the Babylonians, Gemini represented the gateway to Heaven. If we do indeed view the notch as a doorway or entrance we can see that an interpretation of the symbol as some sort of celestial gate is also feasible. In northern Europe in the third millennium BC, Gemini rose heliacally with the Sun at the spring equinox, and this was still the case in Pictland even in the second half of the first millennium AD at around *Beltane*. We will explore further the idea of a 'door to the heavens' in the section on the Arch symbol.

The Snake
This symbol seems to be hard to identify in the sky; this is not because of an absence of snake imagery among the stars from different traditions, but rather because of the number of snakes that different cultures have visualised in the sky. If we examine the classical view of the stars and constellations, then we find two snakes that are visible in the northern hemisphere. Firstly, there is the snake that Ophiuchus holds. This is actually described as two constellations, Serpens Caput and Serpens Cauda (the head and tail of the serpent). Secondly, there is the water-snake, Hydra, which we have postulated might be represented on the Golspie stone as the two intertwined snakes complete with fins and fish tails.

The Pictish 'snake' symbols can occur in several forms, the most obvious being rodded and non-rodded versions. The most common form is most obviously serpentine, carved with two major loops. There are also, however, two examples where the snakes both have three loops. The rod used is usually a z-rod, except in the above two cases, where unusually the rod appears to be straight. These two examples could constitute a variation in snake motifs (perhaps they are older examples) or could even signify two distinct symbols; at present there is no way of distinguishing between these possibilities.

On the Class I stone from Newton House (picture 7), the carving of a rodded snake has an unusual feature associated with it. In the middle of the snake there are two circles, one within the other, positioned just below the diagonal of the z-rod. Within the inner circle is a dot. Could this detail represent a star or planet associated with the snake? If we assume for a moment that the snake symbol represents a significant zodiacal constellation or star, then starting with the brightest fifty stars in the sky (those with a magnitude of 2.0 or less), the following stars lie close to the ecliptic: Regulus in Leo, Pollux and Castor in Gemini, Aldebaran in Taurus, Nunki in Sagittarius, Antares in Scorpio and Spica in Virgo. We have theorised that four of these (Regulus, Pollux, Castor and Spica) may be represented by the double disc (Regulus), the notched rectangle (Pollux and Castor) and the crescent (Spica). So is it possible that these other near ecliptical prominent stars are also represented by rodded symbols? This would leave us with El Nath, Aldebaran, Nunki and Antares. As we explore the stars with magnitudes between 2.0 and 3.0, the possibilities increase substantially with reasonably bright stars, such as Libra Graffias and Delta Scorpio, starting to feature as well as the near ecliptical Zubenelgenubi in Libra. Other stars close to the ecliptic at this magnitude include Zeta Tauri in Taurus, Alcyone in the Pleiades, Hamal and Sheratan in Aries, Ascelia, Kaus Media and Alnasl in Sagittarius, Sabik in Ophiuchus, Sigma, Pi and Tau Scorpii in Scorpio and Porrima in Virgo.

Alphard, the brightest star in Hydra at magnitude 2.0, seems a little bit far from the ecliptic, although Hydra's head is quite close. We will return to Alphard and Hydra later on. In the case of Serpens, only Sabik in the associated constellation of Ophiuchus would seem close enough and bright enough to be displayed so prominently on the Pictish serpent. If these are the only possibilities, then either the Picts saw a totally different serpent in the sky, or our modern definitions of these constellations' boundaries are at variance with the Pictish versions. In the case of the latter possibility, a suggestion for a Pictish Serpens might consist of a larger version of the classical Serpens, starting at the head end (i.e. Serpens Caput with its two eyes – as also seen on the Pictish snakes), swinging southwards towards the ecliptic and taking in the stars of Scorpio, including Antares, then swinging northwards towards Serpens Cauda. This arrangement, though tempting, does not produce a particularly good fit between the stars and the Pictish symbol. Likewise Hydra might also be extended to include stars north of the ecliptic, taking in the stars of Cancer and including one right on the ecliptic (Asellus Australis), but again this arrangement of stars is inadequate. Perhaps the presence of the dotted circle on the Newton House snake provides something of a clue. This circle is placed in the middle of the body of the snake, at some distance from the head, which is reminiscent of the position of Alphard within Hydra. In this scenario, Zeta and Epsilon Hydrae might make reasonable candidates for the snake's eyes and Alphard, at magnitude 2.0, could conceivably equate to the dotted circle found on the body of the snake from Newton House. Clearly at this point we must find evidence that Hydra could be of astrological significance.

In the other symbols we have considered so far, we have looked to the Vedic culture in order to identify parallels. What about a Vedic interpretation of the snake symbol, could this tradition provide any clues? Unlike the Western zodiac, Vedic astrology actually does have a symbol represented by a snake. This is the *nakshatra* (or a lunar mansion) of *Ashlesha* ruled by Sarpa, the snake god, and is represented by Hydra. Here we have our evidence for the constellation of Hydra being of astrological significance, and can confirm that this constellation is close enough to the ecliptic to be considered by Vedic astrology as zodiacal. Ashlesha's symbol is a snake, coiled tightly, unlike the Pictish imagery that seems to depict a snake in the process of moving. The constellation Hydra is therefore regarded in India as being astrologically significant, despite its distance from the ecliptic, and it could be the case that the Picts also recognised the significance of this constellation. Vedic astrology is based on the cycles of the Moon, and the possibility of a snake zodiacal symbol on Pictish stone might suggest a similar system may have been used in Pictland.

The Arch
The arch symbol (picture 18 and picture 4) has also been interpreted as a horseshoe and, although this is not entirely convincing, it is an interesting identification

particularly given the abundance of horses on Pictish stones as well as the still extant folk customs relating to iron horseshoes, luck, and superstition. So what could the arch represent in astronomical or astrological terms? The most obvious arch in the night sky is that formed by the Milky Way, but this identification simply does not fit well with the overall picture that is beginning to emerge, where we are finding the possibility of a focus on individual stars or constellations and Pictish imagery. In astrological terms, the main focus of interest is on stars and constellations on or close to the Sun's path. The Milky Way crosses the ecliptic at two points. The first of these points lies between Taurus and Gemini, with most of Gemini lying within the band of stars. The second point lies between Scorpio and Sagittarius, with most of these two constellations lying within this galactic arch. Therefore, if the arch symbol is related to a particular constellation, we would already have a choice of three. Other constellations lying on the Milky Way, but not on the ecliptic, might also potentially be candidates for the symbol including Cassiopeia, Cygnus, Aquila, Perseus and Auriga. However, one piece of evidence that might help us identify a candidate constellation for the arch is from Miranda Green's book *Dictionary of Celtic Myth and Legend*. In it there is a passage that relates to the Celtic festival of *Samhain*, celebrated notably in Scotland and Ireland. Here she points out the relationship between this festival and the stars of Scorpio:

> The Celts celebrated the Sun's entry into these stars with the feast of Samhain, a great gathering at Tara to celebrate the end of summer. But the eve of Samhain was considered a night of darkness in which the souls of the dead would roam the earth, for it was on that night that the Celts believed the gateway between the other world and the world of the living was open.

This festival survives to this day as Halloween, or more correctly Hallowe'en, a word derived from the Scots phrase 'Hallow's e'en' meaning the evening before All Hallows (All Saints' Day). If we consider Miranda Green's insight into Irish customs at *Samhain*, in the sky on this date (on or around 31 October) during the period of time we are interested in (around AD 700) we would find that in northern Scotland the Sun would start to cross in front of the Milky Way in the constellation of Scorpio. This intersection between the ecliptic and the Milky Way could well have been viewed as a route along which souls could move between the heavens and the Earth. The celestial intersection between the ecliptic and the Milky Way, close to Scorpio, would become particularly important at sunrise or sunset when the Sun would appear to be momentarily in contact with the earth – therefore providing a gateway for souls to pass in either direction. It also makes perfect sense, then, that the Sun's second encounter with the Milky Way occurs six months later at *Beltane* (around the 1 May in AD 700) with the Sun rising with Gemini. This intersection between Gemini and the Milky Way could explain the notched rectangle's doorway. These two events would add further evidence to the suggestion that both *Samhain* and *Beltane* were festivals linked to special and particular astronomical events.

So are we any closer to deciphering the arch symbol? Perhaps yes, if we particularly focus on the idea that the intersection between the ecliptic and the Milky Way

18. Percylieu stone (arch and partial fish symbols), Kennethmont, Aberdeenshire. (© Crown Copyright: RCAHMS. Licensor www. rcahms.gov.uk)

represented some sort of supernatural gateway for souls. Could the arch actually represent this gateway, in some way incorporating both the notion of a gate and also the Milky Way? If we assume for a moment that the arch symbol relates to *Samhain* and not to *Beltane*, then our search narrows to the zodiacal constellations lying on or close to the Milky Way. The most obvious place to look is at the point where the Sun appears to first come into contact with this galactic band of stars. As Miranda Green points out, this point of contact coincides with some of the stars of the constellation Scorpio, in particular Dschubba and Graffias, two prominent stars that make up part of the head of the Scorpion. However, just prior to this the Sun leaves the constellation of Libra. The boundary between the Celtic summer and the winter therefore lies not only where the ecliptic crosses the Milky Way but also on the boundary between Libra and Scorpio. This possible identification might also have a bearing on the interpretation of the notched rectangle as a sort of Gemini doorway or entrance associated with the spring equinox in the Neolithic period and later with *Beltane* in the Iron Age.

Apart from the possibility that the arch symbol represents a metaphorical gateway, could the arch also represent a particular asterism? If we look at star charts for the Libra/Scorpio boundary, an obvious asterism jumps out – that of the main part of the zodiacal constellation of Libra. The three principal stars of

Libra form a beautiful triangle lying straddled across the ecliptic with the central star, Zubenelgenubi (magnitude 2.75), sitting almost on the ecliptic itself. The two other stars that form this triangle are of similar magnitude, with the northern point of the triangle formed by Zubeneschamali (magnitude 2.61) and the southern point formed by Brachium (magnitude 3.25). In terms of the classical zodiac, Zubenelgenubi represents the fulcrum of the celestial scales and the other two represent the ends of the scale's beam. Classical astronomers envisaged, dropping down from the ends of the beam, the strings that hold the pans of the balance running parallel to the ecliptic, and the pans themselves represented by several stars with magnitudes of around 3.0 or 4.0. However, this arrangement of stars could also be envisaged as forming a well-proportioned arch that terminates at the boundary between Libra and Scorpio. Could this be the celestial gateway and also an explanation for the arch symbol? The seemingly unrelated concept of a gateway and that of a pair of scales may actually not be as far apart as one might imagine. We should consider the Celtic notion of souls travelling through a gate between this world and the next and marry this to the notion of divine justice and the weighing or judging of souls on their journey to the afterlife. Perhaps the idea of judging or weighing souls actually gave rise to Libra being seen as a set of scales or even *vice versa*.

If we carefully re-examine the various arch symbols found in Pictland, while bearing in mind the notion that the arch could be a Pictish Libra, a number of features spring out. On the Percylieu stone at Hillhead of Clatt in Aberdeenshire, the arch, which is missing part of its left-hand limb, clearly shows a small hole at the very top of the arch. Could this represent Zubenelgenubi? A further hole appears at the bottom of the right-hand limb, and similarly could represent the star Upsilon Libra (magnitude 3.6). Given the obvious symmetry in the design, presumably there was also a hole on the left limb, and this correspondingly could equate to Theta Libra (magnitude 4.13). A pattern of repeated marks is carved at intervals from the central hole, at the top of the arch, to the hole in the right limb – what remains of the left limb also seems to mirror this arrangement. Could these markings represent the cord or chain depicted in the classical 'scales'? Similarly, the arch on the stone at Strathpeffer in the Highlands has three circles (within which are dots) in the same arrangement as the Percylieu stone, this time linked by curved lines, and these divide into two in the same way as the cord or chains used in scales divide above each pan. Each divided line then meets a circular structure, and it does not take a lot of imagination to realise that we may be looking at a two-dimensional rendition of a classic pair of scales carved into the arch. There is even the hint of a notion of a fulcrum above the central dot and circle. If this interpretation was accepted then this could provide some weight to the idea that the arch might represent the zodiacal Libra, or at least part of it, and that the Picts were not only aware of the classical view of the constellation, but saw the arch as more significant. We would therefore have only the problem of linking the arch to the notion of a gateway.

There seems to be no extant record of a Celtic arch substituting for the classical scales, although we have explored the idea of a Celtic gateway that might have coincided with the boundary between Libra and Scorpio. Can we find any other evidence for any other civilisation seeing Libra as a gateway or arch? Once again the answer is surprisingly yes and again the evidence lies thousands of miles away within the Vedic culture of the Indian subcontinent. The Vedic *nakshatra* or lunar mansion that corresponds to the Libra/Scorpio boundary is *Vishakha*. Amazingly, this lunar mansion is symbolised by the arch or triumphal arch and, despite including the principal stars of Libra, is not symbolised by the scales familiar to us in the West.

It would seem that with each symbol we examine, further evidence is uncovered linking Pictish symbolism to mainstream Celtic beliefs and mythology as well as some evidence linking it, in part at least, to the far distant Indo-European Vedic tradition.

The Z-Rods and V-Rods

Perhaps the most puzzling aspect of the above highlighted symbols is that they are often accompanied by the so-called z-rods or v-rods. This apparent embellishment lends another layer of complexity in attempts to understand the meaning being conveyed. These have been seen in the past as being reminiscent of forks of lightning, or perhaps as broken arrows or spears. It has therefore been suggested that these might be symbols representing the death of a warrior. However, if we are attempting to view Pictish symbols in terms of astronomical, calendrical or astrological events, could the z-rod's form and function also be explained in these terms? There is variation in the form that the rods take, but these fall within a quite narrow range of possibilities. For example, the rods are usually not entirely symmetrical, but typically have a 'tipped' end and a 'trailing' end. Sometimes the tip of the rod takes on a spearhead or arrowhead appearance, or sometimes the tip appears to be more organic in form, perhaps reminiscent of parts of a plant. The trailing edge of the rods often appear to be plant-like, or end in a bulb-like structure, or can appear to be resemble a fish tail or perhaps even arrow flights. Simple embellishments often decorate the shafts of the rods, and these again have an organic quality to them, perhaps reminiscent of tongues of fire. The rods, when they appear with the double disc, tend to start below the left-hand disc, run parallel with the axis of the symbol, cross backwards over the axis and then continue above the right-hand disc (again in parallel with the axis), therefore taking a form similar to a letter 'z' when seen in a mirror. However, in a handful of cases the rods appear to be in the opposite orientation therefore actually resembling a 'z'. This phenomenon occurs with other symbols and we will explore its significance later.

The z-rods found bisecting the double discs tend to show relatively small terminal decorations in relation to their length. This is in contrast to the other type of rods, found associated with Pictish symbols, the v-rods. Typically v-rods, which usually are found only with the crescent Moon symbol (there is one example of a v-rod with an arch), have terminals that are relatively large and have shorter rods. With this difference between the two types of rod in mind, it is probably worth considering the possibility that the v-rod may represent an arrow and, in the context of the night sky, perhaps we should view this not as any common arrow but rather a celestial arrow with further information embedded in the image. Similarly, the z-rod of the double disc symbol may represent not an arrow but a spear, with its longer rod and smaller terminals, and if they too are associated with possible astrological symbolism then again we may want to consider the possibility that these spears have a celestial or supernatural aspect.

There are, however, problems with the identification of the z-rod with a spear, not least the 'z' shape of the rod, but also the fact that a spear usually has only one obvious terminal in the form of the spearhead. However, in the National Museum of Scotland, in Edinburgh, there are spears from the Pictish period that have a metal addition to the 'trailing' edge. This addition was well described by Dio Cassius (prior to AD 229), who made the following observations on the tribes in northern Scotland: 'For arms they have a shield and a short spear, with a bronze apple attached to the end of the spear-shaft, so that when it is shaken it may clash and terrify the enemy.' This type of spear is also depicted on a Pictish stone from Collessie in Fife. The so-called Collessie man is a naked warrior carrying a spear and at the trailing end of the spear can clearly be seen the sort of 'apple' described by Dio Cassius. The apple may have functions other than generating an intimidating din. One suggestion, in the book *Celtic Warriors*, is that the apple was to aid the balance of the spear in flight. Is it also possible that this type of spear was suitable for use with a sling, therefore increasing its penetrative ability and range. Could the trailing terminal shown on many of the z-rods actually represent these apples?

If the tip of the rod represented a spearhead, then we would also have to come up with an explanation for the almost organic feel to the shape. However, it turns out that there were a myriad of designs for both arrowheads and spearheads. These variations may have reflected cultural differences, variations in the favoured material or, perhaps more importantly, they may have reflected differences in the use of each type of spear or arrowhead. Spearheads may have been designed to penetrate different types of protective clothing or armour, or to be easy or difficult to remove, as well as a host of other reasons. Spearheads that have been found in the British Isles, therefore, may not only be from spears but also from javelins, thrusting spears, lances or pikes. Two main types of spearhead seem to be common in Britain and Ireland in the first millennium AD. The first type is the 'shouldered' spearhead, which was apparently typically Germanic, although it seems to have also been quite common in Ireland. The most common type in Britain was the 'leaf-shaped' spearhead. Could the leaf-shaped spearhead explain the almost organic feel to the leading edge of so many rods? The Collessie man's spear sports a small leaf-shaped spearhead, very reminiscent of the rod.

There is so far some evidence that might indicate that the double disc represents the constellation Leo, the Sun's house, or at least part of that constellation (probably the alpha star Regulus) due to its position among the other figures and symbols on the Golspie stone. In addition, we have the circumstantial evidence that the name of the Welsh god of light, Lleu, has been interpreted by Welsh-speaking scribes when translating into English as either 'light' or 'lion', and perhaps as a pun (*Lleu llew gyffes*

– light or lion of the long hand). We have also seen that in the first millennium the Irish festival of *Lughnasa* (named after Lugh, the Irish equivalent of Lleu), occurred when the Sun rose with Leo's alpha star, Regulus, with both star and constellation having very strong associations with the Sun. In the context of this Celtic god, the appearance of the z-rodded spear associated with some of the double discs throws up a fascinating possibility. If we further examine the mythology surrounding this god of light and in particular the Irish version, Lugh, we find that the object most closely associated with this character is in fact a spear. This is no ordinary spear. This weapon almost has a life of its own, seeking out its intended target rather like a modern homing missile – even Lugh has trouble calming its bloodthirsty tendencies. The weapon comes to the fore when Lugh slays the monstrous Fomorian King Balor, by throwing the spear at his single malevolent eye. This spear has another aspect; it is alive with flame, as would befit a weapon associated with the Sun god. To keep the spear from doing harm when it is not being used, Lugh keeps the weapon in a bucket of water, only removing it when he intends to use it. Such a fiery spear should remind us of a sunbeam or the Sun's rays and we should therefore see the spear itself as a solar motif and, in the context of the Pictish symbols, perhaps enhancing the meaning of the individual symbols it is associated with. But what of the fire aspect of Lugh's weapon? If the z-rod is to be viewed as a solar symbol then is it possible that it is in some way related to Lugh's spear or at least a Pictish equivalent? In order to answer this, we need to turn to the many depictions of the rod. Emanating from the shaft of many of the rods are small curly decorations. Is it possible that these decorations actually represent flames, perhaps mirroring the Irish mythological notion of Lugh's fiery Sun spear? It is certainly a tantalising possibility and would fit with solar symbolism.

If some of the symbolism hints at parallels between the Pictish rods and the Irish Sun god's weapon, this still doesn't explain the reason why the rod is bent into a 'z' shape nor does it tell us if the rod is conveying some further information. Let us for a moment consider the relationship between the double disc and the z-rod. In the majority of cases the apple-shaped termination of our potential spear is found below and to the left of the double disc. We can then follow the shaft as it travels from left to right until it doubles back, crossing the axis between the two solar discs, before once again continuing on its original left to right path. It therefore describes a backward 'z'. The left to right orientation of these rods fits well with the notion of solar symbolism, in that the Sun's daily path from east to west is in effect (to an observer) a movement from left to right. This, however, does not explain why the rod crosses diagonally backwards across the axis of the double disc. However, as well as a suggestion of the Sun's daily course from east to west, the z-rod could also be explained in terms of the path of other bodies in the solar system. If we turn back to the ancient science of astronomy, one of the first phenomena that the earliest astronomers must have noticed concerned the behaviour of a small collection of celestial bodies that followed the Sun's path through the sky. To early observers, these bodies generally stayed close to the ecliptic, but had the curious habit of occasionally coming to a halt and wandering away from their original path. This behaviour, which was in contrast to the 'fixed' stars, partly gave rise to their Greek name *planetese* and originally meant wanderer. This word of course gave rise to our own word 'planet'. This peculiar 'wandering' behaviour is technically called retrograde motion, and is a function of our observing planets orbiting the Sun from a planet (Earth) that is also moving around the Sun.

The combination of these two orbits gives us the illusion every now and again that the planets slow in their path in the night sky, appear to stand still, and then for short time move backwards, before once again returning to their original direction. This retrograde motion, which is most obvious in the motion of Mercury, Venus and Mars, when traced out appears to take the form of either a loop or can actually approximate to a 'z' shape or to a mirrored 'z'. It is therefore possible that the z-rod, as well as conveying solar imagery linked to the mythology of a Sun god, conveys the notion of the ecliptic or even relates to information on the motion of a particular celestial body. The two mirror-image versions of the z-rod could therefore be attributed simply to artistic variation, but also might relate to the artist depicting two different circumstances. So for example, the 'z' version of the z-rod and its mirrored counterpart may simply reflect two possible forms of retrograde motion, which can trace out 'z' shape or a mirrored version of this. The planets Jupiter and Saturn also display apparent retrograde motion, with considerable backwards movement, but with little vertical motion away from their path. This apparent backwards motion of all the planets is not a rare occurrence, nor viewed as unimportant, but is used sometimes in both Western and Eastern astrological predictions, where it is regarded as having a profound influence. The two visible giant outer planets spend about a third of their time in apparent retrograde, Mars about 20 per cent of its time, Mercury about 10 per cent and Venus about 7 per cent. The Picts would have certainly known, if observing the nightly motion of the planets, about the existence of this phenomenon.

In the case of the notched rectangle z-rods, seven show the rod traversing the symbol from the bottom left-hand corner to the top right-hand side of the symbols; in other words it diagonally ascends from left to right (forming a mirrored 'N'). In the two other rodded examples, the rods are drawn in the opposite orientation, in effect a mirror image of the other seven, with the rod traversing the symbol from the top left to the bottom right (a descending rod). Rotating the symbol through 90 degrees reveals that these z-rods take the same two forms as the those found with the double disc – the mirrored 'N' is simply a 'z' rotated, and likewise the more common mirrored 'N' is a mirrored 'z' rotated. If we also take cognisance of the leading tip of these rods, and the direction they point, the mirrored 'z' or 'N' rods of the double disc and notched rectangle may actually be indicating rotational direction, rather like a Catherine wheel. The vast majority of the mirrored z-rods of the double discs point to the right, indicating perhaps clockwise rotation; likewise the mirrored 'N' of the notched rectangles points perhaps also indicates clockwise movement. Even if the tip of the rod pointed to the left it would still indicate a clockwise direction. The less common rodded double discs have rods that describe a true 'z' shape. These rods tend to have their tip on the lower arm of the 'z' pointing to the right, suggesting anticlockwise movement, likewise the two N-shaped rods of the notched rectangle.

This potential mirroring of the symbol is given further credence if one examines the internal circles or notches on the vertical sides of the notched rectangles that frequently occur. Seven of the rodded symbols, plus the unrodded symbol, have circles or notches. In the case of the mirrored 'z' or 'N' rods (clockwise), the left-hand notch or circle appears above the rod, and the right-hand notch or circle appears below the rod. In the example from Arndilly, with its rod presenting as an 'N' (anticlockwise), its left-hand circle is below the rod and the right-hand circle above the rod – in other words the circles could support the notion that the Arndilly rectangular notched symbol is a deliberate mirror image. This would also parallel the situation with the double discs, where there also appear to be mirrored symbols. The mirroring of not only the rod but key internal features would seem to suggest that the mirroring may well be deliberate and constitute a further level of complexity in terms of the symbols' message. This would also apply to the rodded double disc.

Within the main group of snake symbols, whether rodded or non-rodded, there appear also to be left-facing and right-facing forms. Within these two groups the rods themselves, as in the case of the other z-rodded symbols, can be clockwise or anticlockwise. The largest group is the left-facing snake, with the majority of examples of these being rodded clockwise. The left-facing snakes also make up the majority of non-rodded examples. Meigle 1 and the St Vigeans 2 stones show examples of left-hand anticlockwise rodded snakes. The Aberlemno 1 stone (picture 1) has an example of a non-rodded right-facing snake, while the right-facing snake on the Newton House stone has an anticlockwise rod. It is possible that these variations in snake and rod orientation convey some particular information which is vital to the interpretation of the pairing.

Within the context of religion and in particular Eastern religion (notably Vedic), motion to the right or clockwise motion is seen as auspicious and male, representing the daily motion of the Sun, stars and planets. Left-handed or anticlockwise motion is seen as inauspicious and female. It could therefore be the case that the two forms of the z-rods are communicating information as to whether the timing of the event commemorated by the stone is auspicious or inauspicious. Interestingly, the clockwise rods far outnumber the anticlockwise rods. It is even possible that the clockwise form is linked to males in some way and the anticlockwise to females.

The v-rods are associated primarily with the crescent symbol, although there is one example of a v-rodded arch. Unfortunately the rodded arch symbol is badly worn, and cannot be analysed with any great confidence. The rodded version of the crescent is extremely numerous in comparison and there are many well-executed examples, with those with rods outnumbering those without by about ten to one. It is the most commonly found symbol in the symbol pairs. The arrow-like v-rods, in contrast to the spear-like z-rods, only appear in two main forms: arrows with a left-hand direction and arrows with a right-hand direction. The right-facing form is approximately five times more numerous than those pointing leftwards. In addition there are a handful of v-rods with indeterminate direction. There is no obvious rotational aspect to the v-rods, no clockwise or anticlockwise forms as we found with the z-rods. This difference could be simply put down to the practicalities of design; in the case of the double disc there is symmetry in two planes, but in the case of the crescent (and arch) just one. It may have been aesthetically unpleasing to the Picts to utilise a z-rod with a crescent as it would be divided by the rod in an asymmetric manner. However, it could also be argued that a z-rodded notched rectangle or the rodded snake are not perfectly divided symmetrically by z-rods either, although the result is considerably more pleasing to the eye than an attempt to use a z-rod with a crescent symbol. Indeed the z-rods utilised in the case of the snakes and notched rectangle are usually orientated with the 'spear' tip pointing upwards or downwards rather than left or right, as is the case with the double disc's z-rods. This would suggest that some importance was placed on the aesthetic impact of the symbol.

If the symbolism of z-rods has some possible connection to the fiery spear of Lleu or Lugh, the Sun god, we might ask whether there is a possible parallel to a lunar god or goddess that could help explain the particular form of the v-rod. As mentioned previously, in Welsh mythology, Lleu has a brother known as Dylan. Both brothers are the sons of Arianrod, a goddess sometimes associated with the Moon (her name probably translating as 'silver circle'). Dylan, referred to as 'the son of the waves', is, however, is very much associated with the sea, diving into the sea at his birth, perhaps indicating that he was god of the sea or the tide – a phenomenon very much governed by the Moon. His ability to swim like a sea creature or fish could potentially be linked to the 'fish tail' motif of the v-rods, but this is purely speculative. The two brothers, Lleu and Dylan are sometimes seen as opposites, a recurring theme in Celtic mythology, with Lleu representing light and Dylan darkness.

Both the z-rods and the v-rods exist in essentially two forms. In the case of the z-rods there are clockwise and anticlockwise forms, with the speartips pointing upwards or to the right, with the clockwise form predominating. In the case of the v-rods, there are left-hand and right-hand forms, with the arrowheads pointing upward and to the right predominating. It could therefore be the case that the rods are conveying information essentially in two 'states'. There are of course many possibilities as to what these two states might be. One possibility is that they are indicating an auspicious or inauspicious event, for example an event predicted by a planet entering a particular constellation or leaving a constellation, or perhaps whether or not a specific planet is in conjunction or opposition with a particular star. Another possibility is that the two 'states', in the case of the z-rod, are indicating something about retrograde motion of a particular body. If this were the case then we would also have to account for the v-rod's rather different form. The 'v' shape may relate to the sinusoidal path that the Moon takes through the night sky. The northern part of this path is referred to in astrology as the 'north node' and the southern extreme being referred to as the 'south node'. In Vedic astrology these two nodes are treated as two 'shadow' planets (Ketu and Rahu), which are regarded as of the same importance as the more conventional planets.

A clue to the function of both the z-rods and v-rods may also lie in the form their decoration takes and, in particular, variation in the tail of the rod. It is interesting that there seems to be a small number of set forms for the rod's tail. For example, by far the most frequent tail motif for the v-rod, associated with the crescent, is the fish tail, which by contrast is found in only one clear-cut example of a z-rod from a double disc. If the tails were simply related to a particular Pictish school of sculptors and their trademark designs, then we would not expect to find two different tail designs within the same rodded symbol pair, yet we find that they are often mixed. In the context of an astrological explanation of the symbols, could the tails and other features of the rod be indicative of a particular planet or associated with a particular deity? Are they the Pictish equivalent of the Western astrological symbols for the planets? Perhaps they could be related to the astrological elements of earth, water, fire, and air? If we re-examine the rodded symbols, there may be hints of this sort of symbolism. The double disc with its solar and fiery components might represent fire, the crescent Moon is a symbol for the element air, the snake has a strongly chthonic aspect and therefore represents earth and if we consider the concept of a fifth element that is sometimes described as the sky, then the arch might well also fit with this. Unfortunately the symbolism of the notched rectangle does not seem to fit with this hypothesis, and it is difficult to see how it might represent the remaining element of water. Certainly, it is, however, possible that there would seem to be a whole other level of complexity in meaning, demonstrated by the decoration found on the rods.

CHAPTER 11

NON-RODDED SYMBOLS

While at first glance these symbols seem rather more mundane than their rodded counterparts, they too have the potential to provide information that might relate to an astronomical, calendrical or astrological function. In some cases, they appear more frequently on symbol stones than some of the rodded symbols, and this might suggest that these particular common symbols were regarded as being of some significance.

Animal Symbols

Elephant / Beast
This symbol resembles no known animal and therefore most likely represents some sort of mythological creature. (Examples of the Pictish beast can be found in pictures 3, 9 and 14.) The symbols are surprisingly uniform across Pictland, exhibiting the same or a very similar set of features. There are a number of these features that stand out. Firstly, the legs do not end in well-defined feet or paws, there is no evidence of claws, but rather they end in swirling patterns; clearly this is no ordinary animal. Indeed, the swirling patterns that terminate the feet might suggest that this animal is nebulous in nature, perhaps blown along cloud-like by the wind. The second feature that stands out is the horn or crest that in most of the examples typically curls back from the top of the head. This bears no obvious resemblance to any trait of any native animal – it could represent a single horn, or perhaps a mane-like structure. However, there are some examples of Pictish beasts where this feature clearly arises not from the top of the head but from the side, in approximately the same place as one might expect horns to appear on other animals, suggesting that this is more likely to be a horn-like structure, although highly stylised. Thirdly, the shape of the head and snout are quite distinctive and have given rise to the description of the symbol as an 'elephant' although, unlike an elephant, the snout clearly has a mouth incorporated within it.

It has been suggested that the Pictish beast is some sort of aquatic creature, and primarily, because of the shape of the snout, a dolphin, or dolphin-like beast. As we have seen before, a dolphin constellation is actually present in the night sky (Delphinus). However, only the head would seem to bear even a passing resemblance to that of a dolphin.

Another fascinating explanation is that this obviously mythological animal represents an aquatic spirit. This idea is based on the possibility that legends have percolated down from the Picts to modern Scotland as tales of water spirits, or kelpies, perhaps even giving rise to the legend of the Loch Ness monster.

Perhaps the most intriguing connection, however, requires an examination of the symbolism of Capricorn, one of the classical signs of the zodiac. We have already discussed the possibility that the beast symbol on the Shandwick stone could well be associated with the winter solstice, and therefore Christmas in a Christian context. Furthermore, the likeliest candidate is the constellation of Capricorn. However, the imagery of the classical representations of this zodiacal sign does not match particularly well with the beast symbol. It is now pertinent to revisit the notion that the beast might represent the constellation of Capricorn.

That Capricorn is represented by a goat is, as we have seen, a modern invention. This sign of the zodiac is actually a sea-goat, classically portrayed, by the Greeks, Romans, Assyrians and Egyptians, as having the head and front legs of a goat, and the tail of a fish. The constellation of Capricorn occupies that portion of the night sky associated with water and therefore has an aquatic aspect to it. While a sea-goat would seem a long way conceptually from the beast, there is a fascinating connection. The Indian zodiac also has its own version of Capricorn, which shares little in common with the goat-fish, but bears more than a passing resemblance to the beast. This creature is the fearsome 'Makara' which, like the Western Capricorn, is aquatic but also considerably more sinister. Depictions vary considerably, but at its most simplistic it is shown with the head of an elephant and the body of a crocodile, sometimes with the tail of a peacock. A number of older carvings show the head as rounded like an elephant, but with a long snout, which like the Pictish beast incorporates a mouth. In the case of the Makara the mouth is armed with sharp teeth. The creature's legs vary considerably and can resemble those of a lion, a crocodile, or an elephant. In some cases the body ends in a flourish of ethereal swirls which, like the nebulous terminations on the beast, may emphasise that this is a supernatural creature. In mythology, the Makara seems to have both an aquatic and sky aspect, being associated with rivers and pools (in a similar way to the kelpie), but was also ridden through the air by Varuna, who is both a sky god and a god of the ocean. Although there are obvious differences between this Indian creature and the Pictish symbol, there are a number of features that the Makara and the beast seem to share – perhaps most obviously the long snout and rounded head. In some of the images and sculptures of the Makara, the upper portion of the snout (despite the incorporation of the mouth) is reminiscent of the elephant's trunk with its bands of muscular tissue that allow the animal to articulate the structure. However, in common with depictions of the Pictish beast, the length of the Makara's snout varies and can be quite a bit shorter than one would expect to see on an elephant, and the tip seems also to end in a tight curl. Examination of the beast found on the Shandwick stone reveals that the upper portion of the snout also ends in a tight curl. Clearly, the beast does not have any defined feet, whereas most examples of the Makara do indeed have feet, although these vary considerably (some Makara have four and some two, ending with a swirling tail). The two-dimensional Pictish beast appears to be four-legged with a rather simple tail, although both legs and feet end in a swirling pattern suggesting it is of supernatural origin. Some Makara also exhibit a small beard-like feature below the lower jaw, reminiscent of the goat-like

Western Capricorn, and in addition have a crest on their heads, reminding us of both the beast's crest and the horns of Capricorn (which typically sweep backwards in the same manner as the Pictish beast's crest).

A further connection can be made between the beast and the Makara, if we consider the possibility that the beast could well be representing, on the Shandwick stone, not only the constellation of Capricorn but the winter solstice and by default the Nativity. In India, the winter solstice festival is referred to as *Makar Sankranti* and marks the day the Sun enters the sign of Capricorn. It is seen as highly significant, symbolising the dawn of a new day for the gods (a year was said equivalent to a day and a night to the gods in Hindu tradition). This to the Hindus also marks the point in time where the Sun begins it journey northwards again and the turning point in the year. Today it is celebrated, not at the solstice but on or around 15 January. In AD 700 we find that, due to precession, the Sun would have already traversed much of Capricorn by this date. In effect, *Makar Sankranti* would be expected to have started on 25 December, Christmas Day. If the Makara and the Pictish beast both represent Capricorn, then this would seem to reinforce the theory that the Shandwick stone is proclaiming the Nativity, using a long forgotten symbol for midwinter, the constellation Capricorn. The month prior to this event in India is seen as very inauspicious; by contrast *Makar Sankranti* is seen as highly auspicious. Perhaps the Picts also regarded 25 December in the same way, a state of mind that would be very useful to the Church as it gradually imposed Christianity on the population. What better symbolism for the Nativity than a proclamation of the dawn of a highly auspicious period of time?

If the beast really does equate to the Makara of India, then the mythology of the Makara – a monster that drags people, or even other mythical creatures, into his watery lair – might find parallels in tales that have survived in Scotland from Pictish times. As previously mentioned, the most obvious tales are those of the kelpies, or water horses, that are associated with specific Scottish lochs. Like the Makara in legend, they too lie in wait, ambushing their victims and dragging them into the depths. It is perhaps also pertinent to mention that a common translation of the word Makara is 'water horse'. Viewing the kelpie as a Makara-like mythological figure also helps to explain one of Scotland's most famous tourist attractions, Nessie. This legendary monster is not, contrary to many people's belief, a modern invention, but has a well-attested mythology going back to the age of the Picts. St Columba, who is credited with bringing Christianity to the northern Picts, was travelling through Pictland in AD 565. On reaching Loch Ness he saved a man from a water monster, banishing the creature with his staff. The loch has been inextricably linked with a monster – or as some locals prefer, a kelpie – ever since. Perhaps, in a mirror to Hindu tales of the Makara, the Picts originally had a myth or legend linking such a monster to the loch, a monster that was stopped in the process of drowning a person by divine intervention. Maybe this intervention originally took the form of a Pictish god, interceding directly as Vishnu is credited with doing in Indian Makara mythology, but this myth was later 'appropriated' by Columba's biographer Adamnan as a miracle by the Christian missionary in order to boost his status. A story relating to the banishment of a monster, which is in the process of drowning a righteous man, is transformed into a story where the monster is banished by the power of Christ through his servant St Columba.

There is one more piece of visual evidence that, to say the least, is startling and is not easy to explain unless the Pictish beast symbol is indeed the Makara. If we return to the fine example of the beast on the Shandwick stone and take another look at the head and snout, as we have previously noted, there appears to be some resemblance to the Makara. There is the rounded elephant-like head, the crest, the long snout and the end of the upper jaw appearing to end in small swirl reminiscent of some of the older Makara carvings. However, we must remember that the Shandwick stone has been badly weathered in the past after many years of exposure to the salt air of the North Sea. The question is, then, are there any features that were apparent in the past, which have faded with time, that could back up the growing evidence that the Pictish beast and the Hindu Makara are one and the same? There are early drawings and photographs of the Shandwick beast, from the late nineteenth and early twentieth centuries, that appear to show more detail than is apparent today. These clearly show that the beast's snout bears all the same hallmarks of the Makara's trunk, with the classic muscular banded features of a typical elephant's trunk. Amazingly this was an integral feature of the beast symbol displayed on a stone in northern Scotland and created in the so-called Dark Ages. The trunk of the Pictish beast does not just vaguely or accidently incorporate some trunk-like features, but it would appear that an elephantine resemblance may have been deliberately sought, in much the same way as in the depictions of the Makara. However, both the Hindu and Pictish sculptors are also obviously aware, at the same time, that this is not an elephant and do appear to have a very clear, similar and well-defined creature in mind. We can therefore say, with increased authority, that both the Pictish symbol and the Indian version of Capricorn both display the same bizarre and almost identical snout-like feature, which is modified in both cases by being shortened, curled tightly at the end and incorporating a mouth. How this incredible similarity could possibly come about creates more questions than it answers, questions that probe the very relationship in space and time between the Celts of North West Europe and the Hindus of India. While the Makara represents the whole of Capricorn in Indian solar astrology, the equivalent *nakshatra* in Vedic lunar astrology is represented by the front portion of the constellation, the 'elephant's trunk'. We therefore have the possibility that the beast could either be equivalent to the entire constellation or solar zodiacal sign of Capricorn or a Pictish version of the much smaller lunar *nakshatra, Uttarashadha*.

Deer's Head and Stag

The deer's head is at first glance a most peculiar symbol. Why the head of a deer and not the whole body? If we consider the hypothesis, presented earlier, that the Picts and the Celts, as well as other Indo-Europeans, visualised a stag constellation (Scorpio), then perhaps the stag symbol might represent a portion of Scorpio. Turning to the Vedic *nakshatras* once again, a potential identification for the deer's head symbol becomes not only obvious, but once again the connections between the Vedic and Pictish symbolism are simply astonishing. The fifth *nakshatra* corresponds to roughly the boundary between Taurus and Gemini in the Western zodiac and is called *Mrigashirsha*; its symbol is not just a deer but specifically a deer's head. Could such a direct correspondence with the Pictish symbol be simply put down as a coincidence, or are we witnessing evidence of a clear relationship between cultures separated by distance and time? *Mrigashirsha* is probably represented in the sky by the star Lambda Orionis and lies directly opposite in the night sky to the star Antares, in Scorpio. This star is the basis of another *nakshatra*, *Jyeshta*. Its symbol is, rather bizarrely, the umbrella, but the animal associated with this particular mansion is the stag. Perhaps this is no coincidence and again leaves us with the possible candidate for the Pictish stag symbol.

Horse's Head

In a further twist, it has been suggested by some authors that two of the deer's head symbols may not be deer at all but may actually be horse heads. We must exercise some caution when deciding whether this truly represents a separate symbol. There is no obvious modern Western zodiacal sign or constellation that would appear to relate specifically to a horse's head. However, there is a possibility that this may represent the constellation Equuleus (the foal), seen by some classical authors as a horse's head, although there is no evidence of this being zodiacal. The Vedic *nakshatras* also offer a possible identification. The first *nakshatra* in the Hindu astrological system corresponds to the initial portion of Aries, termed *Ashwini*; its symbol is the horse's head.

Salmon / Fish

Examples of this symbol can be found in pictures 3 and 9. As there is some variation in body shape and number of fins, the fourteen known examples of this symbol could possibly represent more than one species. Although the consensus is that they are depictions of the salmon, these differences should not rule out the possibility that the Picts were interested in a generic rather than a specific depiction and that the variation in species simply reflects local interpretation as to what constitutes a fish. Ambiguity in the fish's identity would not be unique in terms of symbolism and is mirrored by the zodiacal constellation recognised by modern Western astrologers as Pisces. This pair of fish, which spring from the water poured from Aquarius's pitcher, also lack specific identity and it is possible that the Pictish fish symbol represents a variation on this constellation; indeed several cultures in the past depicted Pisces as a solitary fish. It has been suggested that, even prior to the constellation of Pisces being recognised as a fish, the constellation Piscis Austrinus was the only such animal represented in the sky and had the same role Pisces has today. Its bright star, Fomalhaut, is by far more spectacular than its more famous zodiacal near neighbour. However, we should also be mindful of the fish displayed on the Golspie stone and the possibility that it could represent either Delphinus, 'the sacred fish', or perhaps Canis Minor.

The fish in general has many symbolic meanings, with perhaps the best known in the Western mind being the symbol of the fish representing Christianity. The derivation of this symbolism originates from the period of persecution of Christians in ancient Rome and arises from the phrase *Iesu Christos Theou Uios Soter*, translated as 'Jesus Christ God's Son Saviour'. Taking each starting letter in Greek from each word, the Greek word *icthus*, meaning fish, is formed. In addition, of course, Christ is described as a 'fisher of men' in the Bible.

There is another level of symbolism regarding fish that probably would have been known to the Picts, and certainly seems to have been known to the Irish and Welsh, which is that of the fish as a symbol of knowledge. We are still familiar today with this concept when people refer to fish as 'brain food', an idea that seems to hark back to our distant past and certainly pre-dates our understanding of Omega 3! In Celtic tradition, the specific fish associated with knowledge is the salmon and this fish appears in a number of Celtic stories, notably the Irish story of *Macgnímartha Finn*. The young boy, Fionn, is expressly forbidden by his tutor from eating the 'salmon of knowledge' he was cooking. Fionn, however, accidentally tastes the flesh of the fish after licking his fingers. This act leads to the boy gaining all the knowledge of the world. The fish's association with knowledge is not confined to the Celts but surprisingly, or perhaps not so surprisingly in light of other connections outlined so far, the fish plays a central role in the creation of Vedic belief. The Indo-European root word 'vid', which we have seen gave rise both to the word 'druid' and the word 'Vedic', means knowledge, and in parallel with the 'salmon of knowledge', it was a fish (*matsya*) that brought the 'Vedas', or sacred knowledge, to Manu. Vedic astrology also recognises Pisces as a fish.

Eagle and Goose

From the analysis of the Shandwick stone panel, it is likely that the eagle symbol represents the constellation of Aquila (the eagle), or at least its most prominent star Altair. The goose symbol appears to be quite distinct and is probably unrelated.

Rams

The two small rams that appear on the Shandwick stone underneath the Pictish beast symbol could perhaps represent Aries, or the stars Sheratan and Hamal.

Boar

We have spent a considerable time investigating the wild boar not only as depicted in the context of the Shandwick stone, but also in the context of Celtic and Greek mythology. From these investigations it would seem likely that the boar represents either part or whole of the constellation of Libra, or Ophiuchus. If it represents the zodiacal constellation of Libra, then this would clash with the possibility that the arch symbol might represent this same constellation, but it is possible that it represents a particular star or portion of Libra, rather than the whole constellation.

Wolf

The night sky contains a wolf constellation, Lupus, which, although not a zodiacal sign, is found close to the ecliptic. This constellation probably originally represented a more general beast.

Sea Horse / Fish Monster

There are no obvious constellations that can be matched with any certainty to this particular symbol or symbols, but their aquatic nature might suggest a constellation or constellations below the ecliptic as being the most likely location.

Abstract Symbols

Flower

Two examples of this symbol are shown in picture 3. Most researchers investigating Pictish symbols seem to recognise a plant-like feel to this symbol, but it has also been interpreted as a decoration from a horse harness.

In the discussion on the Golspie stone above, we considered the position of the flower symbol relative to the other figures and concluded that it might represent the star Arcturus in the constellation of Bootes. Among all the various examples of the flower symbol, the version found on the Golspie stone is perhaps the least typical. While it possesses the triangular base and two 'limbs' extending to the right, these features are coarse compared to the delicate tendril-like features of other examples.

The constellation of Bootes is a very ancient constellation usually representing an agricultural figure. The star Arcturus is the third brightest star in the night sky, with a magnitude of 0.0. It is perhaps no coincidence that such a bright star, close to Virgo and its own alpha star Spica, should be associated with agriculture and be portrayed as a male figure to its close female companion Virgo. In classical legend, Bootes is the son of Demeter (the goddess of agriculture), and is credited with the invention of the plough. The constellation has also been seen as a herdsman, driving the oxen that pull the plough, or is sometimes seen as a bear keeper to the Great and Little Bears and as such has been associated with the Celtic figure of Arthur (literally 'the bear').

What information can we glean from Vedic astrology that might help us with our identification of the flower symbol? Interestingly enough, there is some tentative evidence for the identification of Bootes as the flower symbol. We have seen that there are possible connections between other Pictish symbols and Vedic symbolism and perhaps, as the number of apparent coincidences mount, we should not be totally surprised that the flower symbol does actually have a potential parallel within Vedic astrology. The name of the fifteenth Vedic symbol of *Swati* (or *Svati*) is thought to be derived from ancient Sanskrit, with *sva* thought to denote the soul or self, and to represent the star Arcturus. Its Vedic symbol is a 'coral' or a 'young plant agitated by the breeze'. The description of the young plant seems to me to fit very well with the Pictish pictograph, whose flowers seem bent over by the breeze. Similarly the unconventional triangular shape of the 'flower' symbol suggests a young sprouting plant rather than a large mature specimen.

The Bow / Helmet

This symbol is normally interpreted as a bow, but has also been seen by some as a helmet, with the arrow seen rather unconvincingly as a helmet spike. The bow is a peculiarly extravagant shape; what else would we expect from a celestial bow? This could not be an ordinary run-of-the-mill hunting bow, but had to be something fit for the gods. From our exploration of the Shandwick stone, we have suggested that the Picts probably had their own equivalent of Sagittarius, the archer, and we have discussed how the imagery of the classical Sagittarius developed. The oldest symbol for this sign was simply a bow. It is known that the Persian Sagittarius was known as *Kaman*, translated as 'the bow'. The Turkish version of the sign was known as *Yai*, also translated as 'the bow', and likewise the Syrian Sagittarius, *Kertkoalso*, meant 'bow'. If the Pictish bow really is Sagittarius then this would imply a very ancient origin for this symbol, an origin greatly distant in time from the traditions of the Romans and Greeks.

In the Vedic tradition Sagittarius is called *Dhanus*, which again translates as simply 'the bow', with the symbol comprising a bow and arrow. The bow is thought to represent a rainbow and the arrow represents lightning. In the Western zodiac, Sagittarius is of course a centaur with bow and arrow.

If the bow symbol is indeed a true rodded symbol then, as we have speculated previously, the rod could be denoting that the principal star of a constellation represented by the bow is close to the ecliptic. The best candidate (but not the only one), in terms of brightness and proximity to the ecliptic, is Nunki in Sagittarius; with a magnitude of 2.0, it would be an obvious fit.

Triple Disc and Cross Bar

This symbol is sometimes interpreted as a cauldron or alternatively a flattened chariot (examples can be found in picture 3 and picture 10). In the classical view of the night sky, Auriga, a constellation close to Taurus and Gemini, is 'the charioteer' and once represented both a chariot and driver, so it is possible that if this symbol represents a chariot then it may be cognate with Auriga.

In Welsh mythology there are hints that there may well have been a Celtic 'cauldron' constellation. This is referred to as 'Cerridwen's Cauldron' and is mentioned along with 'Arthur's Wain' or 'Arthur's Plough' (Ursa Major, also known as the Great Bear or the Plough) and other constellations and heavenly objects. However, which constellation this cauldron might correspond to is not known. Similarly, in Irish mythology, the god Dagda owned a cauldron that provided never-ending sustenance, although there is no surviving evidence of an associated constellation. Given the importance that cauldrons clearly had in Celtic society, and the magical folklore still surrounding them, these objects were clearly of great significance and most likely had a sacred function. Other stories involving cauldrons often signify rebirth or immortality and some of these vessels were clearly involved in sacrificial rites, perhaps having been used to drown victims.

We know that cauldrons were not only common objects across Europe but that some, such as the 'Gundestrup cauldron', were probably of ritual significance. If there was a Pictish or Celtic constellation depicting a cauldron, are there any constellations from classical astronomy that depict similar vessels? The nearest object to a cauldron visualised in the heavens as a constellation, by the Greeks and Romans, is Crater or the 'cup' found just below the ecliptic close to Virgo and Leo. While Celts saw cauldrons as magical and sacred, their counterparts in the classical world saw the cup or chalice as its equivalent. We therefore also have cups or horns of plenty (*Cornu Copiae*) and cups of immortality. The legends surrounding the stories of Arthur and his knights, and the Holy Grail, contain notions found both in the classical world and in the pre-Christian Celtic world which involve such vessels. In the case of the constellation Crater, the cup in question is none other than Apollo's golden cup that Corvus the crow was supposed to have used in order to bring Apollo some water from the foot of Mount Olympus. Given the strong parallels between cups or chalices and cauldrons, it may not be too far-fetched to suggest that the constellation Crater may also have been seen by the Celts, and therefore possibly the Picts, as a magical cauldron, although there is no direct evidence for this.

There is another possibility; the alpha star of the constellation Auriga is a brilliant star called Capella, meaning 'the little she goat'. It is actually a complex system comprising two pairs of binary stars, but appears to the naked eye as one star. In classical depictions of Auriga, the charioteer carries a small goat under his arm, which corresponds to Capella. However, according to Richard Hinckley Allen in his book *Star Names: Their Lore and Meaning*, Capella also represented the *Cornu Copiae* or horn of plenty. Given the parallels between the concept of the classical *Cornu Copiae* and the Celtic cauldron of plenty, could Auriga have represented a cauldron to the Picts?

Tuning Fork

The so-called 'tuning fork' symbol does not seem to match any known artefact from the period, and has earned this title simply as a convenient description. What could it actually represent? Is it an abstract figure, or is it highly stylised yet unidentifiable object that the Picts would have been familiar with? Any attempt to identify what the tuning fork actually represented is going to be difficult. One remote possibility is that it could represent a Y-shaped divining or dowsing rod; if this were the case then it might be linked to druidry. This particular design of divining rod seems to have a long history, and at its most basic took the form of a forked twig from a hazel tree. The two flexible 'legs' of the fork would be held by the 'diviner' and bent outwards, with the handle-like part of the fork pointing away from the person. If the tuning fork was a forked divining rod, then the form it takes on Pictish stones would suggest a much more sophisticated version than a simple twig. The Vedic *nakshatra Vishakha* is translated as 'forked branch' and it is of course a jump in logic to suggest that this is connected to either the Pictish symbol or divining rods, but it is a possibility that we should nonetheless bear in mind. The recent discovery of a possible 'druid's grave' at a site in Colchester in South East England, dating from around 50 BC, has led to speculation that some of the objects discovered might include divination rods, therefore opening up the possibility that druids did indeed use such rods.

Triple-Oval

This pictograph could represent three links of a chain viewed two-dimensionally, and may therefore relate to the large silver Pictish chains that have been found in a number of locations in Scotland. These silver chains appear to be some sort of symbol of power. Another possibility is that the symbol represents a belt and therefore, in our hypothetical celestial context, Orion's belt or Andromeda's girdle may be candidates.

Mirror Case

The usual identification of this symbol as a mirror case (see picture 3), it would seem, is based on interpreting it as essentially a two-dimensional object. However, it is also possible that the Picts represented three-dimensional objects in a stylised two-dimensional manner. Such an approach would lead to some everyday objects being rendered almost unrecognisable to our modern eyes. For example, the triple disc and crossbar, mentioned above, while displaying clear cauldron-like attributes (such as the bowl as a circle, two handles off to the side and the bar to suspend the cauldron from), is portrayed in a surprisingly simplistic two-dimensional 'flattened' form. It therefore may be necessary to try and view the other abstract figures in the same way. Applying this to the mirror case, we should look for different components within the symbol that may give a clue to the identity of the original object. The common feature of the various versions of the mirror case is the circular form at the top end, with a smaller circle often placed inside. Extending downwards is a shape that approximates to a rectangle, which on some examples tapers out the way towards the bottom of the symbol. If we view the top part of the symbol as a circular table top or something similar, orientated on the symbol to face the viewer, then the bottom half of the symbol becomes the base of the table. An object that would fit with such an interpretation is an altar. In this case the smaller inside circle would represent a carved and indented offering bowl, with the base represented below this. The constellation Ara, to the ancient Greeks, represented the altar set up by the Cyclopes.

Miscellaneous Symbols

There are a number of other symbols that are not easy to identify, including the ogee (a ribbon-like design), the double crescent (two crescents back to back with a small circle and dot in the centre), the step, the rectangle, and the disc. As we discussed in the context of the triple disc and crossbar, and the so-called mirror case, these objects might represent real objects familiar to the Picts but 'flattened' into a two-dimensional symbol. Some of these more abstract pictographs could also potentially relate to some of the more obscure and abstract Vedic *nakshatras*.

CHAPTER 12

A PICTISH ASTROLOGICAL SYSTEM

Overview of the Symbols

The hypothesis, derived from our exploration, is that the Pictish symbols may have an astronomical and calendrical significance, and in particular an astrological function. This working hypothesis has been suggested by a number of strands of evidence. Firstly there is obvious solar and lunar symbolism found in the crescent and double disc designs, which have been recognised to a limited extent over the last one hundred years or so. However, the significance of this has apparently gone largely unnoticed. Secondly, we have seen that the additional mirror and comb symbols are connected with divination and the 'other world' in many cultures across Europe and Asia. Thirdly, some of the symbols are found associated with figures that seem to match constellations. Fourthly, in addition to the more obvious relationships – between the Western astrological symbols for the Sun and the Moon and the Pictish double disc and crescent – some symbols have shown quite extraordinary parallels with the astrological symbolism of other cultures, notably the Vedic tradition of India. The beast symbol, for example, shows a great deal of similarity to the Vedic version of Capricorn (the Makara), despite the distance in both time and space between the two cultures. From the understanding that the Shandwick hunting panel could represent a calendar, there is strong possibility that the beast symbol above it relates to midwinter – a role played in India by the Makara. Overall a number of the Pictish symbols also seem to bear similarities to Vedic astrological symbols, including the deer's head and the horse's head. It would certainly be a startling coincidence if a putative Pictish astrological system had independently adopted these symbols. If this was no coincidence then we have the possibility that we could actually match Pictish symbols to Vedic *nakshatras*. For example, the Pictish deer's head might therefore be cognate with the *nakshatra* of *Mrigashirsha* and therefore represent a star or asterism approximately level with the Taurus/Gemini boundary. Likewise the putative Pictish horse head symbol might represent a star or asterism in Aries (*Ashwini*).

Other symbols that might have parallels with Vedic symbols include the snake, the arch, the notched rectangle, possibly the flower symbol, the bow, the stag and the tuning fork. If these parallels were proven to reflect an actual correspondence, then a possible maximum of ten out of some twenty-three to thirty potential symbols might show some sort of relation to Vedic *nakshatras*. Some of the symbols may in addition correspond to Western constellations, with a few perhaps showing a relationship to Western astrological symbols – the double disc, the crescent Moon, the bow (an older version of Sagittarius) and the fish (perhaps Pisces). In addition, it is possible that the cauldron symbol might equate to Auriga. We therefore have the possibility that over half of the symbols have some evidence of an astrological or astronomical connection.

Understanding the Symbol Pairs

While it is one thing to recognise images or symbols that relate to astronomy, we still have to answer the question of why the Picts would use astronomical imagery or symbolism on their stones. In the case of the Shandwick stone it is possible that the progression of figures from left to right could symbolise the progression of rising stars on a particular night, or represent the heliacal rising of key stars over a period of time that relates to the context of the rest of the stone. The heliacal rising would seem to point to a progression of rising stars from spring to midwinter. In the context of the Christianity expressed by the stone as a whole, it is therefore likely that the panel is deliberately pointing to a specific date, the most likely being Christmas Day. Similarly, the alternative hypothesis that the panel relates to the movement of the stars on a particular night would also point to Christmas Day. The use of astronomy on the Shandwick panel therefore provides an important clue as to why the Picts might have had an interest in the heavens; they were very aware of the night sky as a calendar. The probability is that they were proclaiming, in symbols, how major important celestial events indicated the divine significance of Christmas Day, much as the Star of Bethlehem proclaimed the Nativity in the Bible.

The Golspie stone may also be conveying the notion of a specific period of time, but probably not within a Christian context. It is possible that the arrangement of the figures on the stone may also point to a specific winter event, perhaps *Samhain* or midwinter, but this is less clear. Unlike the Shandwick stone, however, the Golspie stone also incorporates classic Pictish symbols into the scene, providing us with the crucial clue to the nature of the symbols. By being placed within this specific setting, there is a strong possibility that the symbols would also represent constellations, or even individual stars, although selected from a set of designs distinct from the human and animal figures in the scene. If we take a broad view of the other Pictish stones, there is also some evidence that a number of Pictish symbols on further inspection appear also to have astronomical meaning incorporated into their design, and perhaps symbolism related to mythological characters that have celestial connections.

It would appear therefore that we have two categories of Pictish astronomical symbolism being used on the stones. Firstly, we have naturalistic figures, some of which resemble classical depictions of constellations and others that are not so obviously related but nonetheless probably represent how the Picts perceived particular constellations or groupings of stars. It is possible that ordinary Picts viewing these figures would be able, without any difficulty, to recognise their identity and perhaps relate these to mythological stories in much the same way as we do today when looking at Greek constellations, such as Orion or Perseus or many of the other such asterisms, in the night sky. Secondly, we have Pictish symbols which seem to be much more abstract in design, with their meaning appearing to be less or not at all accessible, suggesting a much more serious and perhaps even secretive or sacred purpose.

An important question that needs to be asked is why did the sculptor of the Golspie stone not represent all the constellations as figures? Furthermore, why are the symbols represented at all on the panel amid the figures? A working hypothesis might be that the symbols represent constellations or individual stars that were particularly important to the Picts, in the context of the panel's timeline. However, the constellations or stars that these symbols represent, for some reason, did not fit well with the more naturalistic figures in the panel – the sculptor opting for an alternative system of symbolism. It is possible that the figures could represent a visual version of a mythological narrative, instantly recognisable to the population, while the symbols might represent important stars that could not be ignored but were outside the thematic context of the rest of the panel. Another possibility is these symbols represent not just a constellation or individual star, but a particular key event associated with these, for example a planet present at that time in that constellation, in other words carrying further important information that could not be conveyed by a more mundane figure.

The notion of having two distinct systems to describe constellations is not at all unusual. For example, modern computer sky atlases allow the user to view a constellation as a group of stars joined together simply by lines, or to view the constellation as a drawing of whatever person, animal or object it is supposed to represent. In addition, in Western astrology, the key zodiacal constellations are depicted as figures in the sky but are also represented by symbols, which do not at first glance seem to bear much resemblance to the realism of the art usually used to depict these groups of stars. For example, Gemini, the twins, is represented by the Roman numeral II and Aquarius by two wave-like lines, one placed above the other and representing water. Similarly, symbols are used to represent the *nakshatras* of Vedic astrology. The basic symbol in Western astrology for the Sun, a disc with a dot in the middle, resembles part of the Pictish double disc. The crescent Moon is also a long-established astrological symbol and has obvious similarities to the Pictish crescent. Perhaps also the notched rectangle displays similar proportions to the classical symbol for Gemini and indeed the constellation itself.

Fundamental to this hypothesis – that the Picts were familiar with, and indeed practised, a form of astrology – is the question of what form this took and how it would relate to other systems practised, both in the past and today. If the Picts used a form of solar astrology, similar to that first attributed to the Chaldeans (Babylonians), then we would expect to see some twelve symbols, each representing a sign of the solar zodiac. As there is also a little evidence that Ophiuchus may also have been used as a solar zodiacal constellation, then we have a theoretical upper limit of thirteen symbols. Clearly there are more Pictish symbols than this. However, we know that the ancient thirty-day month could be subdivided into portions of ten days. We could therefore have a potential astrological system of thirty-six time segments, equating to a division of the ecliptic into thirty-six portions of exactly 10 degrees. Each zodiac sign would therefore have three such segments, each presumably with the possibility of different planetary 'influences'. These ten-day periods, or decans, were once a mainstream feature of Western astrology and are represented, for example, in the famous Denderah zodiac found in Egypt. Therefore one possibility is that the Pictish symbols are solar in nature and represent divisions that are similar, or directly equivalent, to decans.

We have seen that counting the number of Pictish symbols is open to interpretation, but the likely number of symbols is around twenty-three to twenty-eight. However, it is possible that some other symbols have not yet been discovered in paired form, so the number may well be greater. The subjectivity in defining what constitutes a symbol is of course only natural and illustrates the point that we will probably never be able to draw up a definitive list of symbol pair components that is not open to challenge. We therefore unfortunately cannot use these lists as reliable indicators of the type of astrological system in use.

If the Picts used a system of decans, then what information would the symbol pair actually convey? Since the decan system is intrinsically linked to a solar astrological system, then it is possible that the first symbol in a pairing would represent the position of the Sun at a particular time of year within a specific decan. The second symbol could therefore refer to the position of one of the planets or the Moon at the same time. This system could therefore carry a simple message that might express, for example, that the Sun is in the second decan of Aries, the Moon in the third decan of Sagittarius. Presumably a druid or astrologer could select, from planetary positions observed in the sky, the appropriate combination of planets that was relevant to the occasion. This type of system is familiar to those who read horoscopes, which often base their predictions on charts that might pick out specific combinations while ignoring others. Therefore an astrologer might place emphasis on the position of just one or two heavenly bodies. For example, a prediction might state that the Sun is in your birth sign and Jupiter is in Aquarius, while ignoring the position of the Moon, and the remaining planets, seen as less important. In this situation an astrologer would state whether or not it was a good thing to have Jupiter in Aquarius at the same time as the Sun in a person's birth sign and then offer advice on that basis. We might envisage a decan-based astrological system as being similar, except that each portion of each of the twelve zodiac signs would have particular planets that would be beneficial or malign if found within them. This would of course create many more permutations. There would, however, seem to be no obvious link between traditional decan symbolism and the Pictish symbols.

Which other basic systems are possible in explaining the symbols and their pairings? A possibility is that the system used was not solar but lunar based, or a combination of both. As we have seen, the Moon's progressive path each night across the sky does not follow the ecliptic exactly, but traces a sinusoidal pathway. This path takes the Moon not only through the more conventional solar zodiacal constellations, but takes it close to stars that are part of other constellations. As the Moon takes approximately (just over) twenty-seven days to complete one cycle around the sky, a convenient method to keep track of its movements is to divide the sky into twenty-seven or twenty-eight portions and allocate a particular bright star within each segment as a sort of marker. Some of these star markers would therefore coincide with prominent stars within the solar zodiacal constellations, as well as stars from constellations beyond these basic twelve. This type of system is precisely the type used by Vedic astrology, with each marker star being termed a *nakshatra* or 'star wife'. We have also already established that there may well be similarities and parallels between some of the Pictish symbols and the symbolism behind Vedic *nakshatras*, which might suggest that there may be some sort of relationship between them. Furthermore, as discussed in chapter five, the writer Peter Beresford Ellis noted that the legendary Queen Maeve of Connaught's husband, King Ailil, had twenty-seven windows in his circular palace and that he used these to watch his twenty-seven 'star wives'. This might suggest a parallel between astrology in ancient Celtic Ireland and the equally ancient Vedic *nakshatras* from India. We have also noted that the giant from Welsh mythology, Rhitta Gawr, defeated some twenty-eight kings over ownership of the night sky. It is therefore possible that the Picts might have recognised a *nakshatra*-like system and indeed may have used a system that was a distant (in time as well as geography) relative of the Vedic astrological system. Such a system could work in a similar way to one based on decans, but with a greater emphasis on the position of the Moon. This might also imply that each Pictish symbol represents the brightest star associated with one of twenty-seven or twenty-eight subdivisions of the Moon's path through the sky.

Whatever the details of the Pictish astrological system, the symbol pairs would therefore most likely convey a message that relates the position of heavenly bodies in the night sky to events on earth. These events might be for example the consecration of a church, and the pair would therefore convey a message along the following lines: planet 'a' is in the domain of star 'b', and planet 'x' is in the domain of star 'y', and this is a positive situation that bodes well for this building. In other words the symbols pairs in this situation would indicate an auspicious set of celestial events. Similarly, a stone that commemorated a victory in battle might be effectively saying that on the day of the battle the stars were in a very favourable position or in other words the gods favoured the positive outcome to the conflict. Equally possible, if a stone commemorated the death of a king or other esteemed individual, the two symbols could indicate planets in key positions that communicate a negative set of circumstances or an inauspicious event. Another possibility along the same lines is that the symbols on a specific stone could represent an individual's specific star signs at their birth; these would not only identify the person to the Picts but could perhaps provide us with information on a birth date, therefore helping to date the stone.

The notion of auspicious and inauspicious events is one often closely associated with Roman astrology. However, the discovery of fragments of bronze sheets, in Coligny in France, dating back to the first century BC has changed this viewpoint. It was discovered that these fragments, when reassembled, formed a sophisticated calendar, inscribed with lists of days and months, and covering a period of five years. The Coligny bronze sheets have therefore provided strong evidence that the Celtic Gauls (at least) used a highly complicated lunar–solar calendar. Days were divided into 'auspicious' and 'inauspicious' or in Gaulish *mat* and *anmat*. The word *mat* is cognate with the Irish and Scots Gaelic word *math* meaning 'good', while *anmat*, although not having a direct equivalent in Gaelic, probably means 'not good'. The existence of these labels would therefore suggest that the Gauls were interested in astrology. Further parallels between Gaelic and the Gaulish tablet inscriptions are also found in the names of two of the months; *Samon(ios)* seemingly corresponding to the Gaelic *Samhain* meaning summer, and *Giamonios* perhaps corresponding to the Irish word for winter – *geimhreadh*. It has also been suggested that small symbols, or sigils, that appear on the calendar marking specific days in the month *Giamonios* (and also in the month of *Elembivios*) might well be indicating the classic Celtic festivals of

Lughnasa and *Beltane*. These parallels of course do not prove that the Celts of Britain and Ireland used the same calendar as the Gauls, but might suggest a significant degree of commonality in the structure of the year.

It is worth noting that if the Celtic festivals were linked solely to lunar events, then this would result in these festivals moving every year without any synchronicity to the Sun. The most likely scenario, however, is that these festivals were celebrated at particular phases of the Moon but also tied to the position of the Sun – in much the same way as Easter is calculated today (Easter Sunday is the first Sunday after the first full Moon after the spring equinox). It may therefore have been a necessity, for a culture that observed and respected the Moon's position and phases, to produce a compromise lunar–solar calendar. Whether the Coligny Calendar represents a specific Gaulish solution to the problem of reconciling the Moon and the Sun's cycles or whether this was 'pan-Celtic' can unfortunately only be speculated on. However, it would be strange if the Celts in Britain and Ireland celebrated key Celtic festivals at very different times of the year from those of the Gauls, especially as Julius Caesar noted that the druids of Gaul had very close associations with the druids of Britain.

In regard to the Picts, since the Pictish language is completely unknown, there is simply no linguistic evidence to suggest that the name of the Pictish months related in any way either to Irish, Gaelic or Gaulish, and therefore it is impossible to speculate on a linguistic basis on the nature of a Pictish calendar. However, if the Picts also marked the key Celtic festivals and at the very least the winter solstice then, combined with a possible interest in lunar astrology, this might suggest that they too could have utilised a lunar–solar calendar. Symbol pairs might represent some aspect of such a calendar, with both solar and lunar components, but, like the Vedic *nakshatras*, the use of lunar mansions may have been used strictly for astrological purposes.

Rodded Symbols and Astrology

If we return for the moment to the puzzling inclusion of rods with some of the symbols, then is it possible that z-rods and v-rods also indicate particular astronomical events that were of particular note to the Picts? Considering the z-rods first, in the case of the double disc and notched rectangle symbols, careful study of the rodded versions of these symbols reveals bias in the use of certain forms of the 'z'. As we have seen in chapter ten, there are four theoretical ways in which a Pictish z-rod could be carved. The 'z' could take the form of a capital letter 'N' with the spearhead on either end; alternatively it could be in the form of a mirrored 'N' with again spearheads on either possible ends. However, only two forms actually appear: predominately the mirrored 'N' with the spearhead on the left-hand side pointing upwards, and a handful of z-rods in the form of an 'N' with the spearhead pointing upwards on the right-hand side of the motif. This apparent exclusion of some of the possible forms of z-rod would strongly suggest that they convey some meaning.

Another way of viewing these two different sorts of rods is to see the spearheads as indicators of direction. If we imagine the z-rod as a device to represent movement, with a central axis, then the spearhead helps us to see clearly which direction of turn is indicated. The vast majority of the z-rodded symbols would therefore be classified as clockwise, the same direction that the Sun, Moon and stars appear to move across the sky. Such a device would not be unique and a very similar symbol that also conveys the notion of solar clockwise motion is the swastika. This symbol also has an anticlockwise counterpart, the sauvastika, and both are found across Eurasia. These symbols, which have unfortunately been more recently linked to the Nazis, are in fact very old solar symbols and relate to the solar wheel. They have a history stretching back to the Neolithic period, and appear in many Indo-European cultures, past and present. In particular in Buddhism and Hinduism both the swastika and sauvastika (both these words are derived from the ancient Indo-European language Sanskrit) are commonly used, decorating temples and even in the case of Buddhism appearing as a symbol on the body of the Buddha. In general the swastika is considered a very beneficial symbol, and is seen as a symbol representing 'good luck' or an auspicious event or situation. Prior to the Second World War the symbol was even used as a lucky charm in Europe. The swastika was also a common motif among the Celts, and even appears twenty-seven times (the same number of days in a lunar month or the number of *nakshatras* in the Vedic lunar zodiac) on the Battersea shield, a masterpiece of Celtic art found in the River Thames in London. It would be tempting to see the z-rod itself as a modified and simplified swastika, comprising just one of the two 'spokes' but still conveying the idea of the Sun moving clockwise across the sky and fitting perfectly with astrological symbolism and the concept of auspicious events. The use of a counter-clockwise rod might therefore suggest a particular event was inauspicious.

The v-rod, however, does not have a central axis, and therefore cannot be classified as either being clockwise or counter-clockwise. We have, however, noticed that they can exist in a left-hand or right-hand version. If the z-rod really does have a connection to the solar swastika symbol, then there is some sense in suggesting that it would be inappropriate for the crescent Moon symbol to be associated with a solar motif. Perhaps more simply, in the same way as the z-rod has two forms, the v-rod likewise has two forms: a right-pointing and left-pointing form. This might indicate whether an event is auspicious or inauspicious. Speculatively the shape of the v-rod may reflect the Moon's apparent sinusoidal movement during the course of its cycle.

Mentioned above was the possibility that if individual symbols did actually refer to a specific celestial event, then two or more symbols might have signified a specific date. For example, if one symbol represented the Sun entering a particular constellation then this would tell us the time of year. If the second symbols represented a particular planet present in a specific house, then this event might be relatively rare, perhaps only occurring every few years. This might allow us to actually narrow down to perhaps a handful of candidate dates. We may therefore be able to use this information to test the hypothesis that the symbols formed part of a *nakshatra*-like astrological system, assuming that we can identify the event and match it to any written chronological evidence. While there are stones that bear symbol pairs and Ogham, these inscriptions are largely unintelligible. No stones exist that provide anything as convenient as legible date in Latin or any other language. A further possibility could be that particular stones can be linked to known historical figures, meaning the possible dating information might well refer to an important date in the person's life and therefore be of historical use. Likewise an unusual symbol combination, assuming the symbols system was sufficiently understood, could lead to the identification of a particular time frame that could help place the monument into a historical context.

Deciphering a Specific Symbol Pair: Aberlemno 2 – The Battle Scene

Surprisingly, a stone from the county of Angus, Aberlemno 2 (pictures 2 and 10), does offer a little hope of matching specific symbols to a known date. Although at this early stage we must be cautious, it is perhaps a worthwhile exercise nonetheless. On this particular stone is carved a battle scene surmounted by a symbol pair. The story is laid out rather like a cartoon storyboard and is read from top left to bottom right. What is intriguing about this storyboard is that the protagonists are very different in appearance. The Picts in the scene, who apparently end up the victors, are easily distinguished by their long hair, beards and clothing – elements that are found in other depictions of men on other Pictish stones. The enemy are dressed quite differently, with chainmail and metal helmets with nose guards. These warriors have been identified as Angles, and are almost certainly from the Angle or English kingdom of Northumbria. These two peoples clashed over a long period of time, but one battle was particularly significant. The battle of Dunnichen, also referred to as Nechtansmere, in AD 685 saw the Angles expelled from a major and serious encroachment into Pictish territory. This battle took place below 'Nechtan's fortress' or Dunnichen in a marsh (or mere) in Angus. The battle was fought between King Brude mac Bili and the Northumbrian King Ecgfrid and was recorded by the Northumbrian monk the Venerable Bede as a huge disaster for the Angles. The Northumbrian forces were almost wiped out and Ecgfrid was killed. This battle marked a turning point in Northumbrian territorial ambitions north of the Firth of Forth, and re-established the Picts as major players in the process that was going to lead to the creation of Alba, the country better known today as Scotland.

What is particularly interesting about the battle, apart from its historical significance, is that firstly, thanks to Bede, we have a specific day and date for the conflict – Saturday 20 May 685. Secondly, the scene portrayed on the Aberlemno 2 stone, located a few miles away from the battle site, is generally thought to portray this very battle, although unfortunately it cannot be proven that this is the case. If this stone really does portray the battle of Nechtansmere or Dunnichen, then the accompanying symbol pair might relate to the battle date, and therefore relate to date-specific astronomical events.

The two symbols that appear above the battle scene are the notched rectangle symbol with a z-rod and the triple disc symbol. Given the discussion above concerning the identity of the notched rectangle, the most likely candidate identified so far would be the stars Castor and Pollux, which form the core of the Gemini constellation. The triple disc's identity is less obvious, but we have the possibility that this symbol could be the representation of a cauldron, as seen from above, or perhaps a chariot. If we start with the possibility that the notched rectangle with z-rod represents the stars Castor and Pollux, then whether the system is based on decans or on *nakshatra-*

like symbols, the presence of the notched rectangle would imply something special was happening in the constellation Gemini on the day of the battle. The presence of the z-rod might also imply that this possible astronomical event had even greater significance. Similarly, whatever the triple disc or cauldron actually represents, it is possible that something of astronomical or astrological significance was occurring within its asterism.

With our date, 20 May 685, we could use astronomical software to ascertain the location of the Sun, the Moon, and the planets in relation to the star background on this specific day and see if any of their positions coincided with Castor and Pollux or provide any clues to the identity of the triple disc. If the system used utilised thirty-six signs, then the planet would have to be within just a 10-degree 'slot' in the sky, or if twenty-seven symbols, then within a slot of just over 13 degrees out of 360. In addition the outer planets – Mars, and in particular, Jupiter and Saturn – could be totally absent from a particular area of the night sky for years.

The first observation regarding the symbols on this stone is that the notched rectangle is larger than the triple ring symbol. Secondly, the rectangle has a right-handed or clockwise z-rod. The size of the symbol might suggest that this portion of the encoded information is more important than that conveyed by the smaller triple ring. The right-handed z-rod might also indicate that the astrological event associated with the symbol was particularly auspicious, something that makes sense in the context of a military victory, whether or not it is the battle of Dunnichen that is actually depicted. In Western astrology Gemini is ruled by the planet Mercury and on 20 May 685, the day of the battle according to Bede, we find (using astronomical software) that the planet Mercury was positioned within the narrow confines of Gemini, an area of sky just a few degrees across. Confusingly, however, and in a relatively rare situation, the planet Jupiter is also located in the same relatively small area of sky within the constellation of Gemini. Jupiter would only be within this particular constellation every twelve or thirteen years. Perhaps also of significance is that the Vedic *nakshatra* corresponding to this portion of Gemini, containing Castor and Pollux (*Punarvasu*), is ruled by Jupiter.

We therefore have the possibility that the rodded notched rectangle on this stone is proclaiming the presence of either Mercury (the Western zodiacal ruler of Gemini) or Jupiter (the Vedic ruler of the *nakshatra Punarvasu*), or even perhaps both planets' presence within Gemini. If this hypothesis is correct then this combination may have been seen as having great significance in relation to the battle or probably the outcome of the battle. In other words, this day was foretold in the stars as being particularly auspicious, and the stone, with the notched and rodded rectangle placed prominently and centrally on the stone, may well be proclaiming the significance of these events within Gemini. The triple disc symbol, which is clearly less important than the notched rectangle, may have represented the constellation Auriga. The Sun, on 20 May 685, was immediately below the star Capella in Auriga, as it would be for several days, and it is a possibility that this is the simple message being conveyed. This would of course be an annual event and not at all unusual and therefore the relatively small size of the triple ring on this stone could be reflecting its lesser importance. However, its presence would also suggest that the Sun's position below Auriga was still of some (positive) significance. If we consider the Vedic symbol represented by a chariot, *Rohini*, this symbol corresponds to the portion of Taurus around the star Aldebaran but was unoccupied on the date of the battle.

Our other potential candidate for the triple disc (or 'three ring') symbol, in the previous chapter, was the constellation Crater, which in classical tradition was seen as Apollo's cup, and could be cognate with a Celtic cauldron. Was there any planet in the vicinity of Crater on the day of the battle? Looking at the battle date we find the planet Saturn was directly above this constellation.

We therefore have at least two possibilities for the presence of the triple disc symbol on the Aberlemno 2 stone. Firstly, it could represent the Sun's position on the day of the battle, between Taurus and Gemini and directly below Capella, or it could represent the influence of the planet Saturn on the constellation Crater.

If we were to accept that the symbols on this stone signify the heavens on the day of the battle, then another question to ask in regard to the battle of Dunnichen and the symbols on the Aberlemno 2 stone is whether the Picts, and specifically their druids, retrospectively recognised that the position of the Sun, Moon and planets on that day were favourable, and displayed selected symbols that fitted with that notion? Or did they plan for the battle to take place on that particular day because the day was particularly auspicious? Certainly the evidence would suggest that druids had the power to decide when a tribe could go to war, but would astronomy really have influenced such a decision in reality? More likely, as was apparently the case at the later battle of Athelstaneford, the 'portents' were seen to be favourable on the morning of the battle, and this would be seen as a morale-boosting divine sign that the Picts would be victorious.

On 20 May 685, the other planets were located as follows: the Moon was located between Virgo and Libra, Venus between Gemini and Cancer (above Canis Minor) and Mars was leaving the constellation of Aries (its ruling house).

We must be cautious in accepting that this interpretation of the symbols on Aberlemno 2 is correct. Firstly, as mentioned previously there is no definitive proof that this stone actually depicts the battle carefully recorded by Bede. Secondly, if the Picts utilised a *nakshatra*-like system then we might expect considerably more emphasis to be placed on the position of the Moon than would apparently be the case here. However, if the Moon was located in a position that was regarded as neither particularly auspicious nor inauspicious then it may not have been deemed significant. Nonetheless, it is an intriguing possibility that the symbols on this stone may point at the actual date of the battle.

The Shandwick Symbol Pair

In the case of the Shandwick stone, we have hypothesised that the beast symbol represents, in the context of the hunting tableau, the rising of Capricorn and therefore signals Christmas Day. If this is the case then it might be possible to look at every 25 December, between say AD 600 and AD 900, to ascertain if the positions of the Sun, Moon and planets coincided with constellations that could be matched to the symbols on the upper half of the stone.

As a reminder, the top symbol on the Shandwick stone is a non-rodded double disc, while the lower symbol is the beast. In addition there are two smaller symbols positioned below the beast on the same panel, the twin rams and a badly damaged four-legged animal. If we accept, firstly, that the beast symbol is to be interpreted in this case as meaning that the Sun is in Capricorn (or the Sun is entering Capricorn), secondly that the double disc might represent the constellation Leo, and finally that the twin rams represents the two stars in the constellation Aries (Hamal and Sheratan), then we might be able to come up with a particular reasonable combination of planetary positions that provide us with potential dates for the Shandwick stone. Of course if all or any of these symbols has been wrongly identified then these dates would be meaningless. Nonetheless, it is a fascinating exercise to undertake, although again highly speculative at this stage.

If the Sun was entering Capricorn, then it follows that the inner planets would also be in the same vicinity. This would rule out an inner planet (Mercury or Venus) being found in constellations a considerable distance from Capricorn, Aries or Leo for example. This would also imply that we are interested, in terms of the symbols on the stone, only in the Moon or the outer planets (Mars, Jupiter or Saturn) as being located in Aries or Leo. Furthermore, we might hazard a guess that in a theoretical Pictish astrology system, as in Western astrology, Mars and Aries are linked (with Mars the ruler of Aries). The depiction of the two rams below the beast might therefore signify that the planet Mars on this particular day and year was in Aries. By therefore examining only those years where Mars was in Aries around Christmas we might be able to narrow down potential dates for the Shandwick stone, assuming of course that we are correct in surmising that the Shandwick stone points towards a particular Christmas Day. If we can also locate the Moon or another planet within Leo, then this might add to our confidence. Between AD 550 and AD 900, Mars could be found in Aries on 25 December on approximately nineteen occasions. Examining the region of space around Leo, only in three of these years were other planets, including the Moon, found in this constellation. These years were AD 711, 852 and 869. In the first of these candidate years, we find Saturn in the constellation Leo, Mercury in Capricorn, Venus in Capricorn, while Jupiter was in Virgo and the Moon was in Taurus. In AD 852, Jupiter was in Leo on 25 December, Mercury in Sagittarius, Venus in Aquarius, Saturn in Taurus and the Moon was also in Taurus (below the Pleiades). In the final year under consideration (AD 869) we find the Moon in Leo, Mercury in Capricorn, Venus in Sagittarius, Jupiter between Sagittarius and Capricorn and finally Saturn in Sagittarius.

Which, if any, of these three dates fits with the symbols on the top panel of the Shandwick stone? The two principal symbols, as we have discussed, may represent Leo (the double disc) and Capricorn (the beast). In addition the two smaller symbols could be Aries (the two rams) with the final symbol difficult to interpret due to damage caused when the stone was split in two during a storm. One possibility is that the two major symbols – the double disc and the beast – along with the two smaller symbols represent star signs that on Christmas Day, in a particular year, were occupied by all seven astrological so-called planets (the Sun, Moon, Mercury, Venus, Mars, Jupiter and Saturn).

If this was the case then the first two years, AD 711 and AD 852, would have to be ruled out as, in both of these cases, the seven planets occupied more than four houses. On 25 December 711, the constellations occupied were Capricorn, Aries, Leo, Virgo and Taurus. On the same day in AD 852 the constellations occupied were Capricorn, Aries, Leo, Taurus, Aquarius and Sagittarius. However, on Christmas Day in the year AD 869, just four solar houses were occupied: Capricorn, Aries, Leo and Sagittarius. Could this be the explanation for the Shandwick stone's symbol panel? If this were the case, then the damaged symbol would have to represent Sagittarius or a portion of it (remembering that each zodiac constellation can have three lunar mansions within it). As we have seen on the hunting scene on the same stone, the hunter with the bow is a reasonable candidate for Sagittarius – based on its position on the stone and early depictions of Sagittarius as simply an archer. Even with the damage to the fourth carving on the symbol panel, it would appear that it represents a four-legged animal of some sort and therefore this would appear to rule out the possibility that it represents Sagittarius. It is possible that the figure represents a centaur and this could fit with the constellation Sagittarius. However, we would have to square the two very different versions of this same constellation that appear on Shandwick, although two distinct systems may have been utilised here – a strictly standardised astrological set of symbols setting out a prediction and a naturalistic depiction of constellations which fits in with a hunting scene. Therefore, we have a slim possibility that the stone refers to a specific date, 25 December AD 869, but given the number of suppositions required to arrive at a firm conclusion, we must exercise a great deal of caution, but perhaps it is a start. Finally, we could also ask, does this particular date fit well within the historical Pictish time frame? If this was the correct date for the stone, then it is one that represents the very tail end of the Pictish kingdoms. Around AD 843 Kenneth MacAlpine became king of both Scots and Picts, and although the creation of the Kingdom of Scotland probably took place some time after this, from this point onwards the fate of Pictland was sealed. The Picts, however, continue to be mentioned in various historical entries for at least another thirty of forty years or so, suggesting that the takeover of Pictland was not completed in one quick event. Since Shandwick is in the far north of Scotland, it is possible that this area remained under Pictish influence for longer and therefore the Shandwick stone may represent one of the last examples of a Pictish carved stone. Given this, it is therefore at least feasible that the stone dates from the mid-ninth century.

Basic Framework for a Pictish Astrological System

In the above examples, we have attempted, using the meagre evidence available, to match the symbols found on the Aberlemno 2 and Shandwick stones to particular dates. If these are in any way correct, then we have some opportunity to at least lay down some possible 'ground rules' for a Pictish astrological system.

Firstly, it could be that the 'norm' was to display two symbols on the stones; depicting probably two key events in the heavens that related in the minds of the astrologers to events on the earth. This would echo, although not necessarily mimic, modern horoscopes that focus on the Sun's position within the birth sign and the rising sign and any accompanying planet or 'ascendant' at the actual moment of birth. It is possible that in rare circumstances a single symbol might be displayed if the celestial event it represented was considered important enough without the need for additional 'portents'. Perhaps in these circumstances other favourable planetary alignments may not have occurred. There may also have been rare circumstances when a number or even all of the planets were aligned favourably at a particular key moment. In these circumstances, more than two symbols may have been displayed, with particularly auspicious alignments being given prominence. Such a circumstance may have arisen in the case of Shandwick stone and the Golspie stone. However, the convention may have been to display the most important two symbols and give prominence to these. An astrological solution to the problem of interpreting Pictish symbolism therefore allows for these special cases, while at the same time explaining the multitude of symbol pairs. This hypothesis would explain why certain combinations, which otherwise would be expected based on probability, are rare or absent from stone while others are over-represented.

The second ground rule in a possible Pictish astrological system would be the emphasis on a particular symbol within the pair. One model would be that the first symbol relates to the position of a specific body in the heavens, most likely either the Sun or the Moon. So for example, it might on every occasion be reporting the Sun's position on the ecliptic, with the second symbol relating to another of the planets. If the system placed greater emphasis on lunar astrology, then the first symbol might relate exclusively to the Moon. However, more likely is that the order in which the symbols appear relates to some sort of hierarchy of key alignments. For example, the rodded double disc frequently appears first, suggesting that the event this represents could be highly auspicious, and the second symbol may also be likewise representative of an auspicious alignment, but considered inferior by the druid or astrologer. Particular combinations may have been synergistic, for example the rodded double disc in combination with the rodded crescent. In contrast, some may have been seen to have a derogatory effect on each other in combination. Whether two symbols in combination were always viewed in the same way may have been dependent on other factors. For example, if the event or circumstances commemorated by the symbol pairs differed, i.e. with one stone relating to the building of a church and another relating to the death of a respected individual, a particular astronomical alignment, and therefore symbol, may have had a very different meaning. It is also possible that different druids, or astrologers, may have at times placed different emphasis on different events. In other words there may have been variation due to the subjective nature of astrological interpretation.

A third element, or ground rule, would be the inclusion of the qualifying symbols, principally the mirror and comb symbols that often accompany the main pairs. These may have been a way of displaying the authority of the astrological reading and emphasised further the importance of a particular combination of symbols.

Fourthly, the rodded aspect to a handful of the symbols again may have been a way of displaying confidence in key planetary events or may have referred to an optimal event, such as a particular body in a perfect position or alignment. It also might have denoted an important constellation or star with its ruling planet in residence (maybe signifying the start of a festival or feast).

CHAPTER 13

THE LAST OF THE DRUIDS

A Major Reassessment of the Picts

When we started out in this exploration of the Picts, we were confronted by the overwhelmingly negative views expressed about this northern people by their contemporaries. This is not surprising, given that the commentators who made these remarks saw the Picts first and foremost as enemies, either to be subdued and exploited or to be discarded as frightful barbarians bent on destruction. Historians in the second millennium were not much kinder to them. Within living memory, the Picts were still being denigrated as naked, tattooed 'barbarians' intent only on mayhem, and indeed this was a common description painted by teachers in some Scottish schools. Yet, the evidence in existence suggested a much more complex story. We know now that they had a sophisticated society, manufactured beautiful jewellery and probably contributed to the artistry of illuminated manuscripts, such as the *Book of Kells*. In addition they carved magnificent stone monuments, comprising some of the finest examples of monumental sculpture of their time. Unfortunately, despite their achievements, the Picts did not leave us any written records; or rather none have survived from Pictland. They did, however, leave us the enigmatic symbols and, as we have seen, the analysis of these has led us in unexpected directions.

It would appear that the basis of understanding a little more of the Picts, their society and their cultural relationship to other peoples, lies in a new interpretation of the imagery of Pictish stones and their accompanying symbols. Our journey started with an analysis of the Shandwick Stone from the north of Scotland. This large, ornately carved cross slab not only unquestionably proclaims its Christian credentials, but at the same time displays two of the seemingly unique and previously indecipherable Pictish symbols. Crucially, however, as we have seen, the sculptor has provided us with a key not only to understanding this particular stone but also to the means with which to gain a greater understanding of the symbol pair system. In consequence we can gain some insight into the minds and culture of the Picts. This key is the so-called 'hunting scene' depicted on the reverse side of the monument, a scene at first glance full of apparent anomalies and peculiarities, but one that becomes much more lucid when viewed within the context of a Pictish night sky.

Pictish Druids?
We have also developed during the course of this book a working hypothesis that the Shandwick stone tableau and the complex scene on the Golspie stone in effect display

astronomical constellations which may to relate to specific dates. These are possibly connected to the raising of each of these monuments. By analysing the relationship and imagery of the key components of these stones, we have developed a new understanding of how the Picts might have seen the night sky. This, for the first time, gives us a unique insight into their culture and their mindset, and most importantly forces us to reconsider and reassess their capabilities. We could in the first instance ask what skills were actually required to produce such a pictorial representation of the heavens. Individuals who created the stone would have needed to have knowledge of the constellations in the night sky and apparently recognise these as specific animals, human, or mythological characters. Crucially these constellations have been placed in a very specific order, representing the progressive rising of the prominent stars or constellations. This would imply much more than a casual interest in the heavens; it suggests a detailed understanding of the movements of the stars, presumably through committed observation. There is of course another level of complexity with a requisite set of skills, and these relate to the 'meaning' of the two carvings; they seem to convey a sense of time and a countdown to a specific event – in the case of the Shandwick stone this may well be Christmas. These sophisticated astronomical skills demand a much higher level of knowledge than simply producing a picture of the night sky. They imply that there were individuals within Pictland who studied the stars with interest and not only knew the order in which specific stars or constellations rose, but could relate these to the calendar.

While it is well attested outside Pictland that Celtic society had a druid class who were known to be highly skilled in astronomy, little is known about Pictish druids. All we know is that, according to Adamnan, they did exist and were seen as a threat to St Columba's mission in Pictland. In addition the druids, who have been mentioned as being highly skilled in astronomy, lived not only outside Pictland but hundreds of years before the Shandwick stone was carved. For example, it is generally agreed that Gaulish druids produced the Coligny Calendar, and inscribed on the surviving fragments of its bronze plates data that not only relate to the contents of what we would consider a calendar, but also are unequivocally religious and with a strong astrological flavour, with days designated as auspicious or inauspicious. We should now consider the Shandwick stone in a similar light; its calendrical panel and the symbols above may well be similarly conveying the message that the stone is commemorating an auspicious moment. Our working hypothesis is that, while it is fundamentally a religious monument, within it is inscribed a calendar that does more than point to a date but is a strongly framed 'mark of approval' – the event commemorated by the stone seemingly so important, so auspicious, even the stars are aligned perfectly, forming a procession across the sky, proclaiming the impending event. In this sense it shares much with the Coligny Calendar. Whoever commissioned this Christian cross slab must have felt it necessary, or was expected, to include such an astronomical component. Perhaps this inclusion was deemed necessary and was an essential component in any public endeavour. This strongly hints that the presumably now Christian population at large still relied on the portents of the sky for reassurance.

The discovery that at least two Pictish stones could have a considerable astronomical content, and the possibility of the symbol pairs themselves representing complex astrological predictions, or observations, also contradicts deep-set prejudices that the second half of the first millennium was a Dark Age. In Pictland at least, it would appear that sophisticated skills were still to the fore. We also have the implication that particular specialists skilled in astrology or astronomy were considered important enough to have a major input in the design and rendition of a Christian monument. This presents something of a conundrum but one that is not at all uncommon in the history of the Church in the first millennium. Early Christian missionaries did not set out to completely eradicate previous religious practices, but seem to have been pragmatic enough to have incorporated key parts of the other religions they encountered into a local 'brand' of Christianity. Therefore we find pagan, Roman and Celtic gods becoming Christian saints, thus allowing their adherents to continue praying to them. Midwinter pagan festivals could be swapped for Christmas, and pagan spring fertility symbols represented by the egg could be incorporated into Easter. Even the name 'Easter' is derived from a word meaning 'egg'. Finally the druid class in the Celtic world would appear to have morphed into a priestly class, maintaining their status within society. In Ireland, this seemingly strange mix of druids and priests is well attested. As we have seen, St Columba had his own personal druid, who guided him on the best times to carry out tasks, but spiritually St Columba also found himself at loggerheads with a Pictish druid. Similarly in Ireland, Saint Brigid is said not only to have had a druid foster father, but even before she was born, druids were predicting her future as a holy person. Furthermore, her druid foster father predicted she would be born at the most auspicious time, at sunrise on a particular day, and therefore she would have no equal on earth. There are other strong hints in the *Life of Saint Brigid* that Brigid's foster father was an astronomer/astrologer, with the story recalling his nights of stargazing. Interestingly, druids in the story are not seen as any threat, but if anything add weight and gravitas to the story. It is therefore possible that druids in Ireland did not simply melt away with the coming of Christianity, but continued in key roles and remained respected members of society. As hinted by the *Life of Saint Brigid* and Adamnan's *Life of St Columba*, they may have retained their role as astrologers and astronomers, determining the best time and day to carry out key events. Perhaps therefore it was essential for the survival of Pictish astrology that Pictland was largely converted by Irish missionaries with their own particular brand of Celtic Christianity, one that seems to have had some tolerance for aspects of druidic practice.

Is it possible that Pictish astrologers, or even druids, also survived the coming of Christianity? Certainly we seem to have evidence of a strong astronomical component to the obviously Christian Shandwick stone, but we also know now that a pictorial representation of the heavens also appears on at least one other Pictish monument that is apparently non-Christian – the Golspie stone. If we also consider that symbol pairs occur on stones that have been dated prior to the arrival of Christianity, but also appear on numerous Christian stones, then we would appear to have strong evidence of continuity in the use of astronomy and astrology across centuries despite the introduction of the teachings of the Church. This should not surprise us. After all Roman astrology is still very much with us and was practised even at the height of some of the Church's most turbulent and anti-heretical moments. Individuals such as Nostrodamus seem to have been tolerated, despite his 'craft' being rooted in the pagan world of the Romans. Similarly, we retain a Roman mythological view of the night sky's constellations despite the Church's attempts to change the characters recognised in the sky into Christian figures. The Church, for example, attempted to convince the population that they should see the constellation of Virgo as the Virgin Mary, yet we still have Virgo with her pagan symbol of the wheat sheaf. If Nostrodamus and countless other astrologers through the centuries in Europe could be tolerated by the Church, then it is certainly possible that astrology in Pictland might also have been seen as non-threatening and that some aspects of druidic teaching survived Christianity. Indeed, such continuity may have been seen as beneficial to the introduction of Christianity. This might encourage us to also suggest that Pictish druidism did survive, but probably in a new form. How such continuity between pagan druidism and Christian 'druidism' (if we can use such a term) could actually have been achieved we can only guess at. Did some druids become Christian converts, but carry on their teachings, or was druidic knowledge accessible outside of druidism? Did priests take on some of the traditional role of the druids in society, perhaps even taking on the practice of divination?

A further piece of evidence to consider in the working hypothesis that there is a druidic input into the carvings that appear on these stones is the significance of the inclusion of mirror and comb symbols on many of them. The fundamental divine or magical nature of these objects enhances the hypothesis that the stones are astrological in nature. These objects, particularly when used in combination, seem to have been believed to allow key individuals to 'see' into the other world or gain some knowledge of the future. The mirror may have been viewed as a portal into another world, perhaps by effectively mimicking the surface of the water at holy sites revered by the Celts and other ancient peoples. We know now that the mirror also has a well attested history as a symbol linked to other world spirits. As we have seen, the comb also appears to have links to divination and it too is associated with legendary creatures such as the mermaid and the banshee. However, the most surprising use is in the Church ceremony and in particular high masses where it had, in the past, a key role in the ordination of bishops with ceremonial combing of the hair of the bishop being integral to the process. It is perhaps possible that the comb is an example of a pagan symbol that was transformed and incorporated into Christianity. If this is the case, then it is very possible that druids also used combs in a similar way and along with the mirror it may have been an important part of their divination 'toolkit'. The mirror and combs that appear on the Pictish symbol stones may therefore be druidic marks, some of which are side by side with Christian symbolism in a way paralleled by the stories of druid's close personal (and apparently amicable) links to early Celtic saints. These potential druidic marks therefore, may be the first real evidence that druids played a key role in the creation of the symbol stones and that at least some druidic tradition, not only survived the introduction of Christianity but was an integral part of the early Church in Pictland.

If the Picts really did employ an astrological system that related to that of other cultures, for example a Welsh or Irish druidic astrological tradition, then should we not ask, where is the evidence of similar symbols from these traditions? Were the Picts unique in employing and displaying such symbols? Certainly, in the context of the

British Isles this would appear to be the case, but we must also view the possibility that there may have been very special circumstances surrounding the creation of the Pictish symbol stones. The first people in Scotland known to carve and dress stones were the Romans. They erected various monuments, altars, grave markers and milestones in southern Scotland. Interestingly, some of these monuments bear carvings of zodiacal figures. The Irish, Welsh and Angles carved monuments in the Dark Age; most of these seem to be Christian in context, while the earliest Pictish stones (Class I) are probably not Christian. One potential answer to the conundrum of the uniqueness of Pictish symbol stones lies in the possibility that symbols were originally displayed on materials that have simply rotted away, both in Pictland as well as in other areas. We might speculate that the decline of the druid orders under the Roman Empire (at least in part forcibly), the introduction of Christianity within the empire and continued influence of Christianity post-Roman in the other Celtic areas of Britain, may have led to the extinction of recording astrological symbols on transient materials, prior to the adoption of native themed monumental sculpture. Furthermore, a Roman-centred Church may have been more insensitive to local cultural traditions. In Ireland, the decline of druidry, although the country was Christianised later than Celtic Britain, may likewise have occurred prior to the widespread adoption of monumental carving. Pictland, however, because of its unique position just outside the empire, but in close contact with it, may therefore have adopted monumental stone carving at a relatively early stage, prior to Christianisation, but crucially during a time when the symbol system was still very much in use. What we see with the transition from Class I stones (Pictish symbols only), to Class II stones (Pictish symbols/Christian symbolism), to Class III (Christian with no Pictish symbols) may well represent a gradual takeover by Christians of a well-established tradition of stone carving, leading to the eventual disappearance of the ultimately pagan symbols. The existence of Class I stones suggests that Pictish druids, in contrast to druids in other areas, may have been able to make the transition from recording symbols on organic media to displaying these more permanently on stone prior to significant interference from the new ideas and religion. These permanent displays of symbols on spectacular stone monuments may therefore have taken on a much more public aspect, creating a religious focus for the population, a focus that was subsequently utilised by a culturally sympathetic Celtic Church in Pictland.

One major surprise in this study is that there may well be evidence of similarities between the Pictish symbols discussed here and Vedic *nakshatra* symbolism from the Indian subcontinent. Although the Vedic symbols do not seem today to be employed in the same way as their theoretical Pictish equivalents, their survival may indicate a forgotten function. Furthermore, we must also remind ourselves that Vedic astrology is very much part of the ancient Vedic or Hindu religion and that while modern Western astrologers have little to do with any organised religion, their Eastern counterparts recognise astrology within a broader spiritual context.

What of the mythological tales we have explored? From Celtic tales to the story of Hercules and the widespread 'white stag' tales, we seem to have a significant collection of stories that relate to the night sky. Is it possible that these stories originally had a purpose beyond that of entertainment? These stories may, for example, have been the remnants of sacred tales used to explain an essentially divine night sky, perhaps even an aid to memory for druids and other priestly castes. This might explain the similarities that have been detected between mythological stories originating from India, the Celtic countries and Greece. There may well have been a degree of conservation in the basic message simply because the information was fundamental to cosmological and therefore religious beliefs within these societies – beliefs that at one point were shared across Indo-European cultures. The survival of these myths in this context should be perhaps considered nothing short of miraculous, and has enabled us to gain insight into how ancient peoples in northern Europe and Asia may have viewed the heavenly bodies.

Short of finding a detailed contemporary account of Pictish druidism that we could use, to compare what is known about druidism in Britain, Ireland and Gaul, there is a real difficulty in knowing whether these Pictish astrologers and the druids mentioned by Adamnan were actually druids in the Celtic sense. While astrology is apparently being used in connection with specific events, just as we know it was used by Celtic druids, we must remind ourselves that other societies have used astrology in the same way. If we are to feel confident that the astronomical references we have found on the stones are the work of druids, in the proper Celtic sense of the term, then we must strengthen the case that Pictish culture was essentially Celtic and resembled that of their Celtic neighbours.

Cultural Origin of the Picts

The debate on the nature and origins of the Pictish language, particularly whether they spoke a Celtic language, has hinged mainly on the study of place names. This evidence indicates that the Picts probably did speak a Celtic language, although it is still open to debate whether this was q-Celtic or p-Celtic in origin and also whether there was a non-Indo-European component to this. What can this exploration of the Pictish stones, their carvings and the symbols add to this debate? Interestingly, both the Shandwick stone and the Golspie stone have characters on them that have at the very least a resonance with known Celtic tales from both Ireland and Wales. On the Shandwick stone we have two warriors facing each other with a calf in between them, beside two bulls that also appear to be in conflict. The similarity to the classic Irish tale *Táin Bó Cúailnge* is clear. We also have, on the right-hand side of the tableau, a portion of the night sky characterised by animals/constellations, which bears some resemblance to a part of a Welsh tale found in the *Mabinogion*. On the Golspie stone and Rhynie stone we have hideous giant-like figures with characteristics that are reminiscent of both literary descriptions of Balor, the chief of the giant Fomorians from Irish legend and his potential Welsh counterpart, Ysbaddaden Penkawr. Similarities are also evident between these two Pictish figures and the Greek Orion, as well as between Orion and Balor. A possible link between the Golspie man, the Rhynie man and Balor, would also provide another tentative clue about the Picts' Celtic credentials; Balor was the king of the Fomorians in Irish legend. These were a mythological race people credited with the introduction of the festival of *Samhain*, one of the four key Celtic festivals. In addition the Sun god Lugh (who battles with the Fomorians and Balor) in particular is linked directly to another of these four festivals, *Lughnasa*. In the Pictish double disc symbol, we have a design with strong solar symbolism. Furthermore, the dual solar symbolism contained within the double disc also hints that this symbol related at some point to the constellation Leo (the Sun's house) and therefore in the distant past to the summer solstice at around 2500 BC. As time has moved on, the Sun's position within Leo has shifted away from the summer solstice. By the time the Pictish monuments were being erected, the Sun was level with Leo's principal star, Regulus, on 1 August – a date that seems to have become fixed as the date of *Lughnasa*. Tantalisingly, the z-rod associated with the double disc symbols is in the form of a spear and if we interpret the detail on the shaft of the spear as tongues of fire, then we may also have a visual representation of Lugh's fiery spear on Pictish monuments.

It could therefore be argued that there is indeed a strong Celtic influence on both the Golspie stone and the Shandwick stone, one that would strengthen the claim that Pictish culture was indeed Celtic, and this cultural influence went further than simply a linguistic commonality, including a mythological component and the celebration of Celtic festivals. If this can all be accepted, then it is most likely that Pictish druids shared at the very least some similarities with their counterparts in lands that are generally accepted as being 'Celtic'. However, we should also exercise some caution, in that it is also entirely possible that the Celtic tales of Ireland and Wales have a much older origin and that elements of these stories, as well as the gods and other characters they describe, originate prior to Celtic civilisation. We have seen that there are elements within the myth of Hercules that resemble Celtic tales and suggest perhaps some commonality. Other authors have also noted similarities between Celtic myths and stories from the Vedic tradition. It would be perfectly feasible, therefore, if Pictish culture was derived from an older pre-Celtic Indo-European tradition, that they too would have a mythology with shared elements with that of the Celts. This notion is tempered somewhat by the possibility presented here that the Picts may have observed the Celtic festivals. Another potential problem – with the argument that the Celtic characters, appearing on Pictish stones, imply that the Picts were themselves Celtic – is that it could be the case that the Picts acquired Celtic stories from their neighbours. However, this would also imply that the Picts enthusiastically took up Celtic mythology to such a degree that it permeated even the design and carvings of their sacred stone monuments. While it is still possible therefore that there was some non-Indo-European influence on Pictish culture, on balance the evidence from Pictish stones suggests at the very least an Indo-European influence but most probably a strong Celtic influence on the imagery and cosmology. If we regard the stones as representing ideas at the very core of Pictish society, then we must also accept that 'Celticness' was also at this core. What is still difficult to say is whether their form of Celtic culture was closer to that of the Irish or the Welsh. In line with these new ideas on the function and symbolism of the Pictish monuments and their relationships to other cultures, we are also forced to review the claim that early non-Celtic cultures in Britain and Ireland had an overwhelming or even substantial role in the development of insular Celtic society.

The Shandwick and Golspie stones seem to have resonance with the mythological traditions not only of their Celtic neighbours, but also with tales from ancient Greece. The images from these stones seem to mirror and evoke Celtic and Greek tales from antiquity. For example, the fighting warriors and bulls, from the Shandwick stone, give us a real flavour of ancient societies where wealth was measured in cattle and an elite class were apparently preoccupied with cattle raiding. Perhaps most surprisingly, these images also suggest that the Picts recognised, at least in part, a distinctive understanding and interpretation of the night sky at variance with post-Herculean Mediterranean traditions. This 'Pictish' night sky and its resonance to other European mythological traditions, as well as artefacts such as the Gundestrup cauldron from around 100 BC, and the Saxon Parwich tympanum, suggest that there was a distinctive non-Mediterranean tradition – a tradition with its own constellations and view of the heavens. Perhaps this was once prevalent across northern Europe, surviving within Pictland in the latter half of the first millennium. This tradition, given the commonality between some of the basic elements of Celtic and ancient Greek mythology, could be very ancient. Perhaps it is hinting at an origin prior to the divergence of the Celtic and Greek (and perhaps other) Indo-European cultural groups. Furthermore, the potential for shared elements with the Vedic astrological tradition may even suggest that this alternative tradition could potentially have roots associated with the earliest Indo-Europeans. Perhaps the most surprising aspect uncovered here in regard to the symbols is the possible connections to Vedic astrological symbolism. The symbol that seems to particularly stand out in this connection is the Pictish beast, which as we have seen bears a number of interesting, and at first seemingly perplexing, parallels with the Vedic Makara. This fascinating Pictish symbol, if the interpretation of the Shandwick stone presented here is correct, would seem to relate to midwinter in the same way as the mythological Makara represents midwinter to Hindus. There are also parallels in some of the features, particularly the trunk-like mouths of both creatures which, unlike elephant trunks, have a mouth incorporated into the structure. There may also be common features with the Western zodiacal equivalent of Capricorn (the 'sea goat'), which may hint at a common origin for all three symbols.

The mythology surrounding the Makara also is surprisingly similar to traditional Scottish stories of kelpies or water horses and again these similarities surprisingly may hint at a common origin. If these two beasts really are related then we need to able to explain why a Makara-like creature with a similar folklore was depicted thousands of miles away from India on the northern portion of an Atlantic island. It is known that Pictish artists had access to a wide range of books, including medieval 'bestiaries', which could account for the strange menageries that appear on some Pictish stones. For example, a kneeling camel is carved on the Meigle 1 stone. Could a Makara-like beast have appeared in one of these books? The difficulty with this hypothesis is that the Makara's associations with midwinter and the mythology surrounding this monster would also have to be known to Picts and would seem incompatible with a Christian bestiary. Secondly, the beast symbol almost certainly pre-dates Christianity in Pictland. Further, we would have to explain why the Picts would so readily integrate a foreign mythological creature into an indigenous symbol system. Another possibility is that the similarities between the two figures are entirely coincidental, with both cultures independently creating two mythological creatures with strikingly similarities. These similarities concern structures that are very peculiar and not found in the natural world, suggesting that coincidence, as an explanation, is highly unlikely. Perhaps the most logical explanation is that both the Pictish beast and the Makara (and indeed Capricorn) do indeed have a common origin far back in time. However, the survival of the highly modified elephant-like trunk of the Pictish beast is still highly perplexing and could indicate that this particular symbol was highly conserved over a period of as much as two thousand years, long before it was committed to stone monuments. It is also perhaps timely to remind ourselves that a postulated Makara-like figure in Pictland is not the only example of seemingly inexplicable links between Indian symbolism and Europe; for example the Celtic god Cernunnos is depicted as sitting in a typical Indian 'lotus position' on the Gundestrup cauldron found in Denmark.

If there really are long-forgotten connections between different Indo-European groups in terms of astronomical and astrological knowledge, then their rediscovery offers a significant advance in the understanding of the nature and influence of Indo-European culture from its earliest beginnings. There has been some reluctance until now to view even the label 'Indo-European' as anything other than a linguistic term. Perhaps now, with the growing understanding of the relationships between religious ideas and the parallels in the social structures of seemingly distant cultures within the Indo-European family, it is time to re-examine the broader implications of a distinct ancient Indo-European culture. Part of this reassessment must also take into consideration the strong possibility of a shared and highly sophisticated notion of the heavens and the application of that knowledge as an astrological tool, with the attendant influence this would have on the very structure and fabric of society. Any such reassessment must endeavour to explain the mechanisms involved in the dissemination both of language and other fundamental aspects of culture. In addition, models of the spread of the Indo-European languages must also take into account the possibility that a much larger cultural 'package' became established in places as seemingly diverse and distant as Scotland and northern India.

Can we be sure that an Indo-European astrological system had the same origins as the Indo-European languages? While it would be very satisfying to ascribe a much larger cultural package to a postulated proto-Indo-European people, one that contained the origin of Indo-European languages, social structure, religion, astronomy and astrology, we simply do not have enough evidence for this. It certainly is possible that such a cultural 'package' was transmitted. As early Indo-Europeans migrated from an eastern European/western Asian homeland, both eastwards and westwards, they may well have carried some major technological advantage that allowed them to impose not only their language, but other key parts of their culture on the indigenous peoples they encountered. If Indo-European culture was spread by a more passive mechanism, such as by the domination of trading routes and trading centres, then would we expect our putative Indo-European zodiac also to have spread? We must consider a number of possibilities; for example, aspects of Indo-European culture may have originated in different locations (not necessarily among proto-Indo-European speakers) but spread through established trade routes in different directions. So it is possible that while the Indo-European language group may have had an origin in, for example, southern Russia, spreading westwards through Europe along the great rivers such as the Danube, it is equally feasible that ideas flowed in the opposite direction, a flow that could be made easier if there was a common language in use. Similarly, these ideas could have originated further east, making the journey all the way across the continents to finally reach the British Isles or just as plausibly in the opposite direction. One thing, however, we can be sure of, given the nature of the zodiacal signs we have elucidated, is that this system would seem to be at least in part northern in origin. It is interesting to note that a number of the possible proto-Indo-European root words, reconstructed by linguists, may also reflect a 'northern' European origin.

The two putative constellations that seem to really stand out in this northern perspective are the wild boar and the stag. These are animals of the northern European forests and moors and it is perhaps here that we should look for the origins of this view of the night sky. All of this therefore raises the question, what relationship does this postulated north European astronomy/astrology have to that of the Chaldeans and Babylonians – cultures generally regarded as the birthplace of Western astrology and much of astronomy? Similarities between aspects of a Pictish and Vedic astrological systems, given their great special and temporal isolation from one another, could lead to speculation that once there may have existed a form of astrology at least as old as that of the civilisations of the Middle East. Similarities between all three might suggest that they all have a common, even older origin, pushing back in time our knowledge of the very origins of astronomy and astrology. Another point worth considering is the presence in Europe, in the Neolithic and Bronze Age, of peoples who have left substantial evidence of an interest in astronomy – from the stone megaliths and alignments of Western Europe to the 'Nebra Disk' and the bronze conical 'wizard' hats of central Europe. Could Europe be the ultimate origin of our view of the night sky and at least some of the constellations, with ideas spreading to Babylonia and India from the West? We tend to think of innovations and ideas in prehistory as flowing from the Middle East outwards, spreading westwards into Europe, eventually reaching the fringes of the continent. These ideas are based on our assumption that the civilisations of Rome and Greece, as well as those of the Middle East, represented the zenith of intellectual thought in their respective time periods, whereas the 'barbarians' to the north, in sharp contrast, represented the nadir of human endeavour. Of course this viewpoint has been formed largely by commentators from some of these civilisations telling us that this was the case. Even the word 'barbarian' derives from a Greek word lampooning other people for speaking languages that sounded unintelligible to the Greeks; to them, foreigners made primitive noises when speaking that sounded like 'bar bar'. Perhaps we should start to seriously consider the possibility that the people of western and north-west Europe had their own contribution to make to civilisation, one that until now has been largely ignored or forgotten.

Another clue as to the relationship between Pictish and other Indo-European cultures that has presented itself during the course of this study is the light that the Pictish symbols have shed on the origin of the Celtic festivals. As previously stated, the symbolism of the double disc symbol seems to link this particular design not only to the Sun but also to the constellation Leo and its alpha star Regulus. Significantly though, in Pictland (and elsewhere) the near conjunction of the Sun with Regulus would have occurred around 1 August in the first millennium, precisely the time of the festival of *Lughnasa*, the festival of the Celtic solar deity Lugus or Lugh. We have asked the question, why hold a Sun god's festival in August and not at the summer solstice? The answer we have seen to this question may be straightforward. At around 2300 BC the Sun would have been in conjunction with Regulus on the summer solstice, but over the centuries this relationship would have broken down. It is also important to note that the other Celtic festivals are separated by the same time interval that is found between the solstices and the equinoxes but, as we have seen, shifted by a number of weeks from these dates due to the astronomical phenomenon of precession. In other words these Celtic festivals almost certainly originated from festivals marking the solstices and the equinoxes, but became detached from the solar calendar due to precession. If we were to look at the night sky through the course of a year at around 2300 BC we would find the Sun in Leo (the Sun's zodiacal house) at midsummer, when of course the Sun is at its most dominant. At the autumnal equinox in 2300 BC the Sun would have been between Libra and Scorpio (and therefore the Milky Way), at midwinter it would be entering Aquarius, and at the spring equinox it would be entering Taurus (in alignment with the Pleiades). In the last half of the first millennium AD, in the case of the first two astronomical events, these alignments would have occurred at *Lughnasa* (1 August) and *Samhain* (31 October). The original alignment that coincided with the winter solstice in 2300 BC would be replicated in the first millennium at the end of January a couple of days before our current date for the Celtic festival of *Imbolc* (1 or 2 February), and the spring equinox alignment replicated on 29 April, just prior to the current date for *Beltane* of 1 May.

We have also seen, from the Golspie stone, that the constellation Orion may have played a significant role in not only the mythology surrounding key Celtic festivals but also with its prominent stars heralding these events as part of a sky calendar. Greek mythology may also hint at the distant memory of a similar role in ancient Greece.

We therefore have a strong case for the Celts having originally observed the solstices and equinoxes, in the same way as other Indo-European peoples (including modern Hindus). We can hypothesise that whereas non-Celts continued to observe these solar events but forgot the original astronomical alignments that accompanied these (although retaining the notion of the Sun's house and the other houses) the Celts presumably saw these alignments as greatly significant and preferred to hook their Calendar to a sidereal year rather than a tropical year. One example, however, of a non-Celtic people choosing to observe the stars rather than a solstice is that of the Hindus. The date of their great winter festival, the Makar Sankranti, is fixed by the Sun's entry into Capricorn. The festival is celebrated today around 15 January, and marks the start of the Sun's northward journey from its southernmost position at dawn. However, as mentioned previously, this transition today actually occurs at the winter solstice around 21 December. This would suggest that the calculation for the festival has also become unhooked from the solstice, exactly the same way as the Celtic festivals became detached from the equinoxes and solstices although probably at a later date. It would seem therefore that Vedic priests took the decision at some point to base the beginning of the festival on the Sun's position relative to the constellation of Capricorn as more important than observing the true solstice.

Why did some Indo-European groups (the Celts and the north Indians) choose this particular path? The probable reason is that they had attached a particularly strong religious and mythological element to these astronomical alignments and placed a greater emphasis on astronomy than their other Indo-European counterparts. A greater emphasis on astronomy would naturally require a dedicated and well-educated and organised group of individuals capable of making the necessary observations, and relating these to the calendar – in the case of the Celts, a druidic class.

The divergence between Celtic observance of their quarter-day festivals and the solstices and equinoxes must have occurred gradually after 2300 BC. By around 1500 BC the Sun at the summer solstice, for example, would be at the boundary of Cancer and Leo, and any later than this date would be in Cancer at the solstice. Certainly by the time archaeologists argue for the emergence of the Celts, conservatively at around 800 BC, the divergence would have been substantial, and the Celtic festivals and the solstices and equinoxes would have long parted company. This point would support a much earlier emergence of this fundamental aspect of Celtic culture from mainstream Indo-European culture than suggested by many archaeologists, perhaps even prior to the development of the Urnfield culture in central Europe. This divergence and devotional evolution might also suggest that the origin of the Celtic festivals lay with a population relatively isolated from the mainstream. Such isolation might be geographic or isolation as a result of a period of upheaval. It is not beyond the realms of possibility that the location for such a fundamental shift was within Western Europe. The distribution of place names in Western Europe and the British Isles linked to the god Lugh and therefore probably to the devotional festival of *Lughnasa* may be evidence of the origin and evolutionary locus of the distinctively Celtic festivals. Such a possibility would suggest a much more complex development of Celtic culture, particularly if these festivals arose prior to any known distinctive archaeological evidence of the Celts, and also if the locus of the origin of the Celtic festivals did not correspond to central Europe, the supposed 'birthplace' of Celtic culture.

Conclusions

The Sun, the Moon, the planets and the stars have long fascinated mankind, and it is not difficult to imagine our far distant ancestors gazing up at the wonders of the night sky. To them, and for countless generations after their passing, the heavenly bodies must have meant much more than just being a spectacle. The rhythms of everyday life were bound to the rising and setting of the Sun, night-time hunting was dependent on the phases of the Moon and even the human reproductive system seemed to mimic the Moon's monthly cycle.

As hunter-gathering gave way to agriculture in many parts of the world, the Sun's importance to these emerging societies appears to have increased. Then, as now, farmers were dependent on the weather, with success or failure, feast or famine, inextricably linked to the Sun. On one hand it could nurture and ripen crops, but the droughts it could create could also destroy these same crops. Its power therefore seemed to be both fickle and divine. Understanding it was literally a matter of life and death. These early societies also realised that the appearance of stars in the night sky could be used to measure time, and therefore predict both the Sun's course though the year and even the Moon's seemingly erratic behaviour. As cultures became increasingly sophisticated their understanding of the movements of the stars, moon and planets also increased, allowing them, for example, to predict the future and the frightening occurrence of eclipses. In addition, this sophistication allowed the creation of calendars by priestly castes, an invention critical to the smooth running of advanced societies.

It was therefore only natural that belief systems arose that viewed the heavenly bodies as divine or as the instruments of divinity. If the Sun or the Moon could be observed and their positions correlated to observable key events on earth, events such as the seasons, then it must have seemed perfectly logical that the course of the planets across the star background could also affect people's lives. By developing the science of astronomy early cultures believed that by inference you could gain knowledge of the effect the Sun, Moon, stars and planets had on mankind – in other words, the art of astrology. Civilisations across the world have apparently, independently, developed astrological systems and have attached mythologies to the heavenly bodies. Many recognise similar star patterns or constellations and have attributed these to divine beings. In Europe, the Middle East and India, ancient systems of astrology were developed which became widespread and of enormous influence on civilisations such as the Babylonians, the Egyptians, the Greeks and the Romans. However, there remains the question, did the peoples of northern Europe also practice astrology and study the stars? If they did what form did this take and what happened to the knowledge they developed? A significant part of this study has been an attempt to try to understand one of the broader cultural European groupings, the Celts, which almost certainly included the Picts, whom we know from the Greeks and Romans did indeed practise some unknown form of astrology. A strong possibility that has arisen from this examination of Pictish stones is that there may have been a sophisticated form of astrology practised among the cultures of northern Europe, perhaps congruent with Indo-European speech, one that extended as far east as India and as far west as Pictland. This analysis of Pictish stones and their symbols has led to the startling conclusion that the key to understanding these enigmatic carvings lies in astrology. We have also seen that far from being isolated and separate from the mainstream of European and indeed Indo-European culture, the symbols demonstrate that the Picts may have actually maintained some of the core elements of Indo-European culture which were lost elsewhere. Indeed, there would appear to be evidence that a druidic culture may have survived in Pictland long after druids had apparently disappeared from the other Celtic areas.

We have made significant advances in our understanding of the Pictish symbols, but there is a great deal of work to be done. We still have to exercise caution in most cases in attributing specific meaning to specific symbols. It may well be the case that some of the symbols will never be understood and, just as with the Coligny Calendar, we will always have a partial and fragmentary view of Pictish astrology. However, this study concentrating on this aspect of Pictish culture has revealed connections to other peoples that are unexpected and surprising. Further study is therefore absolutely necessary – study that should not be introspective but rather take place in a wider cultural context and crucially recognise that Pictish culture was not isolated and primitive, but rather was related to other traditions both ancient and contemporary.

The Pictish stones are a reminder of distant times when people felt closer to nature and still viewed the night sky with a sense of awe. For us, in the twenty-first century, the stones should not just symbolise the yearly cycle of the stars and planets, but should open a window into the past – a window that reveals not just the uniqueness of Pictish culture, but also the commonality between different peoples separated by great distance in time and space. To be able to gaze up at the night sky and recognise the stars and constellations that the Picts once knew is a profound feeling and allows us to feel in some sense closer to these people. Perhaps as a result of this exploration into the Pictish symbols, some of the veils obscuring the so-called enigmatic Picts have been lifted and the mystery reduced, but what has been revealed can only be a source of wonderment.

Finally after over a thousand years of silence, the stones are speaking to us once more. While we do not as yet understand everything they are trying to tell us, we have made important strides forward, and hopefully as time progresses we will learn more about the people who created them and their place in the world.

Suggested Reading by Chapter

Introduction

General background reading:
A. A. M. Duncan *Scotland: The Making of the Kingdom* Edinburgh History of
　　Scotland vol. 1, 1975, Oliver & Boyd.
Elizabeth Sutherland *In Search of the Picts* 1994, Constable.
Tim Clarkson *The Picts: A History* 2008, Tempus Publishing Limited.
Lloyd and Jenny Laing *The Picts and the Scots* 1993, Sutton Publishing Limited.
W. A. Cummins *The Age of the Picts* 1995, Sutton Publishing Limited.
Stephen Driscoll *Alba: The Gaelic Kingdom of Scotland* 2002, Birlinn with Historic
　　Scotland.
Tacitus (98) *The Agricola and The Germania* 1948, rev. 1970, Penguin Books.
Gildas (540) *The Ruin of Britain and Other Documents* 1978, Phillimore edition,
　　translated by Michael Winterbottom.
Bede, the Venerable (731) *Ecclesiastical History of the English People* 1990, Penguin
　　edition, translated by L. Sherley-Price.
Nennius (830) *British History and the Welsh Annals* 1980, Phillimore edition,
　　translated by John Morris.
Miranda J. Green *Exploring the World of the Druids* 1997, Thames & Hudson.
Peter Berresford Ellis *The Druids* 1994, Constable.
Anne Ross *Druids: Preachers of Immortality* 1999, Tempus Publishing Limited.
Nora Chadwick *The Celts* 1970, Penguin Books.
Edward Sullivan *The Book of Kells* 1920, facsimile reprint 1986, Studio Editions Limited.
Ian Armit *The Towers in the North: The Brochs of Scotland* 2003, Tempus Publishing
　　Limited.
Iain Fraser, J. N. G. Ritchie, et al. *Pictish Symbol Stones: An Illustrated Gazetteer*
　　1999, Royal Commission on the Ancient and Historical Monuments of Scotland
http://www.missgien.net/celtic/gododdin/

Chapter 1

The Indo-Europeans:
Benjamin W. Fortson *Indo-European Language and Culture: An Introduction* 2004,
　　Blackwell.

The Celts:
Nora Chadwick *The Celts* 1970, Penguin Books.

T. G. E. Powell *The Celts* 1958, Thames & Hudson.

John Collis *The Celts: Origins, Myths & Inventions* 2003, Tempus Publishing Limited.

Christiane Eluere *The Celts: First Masters of Europe* 1992, translated into English by
    Daphne Briggs 1993, Thames & Hudson.

Barry Cunliffe *The Celts: A Very Short Introduction* 2003, Oxford University Press.

The Celts in Britain and Ireland:

Lloyd and Jennifer Laing *Celtic Britain and Ireland: Art and Society* 1995, The Herbert
    Press Limited.

Simon James *Exploring the World of the Celts* 1993, Thames & Hudson.

The *Pictish Chronicle*:

Alan Orr Anderson (ed.) *Early Sources of Scottish History* first published 1922, Oliver
    and Boyd, republished with corrections 1990, Paul Watkins.

Matrilineal succession:

The Venerable Bede (731) *Ecclesiastical History of the English People* 1990, Penguin
    edition, translated by L. Sherley-Price.

Origins of the Picts and the Pictish language:

Earl of Southesk *Origins of Pictish Symbolism* facsimile reprint 1999 (originally
    published 1893), Llanerch Publishers.

Paul Dunbavin *Picts and Ancient Britons: An Exploration of Pictish Origins* 1998,
    Third Millenium Publishing.

Katherine Forsyth *Language in Pictland: The Case Against 'Non-Indo-European
    Pictish* 1997, De Keltiche Draak.

Adamnan *Life of Saint Columba: Founder of Hy (Iona)* facsimile reprint 1988, Llanerch.

W. F. H. Nicolaisen *Scottish Place-Names* 1976, B. T. Batsford Limited.

Picts of Galloway:

Alan Orr Anderson (ed.) *Scottish Annals from English Chroniclers* first published
    1908, David Nutt, republished with corrections 1991, Paul Watkins.

Hadrian's Wall and the Antonine Wall:

David J. Breeze and Brian Dobson *Hadrian's Wall* 1976, Allen Lane.

The battle of *Mons Graupius*:

Tacitus (98) *The Agricola and The Germania* 1948, rev. 1970, Penguin Books.

Post-Roman Britain:

Gildas (540) *The Ruin of Britain and Other Documents* 1978, Phillimore edition,
    translated by Michael Winterbottom.

Germanic settlement in Britain:

J. N. L. Myres *The English Settlements* The Oxford History of England, 1986,
    Oxford University Press.

Scottish settlement:
Stephen Driscoll *Alba: The Gaelic Kingdom of Scotland* 2002, Birlinn with Historic
    Scotland.

The Pictish kingdoms:
Elizabeth Sutherland *In Search of the Picts* 1994, Constable.

St Columba's mission to the Picts:
Adamnan *Life of Saint Columba: Founder of Hy (Iona)* Facsimile Reprint 1988, Llanerch.

The battle of Catraeth:
http://www.missgien.net/celtic/gododdin/

The Northumbrians:
John Marsden *Northanhymbre Saga: History of the Anglo-Saxon Kings of Northumbria*
    1992, Kyle Cathie

***Legend of Saint Berchan*:**
Alan Orr Anderson (ed.) *Early Sources of Scottish History* first published 1922, Oliver
    and Boyd, republished with corrections 1990, Paul Watkins.

Chapter 2

Classification of Pictish stones:
J. Romilly Allen and Joseph Anderson *The Early Christian Monuments of Scotland* 1993,
    the Pinkfoot Press (First published 1903, Society of Antiquaries of Scotland).

The *Book of Kells*:
Edward Sullivan *The Book of Kells* 1920, facsimile reprint 1986, Studio Editions Limited.
http://www.visual-arts-cork.com/cultural-history-of-ireland/book-of-kells.htm

Cataloguing and description of the Pictish symbols:
J. Romilly Allen and Joseph Anderson *The Early Christian Monuments of Scotland* 1993,
    The Pinkfoot Press (first published 1903, Society of Antiquaries of Scotland).
Anthony Jackson *The Symbol Stones of Scotland: A Social Anthropological Resolution of
    the Problem of the Picts* 1984, The Orkney Press.
Anthony Jackson *The Pictish Trail: A Travellers Guide to the Old Pictish Kingdoms*
    1989, The Orkney Press.
Alastair Mack *Field Guide to the Pictish Symbol Stones* 1997, The Pinkfoot Press.

Theoretical Scandinavian origin of Pictish symbolism:
Earl of Southesk *Origins of Pictish Symbolism* facsimile reprint 1999 (originally
    published 1893), Llanerch Publishers.

Irish and Anglo-Saxon influence on Pictish art:
F. T. Wainwright (ed.) *The Problem of the Picts* 1955, Thomas Nelson (republished
    1980 The Melvin Press).

Indo-European connections with Pictish art:
Inga Gilbert *The Symbolism of the Pictish Stones in Scotland* 1995, Speedwell Books (Edinburgh).

Function of the symbols:
Elizabeth Sutherland *In Search of the Picts* 1994, Constable.
Anthony Jackson *The Symbol Stones of Scotland: A Social Anthropological Resolution of the Problem of the Picts* 1984, The Orkney Press.

Chapter 3

Rosetta Stone:
http://en.wikipedia.org/wiki/Rosetta_Stone

The Shandwick stone (description):
J. Romilly Allen and Joseph Anderson *The Early Christian Monuments of Scotland* 1993, The Pinkfoot Press (first published 1903, Society of Antiquaries of Scotland).

Irish high crosses:
Hilary Richardson and John Scarry *An Introduction to Irish High Crosses* 1990, Mercier.
Roger Stalley *Irish High Crosses* 1996, Country House, Dublin.

Anglian monumental sculpture:
James Lang *Anglo-Saxon Sculpture* 1998, Shire Publications.

Denderah zodiac:
http://www.all-about-egypt.com/dendera-zodiac.html

Early astronomy:
Christopher Walker (ed.) *Astronomy Before the Telescope* 1996, BCA.
Richard Hinckley Allen *Star Names: Their Lore and Meaning* first published 1899, reprinted 1963 by Dover Publications Limited.

Modern astrology:
Julia and Derek Parker *Parker's Astrology* 1991, Dorothy Kindersley.

Chapter 4

Greek mythology and Hercules:
Arthur Cotterell and Rachel Storm *The Ultimate Encyclopedia of Mythology* 1999, Lorenz Books.
Stephen P. Kershaw *A Brief Guide to the Greek Myths: Gods, Monsters, Heroes and the Origins of Storytelling* 2007, Robinson
http://www.ianridpath.com/startales/hercules.htm
http://www.mlahanas.de/Greeks/Mythology/HeraclesLabours.html

The Nebra disc:
http://en.wikipedia.org/wiki/Nebra_disc

Bronze Age 'wizard hats':
http://en.wikipedia.org/wiki/Golden_hat

Callanish and other stone circles:
Aubrey Burl *A Guide to the Stone Circles of Britain, Ireland and Brittany*' 1995, Yale University.

Chapter 5

The story of 'Culhwch and Olwen':
Charles Squire *Celtic Myth and Legend: Poetry and Romance* 1905, The Gresham Publishing Company.
The Mabinogion c. 1300 – 1425, translated by Gwyn Jones and Thomas Jones 1949, Guernsey Press.

Ursa Major and Arthur:
http://www.britannia.com/history/arthur/kamyth.html
Richard Hinckley Allen *Star Names: Their Lore and Meaning* first published 1899, reprinted 1963 by Dover Publications Limited.

Maponus and Mabon ap Modron:
Peter Berresford Ellis *Dictionary of Celtic Mythology* 1992, Constable & Company.
http://en.wikipedia.org/wiki/Maponos

Heliacal rising of Sirius and the Nile floods:
Richard Hinckley Allen *Star Names: Their Lore and Meaning* first published 1899, reprinted 1963 by Dover Publications Limited.
http://www.ephemeris.com/history/egypt.html

The constellation Delphinus and the 'sacred fish':
Richard Hinckley Allen *Star Names: Their Lore and Meaning* first published 1899, reprinted 1963 by Dover Publications Limited.

***Táin Bó Cúailnge*:**
Thomas Kinsella *The Tain* 1969, translated from the Irish, Oxford University Press.

***Bóthar na Bó Finne*:**
Patrick S. Dineen (ed.) *Foclóir Gaedhilge Agus Béarla: An Irish-English Dictionary, Being a Thesaurus of the Words, Phrases and Idioms of the Modern Irish Language, with Explanations in English* 1904, The Irish Texts Society (available at http://www.ucc.ie/celt/Dinneen1.pdf)

King Ailil's 'star wives':
Peter Berresford Ellis 'Meet the Brahmins of ancient Europe, the high caste of Celtic society' 2000, *Hinduism Today* (available at http://www.hinduismtoday.com/modules/smartsection/item.php?itemid=4274)

Nynniaw and Peibaw / Gwyn ap Nudd / The legend of Math and Goewin / Lleu and Dylan:

Charles Squire *Celtic Myth and Legend: Poetry and Romance* 1905, The Gresham Publishing Company.

Arianrod's Palace:

Richard Hinckley Allen *Star Names: Their Lore and Meaning* first published 1899, reprinted 1963 by Dover Publications Limited.

Lleu and Dylan:

Charles Squire *Celtic Myth and Legend: Poetry and Romance* 1905, The Gresham Publishing Company.

Lleu's name and Proto-Indo:

http://en.wikipedia.org/wiki/Lleu_Llaw_Gyffes

The star Regulus:

Richard Hinckley Allen *Star Names: Their Lore and Meaning* first published 1899, reprinted 1963 by Dover Publications Limited.

Star signs and 'ruling' planets:

Julia and Derek Parker *Parker's Astrology* 1991, Dorothy Kindersley.

Lugh and *Lughnasa*:

Miranda J. Green *Dictionary of Celtic Myth and Legend* 1992, Thames & Hudson.

Peter Berresford Ellis *Dictionary of Celtic Mythology* 1992, Constable & Company.

James Mackillop *A Dictionary of Celtic Mythology* 1998, Oxford University Press.

Chapter 6

The constellation of Ophiuchus and Aesculapius:

Richard Hinckley Allen *Star Names: Their Lore and Meaning* first published 1899, reprinted 1963 by Dover Publications Limited.

The god Cernunnos:

Miranda J. Green *Dictionary of Celtic Myth and Legend* 1992, Thames & Hudson.

Gregory A. Clouter *The Lost Zodiac of the Druids* 2003, Vega.

Gundestrup cauldron:

http://www.unc.edu/celtic/catalogue/Gundestrup/kauldron.html

Ophiuchus as the thirteenth sign of the zodiac:

http://en.wikipedia.org/wiki/Ophiuchus_(astrology)

Meaning of *Damhair*:
Edward Dwelly *Faclair Gàidhlig gu Beurla le Dealbhan / The Illustrated [Scottish] Gaelic–English Dictionary* 1911, Birlinn.

The 'otherworld' and the stag:
James Mackillop *A Dictionary of Celtic Mythology* 1998, Oxford University Press.

Vedic *nakshatras* and the stag:
Peter Marshall *World Astrology: The Astrologer's Quest to Understand the Human Character* 2004, Macmillan.
Dennis M. Harness *The Nakshatras: The Lunar Mansions of Vedic Astrology* 1999, Lotus Press.

Parwich tympanum:
http://www.liverpoolmuseums.org.uk/conservation/technologies/casestudies/3d/parwich/

The 'Legend of the White Stag':
http://www.pinetreeweb.com/stag.htm

Chapter 7

Brigid / St Brigid:
Miranda J. Green *Dictionary of Celtic Myth and Legend* 1992, Thames & Hudson.
James Mackillop *A Dictionary of Celtic Mythology* 1998, Oxford University Press.

Pictish beast – dolphin interpretation:
Elizabeth Sutherland *In Search of the Picts* 1994, Constable.

Origins of the symbolism of the constellation Aquarius:
Richard Hinckley Allen *Star Names: Their Lore and Meaning* first published 1899, Reprinted 1963 by Dover Publications Limited.

Chapter 8

The Golspie stone:
J. Romilly Allen and Joseph Anderson *The Early Christian Monuments of Scotland* 1993, The Pinkfoot Press (First published 1903, Society of Antiquaries of Scotland).

Orion mythology:
Arthur Cotterell and Rachel Storm *The Ultimate Encyclopedia of Mythology* 1999, Lorenz Books.

Mythology and the star Sirius:
Richard Hinckley Allen *Star Names: Their Lore and Meaning* first published 1899, reprinted 1963 by Dover Publications Limited.

The Fomorians and Balor in Irish legend, Yspaddaden Penkawr in Welsh legend:
Miranda J. Green *Dictionary of Celtic Myth and Legend* 1992, Thames & Hudson.

Arthur Cotterell and Rachel Storm *The Ultimate Encyclopedia of Mythology* 1999, Lorenz Books.

Peter Berresford Ellis *Dictionary of Celtic Mythology* 1992, Constable & Company.

Charles Squire *Celtic Myth and Legend; Poetry and Romance* 1905, The Gresham Publishing Company.

The god Bel / Beli:

James Mackillop *A Dictionary of Celtic Mythology* 1998, Oxford University Press.

Chapter 9

Ancient calendars:

David Ewing Duncan *The Calendar: The 5000-Year-Old Struggle to Align the Clock and the Heavens – and What Happened to the Missing Ten Days* 1998, Fourth Estate.

The Vedic *nakshatras*:

Dennis M. Harness *The Nakshatras: The Lunar Mansions of Vedic Astrology* 1999, Lotus Press.

Peter Marshall *World Astrology: The Astrologer's Quest to Understand the Human Character* 2004, Macmillan.

Mirror as a female symbol:

Elizabeth Sutherland *In Search of the Picts* 1994, Constable.

Definition of 'luck' and 'fortune' and their relation to prediction:

Chambers 20th Century Dictionary, 1983, W. & R. Chambers.

The link between mirrors and speculation:

Jean Chevalier and Alain Gheerbrant *The Penguin Dictionary of Symbols*, first published in France 1969, translated by John-Buchanan Brown and published 1996, Penguin.

Jack Tressider *Dictionary of Symbols* first published 1997, reprinted 1999, Duncan Baird Publishers.

Celtic customs and the mirror as an instrument of divination:

Ruth Edna Kelley *The Book of Hallowe'en* 1919, Lothrop, Lee & Shepard Co.

The significance of mirrors and combs in European folk tales:

http://www.online-literature.com/hans_christian_andersen/972/

http://worldoftales.com/fairy_tales/Brothers_Grimm/Margaret_Hunt/The_Nix_of_the_Mill-Pond.html

The role of combs in religious ceremonies:

'The Mystery of the Comb' 9 September 1888, article in the *New York Times*, first published in the *Cornhill Magazine*.

http://www.religionfacts.com/christianity/things/vestments_bishops.htm

Chapter 10

Solar symbolism:

Earl of Southesk *Origins of Pictish Symbolism* facsimile reprint 1999 (originally published 1893), Llanerch Publishers.

Jack Tressider *Dictionary of Symbols* first published 1997, reprinted 1999, Duncan Baird Publishers.

Basic information on astrological practice:

Julia and Derek Parker *Parker's Astrology* 1991, Dorothy Kindersley.

Pictish brochs:

Ian Armit *The Towers in the North: The Brochs of Scotland* 2003, Tempus Publishing Limited.

Gemini as the 'gateway to heaven':

S. Langdon *Tammuz and Ishtar: A Monograph upon Babylonian Religion and Theology'* 1914, Oxford at the Clarendon Press.

http://www.ianridpath.com/startales/gemini.htm

Samhain as a gateway to the other world:

Miranda J. Green *Dictionary of Celtic Myth and Legend* 1992, Thames & Hudson.

Pictish spear shafts:

Cassius Dio *Roman History* Epitome of Book LXXVII, published in Loeb Classical Library edition, 1927.

Retrograde motion:

Geoffrey Cornelius and Paul Devereux *The Language of Stars and Planets: A Visual Key to Celestial Mysteries* 1996, Duncan Baird.

Right or clockwise motion seen as auspicious:

http://www.khandro.net/swastika.htm

The Celtic gods Lleu and Dylan:

Charles Squire *Celtic Myth and Legend: Poetry and Romance* 1905, The Gresham Publishing Company.

Chapter 11

The Pictish beast as an aquatic animal or spirit:

Elizabeth Sutherland *In Search of the Picts* 1994, Constable.

Mythology of the constellations of Capricorn, Sagittarius, Bootes and Auriga:

Richard Hinckley Allen *Star Names: Their Lore and Meaning* first published 1899, reprinted 1963 by Dover Publications Limited.

The Makara and Makar Sankranti:
http://en.wikipedia.org/wiki/Makara_(Hindu_mythology)
http://en.wikipedia.org/wiki/Makar_Sankranti

St Columba banishing a monster from the River Ness:
Adamnan *Life of Saint Columba: Founder of Hy (Iona)* facsimile reprint 1988, Llanerch.
The salmon of knowledge:
http://www.maryjones.us/ctexts/f02.html

Symbolism of the *nakshatra Swati*:
http://en.wikipedia.org/wiki/Svati

'Druid's Grave', Colchester:
http://en.wikipedia.org/wiki/Druid_of_Colchester

Chapter 12

Babylonian solar astronomy and astrology:
http://swadhwa.stormpages.com/hofa/mesopotamia.html
http://en.wikipedia.org/wiki/Zodiac

Denderah zodiac:
http://www.all-about-egypt.com/dendera-zodiac.html

Coligny Calendar:
http://technovate.org/web/coligny.htm
http://en.wikipedia.org/wiki/Coligny_calendar
http://www.maryjones.us/jce/coligny.html

The swastika and sauvastika symbols:
J. C. Cooper *An Illustrated Encyclopaedia of Traditional Symbols* 1978, Thames & Hudson.

Battersea shield (see detail of enamel designs):
http://www.britishmuseum.org/explodetailre/highlights/highlight_objects/pe_prb/t/the_battersea_shield.aspx

Battle of Dunnichen:
Graeme Cruickshank *The Battle of Dunnichen* 1991, The Pinkfoot Press.
The Venerable Bede, (731) *Ecclesiastical History of the English People* 1990, Penguin edition, translated by L. Sherley-Price.

Kenneth Macalpine and the creation of the Kingdom of Scotland:
A. A. M. Duncan *Scotland: The Making of the Kingdom* 1975, Vol 1., Oliver & Boyd.

INDEX